D0024851

SOCIAL
THE ENGLISH ORIGINS
CREDIT

John L. Finlay

Montreal and London   1972

SOCIAL

THE ENGLISH ORIGINS

CREDIT

McGill – Queen's University Press

© McGill – Queen's University Press 1972
International Standard Book Number 0-7735-0111-8
Library of Congress Catalog Card Number 72-75859
Legal Deposit fourth quarter 1972

This book has been published with the help
of a grant from the Social Science Research
Council of Canada, using funds provided by
the Canada Council.

Design by Mary Cserepy

Printed in Canada by Gordon W. Ross Ltd., Montreal

To Rosemarie

contents

This account of Social Credit was written with a primarily Canadian readership in mind. Most such readers will be familiar, in outline at least, with the technical case for Social Credit and will require no introductory description of it. However, there may be others not so familiar with the doctrine, in particular British readers interested not so much in the background to what is still a significant political activity as in a minor yet intriguing strand of British intellectual history. If these readers prefer to familiarize themselves with Social Credit before beginning this account, they will find a description of it in chapter 5.

There are many people whose generous assistance I wish to acknowledge. Those who communicated with me on the subject of Social Credit and whose help is noted in the book are too numerous to list here, but they know, I hope, of my gratitude to them. Special mention, however, must be made of the following: the Canada Council and the Faculty of Graduate Studies of the University of Manitoba, providers of the financial assistance which made the research possible; Miss Carol Clerihew and especially Miss Blanche Miller, most obliging and efficient typists; and Dr. K. Sandiford and Professor W. D. Smith, who offered valued advice and encouragement. To them all I am very grateful. In particular, I wish to acknowledge my debt to Professor W. L. Morton, who suggested the topic of and supervised the research for the doctoral dissertation on which this book is based. But it is not simply that he made possible the writing of the book; he made possible far more than that, and I thank him for his many kindnesses. Above all, I am deeply indebted to my wife, Rosemarie, to whom this book is dedicated.

The material in chapters 3, 7, and 10 appeared in altered form in *Queen's Quarterly,* the *Journal of Contemporary History,* and the *Journal of Religious History,* respectively, and I thank the editors of these journals for their permission to use this material.

chapter one

THE DECLINE OF LIBERAL ORTHODOXY

Towards the end of the First World War an obscure engineer then serving with the Royal Flying Corps, Major C. H. Douglas, began to advocate those ideas which later became known as Social Credit. Notwithstanding successes in Alberta, British Columbia, and to a lesser extent elsewhere in the world, Social Credit has remained part of what Keynes described as "an underworld."[1] This description is apt. It suggests that the doctrine had but a shadowy existence; even in its heyday in the twenties and again in the thirties this was true. Social Credit was never at the centre of things; it always remained on the fringes, and its triumph, the election of a Social Credit government in Alberta in 1935, turned out to be insubstantial. However, the term *underworld* also suggests that, if never exactly vital, Social Credit was never quite lifeless, that it did have a past, that it was part of a tradition, and that it did have its moments of vigour. This study acknowledges that Social Credit was a minor phenomenon and ultimately a failure, and yet, it is hoped, it also shows that the movement's fortunes were not without significance, above all in illuminating other, more major, trends in recent intellectual development.

[1] J. M. Keynes, *The General Theory of Employment, Interest and Money* (London, 1936), p. 32.

What Keynes had in mind when he spoke of an underworld was the economic aspect of Douglas's philosophy, that economic theory which is known as underconsumptionist and which rejects the possibility of other than temporary overproduction. As Keynes himself was interested in showing, such a view had not always been as unorthodox as it became in the first third of the twentieth century; as late as 1831 a commentator could describe Ricardo's conclusions as a "modern paradox."[2] But the seeming triumphs of Manchesterism were such that within some thirty years of this judgement liberal economics had acquired an almost absolute and unchallenged acceptance, so that its sway "must surely represent the most successful and important campaign of intellectual aggression and terminological dogmatism in the history of economic thought."[3] Such a supremacy went hand in hand with the demonstrated blessings of British capitalism, and therefore it was only natural that the questioning arose when that same industrial expansion was checked and its preeminence threatened. The roots of an alternative system are to be sought, then, in this period of uncertainty, and it is in the criticism of the prevailing economic beliefs of the late nineteenth century and after that an examination of the rise of Social Credit must begin.

But Social Credit was not simply an economic doctrine. As Ezra Pound reminded the world, "The surprise on Re-reading is that Douglas seems . . . to deal so little with economics and so greatly and generally with the philosophy of politics."[4] And this reminder underlines the fact that Social Credit was an underworld in quite another sense from that intended by Keynes. The repudiation of economic liberalism demanded a rejection of existing political practices and social arrangements. For the vast majority of critics, this meant some form of socialism. Underconsumptionism itself could tend in this direction, as was indicated by the career of J. A. Hobson, the writer who for Keynes signalled the resurrection of that unorthodoxy. Yet there were those critics who felt that socialism was not a sufficient break with liberalism, that it was a mere tampering with the mechanism. Such critics pointed to socialism's clinging to the Rousseauesque notion of the atomized society of free individuals, to its

[2] This observation by Chalmers is quoted in T. W. Hutchinson, *A Review of Economic Doctrines, 1870–1929* (Oxford, 1953), p. 348.

[3] Ibid.

[4] *New English Weekly*, 2 April 1936. (Subsequent references to this periodical will be abbreviated in this manner: NEW 2.4.36.)

retention of profit as the test of any course of action even if the profit motive itself was abandoned, to its willingness to make use of a purged parliamentary system. Social Credit shared these criticisms, and so in the wider sense was condemned to be a part of the underworld, alienated from liberalism and socialism alike.

This introduction will sketch the crisis of orthodoxy in England and draw attention to the need for a radical break with established practices. It will also suggest why some observers felt that developments pointed to a solution along the broad lines advocated by Social Credit and the rest of the underworld.

Certainly the need to find some drastic alternative seemed very pressing after twenty years of the twentieth century, when Douglas began to put forward his heresies. Since the 1870s the new orthodoxy had taken a succession of heavy blows. The depression of trade which until 1929 would be known as the Great Depression had begun in 1873 and lasted until the late 1890s, when fortuitous gold discoveries allowed a new expansion of currency and so of production. In all branches of the economy there was stagnation, though nowhere were the results felt more severely than on the land, for in the case of agriculture the problems of depression were intensified by technological advances. With the opening up of the North American plains, and with the improvements to transport in other ways, British agriculture was overwhelmed by a torrent of cheaper products and began that calamitous decline which was to be a feature of the next half-century and more. And yet for a country still solidly free-trade this was not considered a disaster; indeed it was fulfilment. Britain was felt to be predestined to be the workshop of the world, and given a revival of world trade Britain would surely go on to make bigger and bigger profits. In its early stages, then, the depression had set some people thinking but had not given cause for general alarm.

In fact alarm did not really develop until the onset of better times, and disquiet arose with the realization that as trade began to revive, Britain's share of it was ever diminishing. By 1913 Britain's lead in the manufacture of iron and steel had long been eaten away, and what had been possible to ignore in the case of agriculture was no longer something to be pushed aside. Britain was being made to realize the difficulties of being a free-trade island in a world increasingly industrialized and tariff-bound, and the rise of Chamberlain's protectionist star was the inevitable outcome.

Faced by the growing problems of a maturing capitalism, the industrialists began to look to their profits. One result was the beginning of an amalgamation movement which, while not approaching the completeness of the American trusts or of the German cartels, was none the less a disturbing element in a system based upon competition. Particularly striking in view of later Social Credit critiques was the amalgamation in banking. In 1890 the Baring scandal had given the banks a push towards bigger, more stable, units, and helped by government sanction, the movement which was to culminate in the emergence of the "Big Five" was under way; the 273 banks of 1890 had shrunk to 157 in 1903, and by the end of the war, only 40 remained. Indeed, so threatening was the situation felt to be that the Colwyn Committee on Bank Amalgamations was appointed in April 1918.[5]

The employers, however, were not having things all their own way. Consolidation among the industrialists and bankers was matched by the growth of a countervailing power among the workers. The old craft unions, run on the lines of friendly societies, had long been accepted as harmless, at times beneficent, institutions. But at the end of the 1880s the emergence of "new unionism," the organization of casual workers, raised very different issues. The numbers involved were potentially so large that they showed only too clearly what was happening—that the free play between individual employer and employee was becoming a thing of the past and that in its place was to be the increasingly violent confrontation of two armies.

The logic of the system itself was bringing about the negation of liberalism. Yet this was not all, for the state was beginning to play an increasing part in the control of economic and social life. There had, of course, been state legislation against freedom of contract before, notably the Factory Acts, but the later legislation was so different in scope as to amount to a difference in kind. The series of reforms introduced by the Liberal government after 1906 was recognized to be revolutionary. That it was Liberal legislation underlined the changed nature of the problems facing society.

This abandonment of classical liberalism by its own leaders was inevitable, however. Liberalism had failed. It was not only that Britain was failing to remain the world's leading industrial power, nor was it that at home competition seemed to be giving way to monopoly.

[5] J. Sykes, *The Amalgamation Movement in English Banking, 1825–1924* (London, 1926), pp. 47, 220; W. Ashworth, *An Economic History of England, 1870–1939* (London, 1960), pp. 166–70; and P. Fitzgerald, *Industrial Combination in England* (London, 1927), pp. 10–12.

A deeper cause for disillusionment was the growing awareness that the basis of liberalism—with its belief, epitomized by Samuel Smiles, that virtue and determination would be rewarded—had long been a cruel myth. The growth of amalgamated businesses whose control of markets and credit was such as to crush any competition was sufficient indication, perhaps. But another approach was even more telling. The researches of Booth and of Rowntree showed that a great proportion of the population lived in such perpetual poverty that any margin for saving and hence advancement was completely wanting.[6] At the same time, as Halévy noted, the decline of the nonconformist ethic suggests that it was possible to look upon poverty as something other than a sin to be kept hidden.[7] Thus, in the decades before the war an increasingly literate public was enabled to look upon its suffering in a new light and prepared to see the possibility of improvement. The willingness to do so was reinforced by a spate of publications which discussed such problems. Such a one was the very popular book *Riches and Poverty* by Sir Leo Chiozza Money, which appeared in 1905 and went through ten editions by 1911. Here, to his own satisfaction and to that of many other people, he showed that "the wealthy classes [had] increased their share of the national dividend, both actually and relatively," for if 1900 were taken as the base year, profits in 1893 and 1908 were 86.8 and 112.5 respectively, but wages were 90.1 and 101.0; at the same time unemployment had risen from 2.77 percent to 5.63 percent in 1910.[8] Another, less polemical, contemporary writer estimated that real wages had dropped from an index number of 179 in 1900 to 161 ten years later.[9]

Conditions both at home and abroad, then, were causing people to repudiate liberalism. The disturbing element, however, in this quarter-century of rapid change was not so much that liberalism and the Liberal party were breaking up as that the dissolution was accompanied by an outburst of anarchical violence. Parliament itself had

[6] C. Booth, *Life and Labour* (London, 1889); B. S. Rowntree, *Poverty* (London, 1901). These studies have been confirmed by more recent investigators; see Ashworth, p. 251.

[7] E. Halévy, *A History of the English People in the Nineteenth Century*, vol. 6 (London, 1952), p. 276.

[8] This information was included in the edition used here—London, 1913, pp. 50, 111, 116.

[9] G. H. Perris, *The Industrial History of Modern England* (London, 1914), appendix VIc.

been the first to experience this changed climate. The obstructionism of the Parnellites had been the first sustained attack upon the almost divine sanctions which protected late Victorian parliamentary procedure. Since then there had been the Bradlaugh affair and the scenes provoked by Hardie, capped by the performance of Victor Grayson, who had been suspended from the House. Irish developments had provided an excuse for the Conservatives to defy the Liberals by emulating the Irish members themselves and had led to the mood in which Halsbury and the Diehards flourished. Further to poison the atmosphere of parliamentary debate were the "mutiny" at the Curragh and the antics of the suffragettes.

The same anarchical wave characterized the wider public life, and in the period before the war the country was rocked by savage industrial unrest. The figure for days lost through strikes, which had averaged 4.25 million a year, suddenly shot up to well over 10 million in 1911 and to the enormous total of over 40 million in 1912. At the same time feeling was ugly, with battleships being brought into the Mersey to cow the Liverpudlians and Mr. Churchill becoming involved in troop movements which still remain a subject of discussion today.[10] This new militancy had its counterpart in organized politics. Many expressed impatience with the newly founded Labour party and refused to consider it as a viable alternative to the established parties. Although the truth of the Lib-Lab electoral agreement was not known for certain at the time, the dependence of the Labour Party on the Liberals could not be disguised. The coincidence of Labour's first appearance at Westminster and a marked drop in real wages had provided a ground for dissatisfaction with the new party which began to be voiced among its own supporters as early as 1907.[11] The result was a resurgence of more definitely socialist feeling, a youthful rebellion which had begun even before 1906. In 1903 the Socialist Labour party was set up, in 1904 the Socialist Party of Great Britain; in 1907 the Social Democratic Federation turned itself into the Social Democratic party;[12] in 1911 a fresh realignment of

[10] Perris, p. 510; R. V. Sires, "Labour Unrest in England, 1910–14," *Journal of Economic History*, 1955; for a firsthand account of these events, see Lord Askwith, *Industrial Problems and Disputes* (London, 1920).

[11] *New Age*, 6 June 1907 and 5 September 1907. (Subsequent references to this periodical will be abbreviated in this manner: NA 6.6.07 and 5.9.07.)

[12] For a survey of these developments see C. Tsuzuki, *H. M. Hyndman and British Socialism* (Oxford, 1961), pp. 138–64.

old groupings around the violent figure of Victor Grayson gave rise to the British Socialist party.[13]

It was into such a society that the Great War exploded. Its effect could not be other than to intensify the mood of criticism, but at the same time it gave a twist to the direction which this criticism was taking.

The war, both at the front and at home, was increasingly a technician's war, and the centralized apparatus to fight such a war was quickly put together. Those who attempted to cling to laissez-faire principles were few (Sir John Simon, the home secretary, who resigned from the government on the ground that conscription was an unjustifiable interference with liberty, was the most notable example), and in general the public was prepared to give the administrators carte blanche.

Armed with wide powers, the authorities achieved striking success in controlling the economy of a country locked in total war.[14] After a shaky start when the Board of Trade issued a list of maximum prices but refrained from making these compulsory, the various ministries, and above all the Ministry of Munitions under Lloyd George, extended the scope of government control ever wider. It was not simply that the population was made to endure the restrictions inevitable in the course of a modern war, or even that in Carlisle, say, where absenteeism was endangering munition production, the drink trade was brought under state control; the important departure was an outright attack upon the sacred efficacy of supply and demand. In the realm of prices this was substantially achieved by 1915 when the government acquired the power to inspect a firm's books and so arrive at a costing estimate. As the war went on and the government was obliged to go to the source of a process to prevent profiteering, more and more use was made of this control over costing, and an increasing number of firms were turned into government agencies acting upon a commission basis. The best example of this process was in connection with sandbags. Relatively early in the war the effort to control prices led to a sudden swoop on supplies lying at Liverpool and the

---

[13] Ibid., p. 175.

[14] Ashworth, pp. 270, 276; S. J. Hurwitz, *State Intervention in Great Britain, 1914–19* (New York, 1949), pp. 76, 109, 158; E. V. Morgan, *Studies in British Financial Policy, 1914–25* (London, 1952), pp. 36, 39, 48; A. C. Pigou, *Aspects of British Economic History, 1918–25* (London, 1947), pp. 107–15, 122, 127–28.

forced sale of millions of sandbags at tuppence each instead of the expected profiteer rate of sixpence. But naturally this did not solve the problem, for the profit-making area was merely moved back to the earlier stages, and so before the end of 1917 the War Office was buying the whole of the jute crop in Calcutta. This bulk buying was to be seen also in connection with the wool clip from Australia and the Canadian grain crop, and by 1918 the Ministry of Food was responsible for the purchase of 85 percent of Britain's consumption. Of course, control was not confined to prices alone. Factory output was controlled by licence, and the Ministry of Munitions, which controlled some two million workers, had the power of directing employment and of settling rates of pay; in some cases outright subsidies were paid. The railways were brought under a single state authority, with profits pegged to a prewar level. And when the McKenna duties were imposed in 1916, protection had been countenanced.

All in all, it was a monumental tribute to coordinated efficiency, so imposing that in November 1918 it was difficult to face its abandonment, and the naval blockade of Germany did indeed run on under its own impetus. It is also to be noted that the critics of these developments accepted the material triumphs which the state had achieved. The guildsmen and the Church Socialists, for instance, feared the emergence of a too-powerful and stultifying state. The left extremists, in particular the Shop Steward movement, attacked the way in which capitalists rather than workers received the benefits. But these were ethical objections, and no significant voice was raised to question the technical achievements of wartime control, a system of full employment and relative prosperity.

The story of wartime finance, however, was quite otherwise.[15] At the mere onset of war the worldwide lack of confidence subjected the London money market to intolerable strain. The position of the Bank of England was particularly vulnerable, and in effect the bank failed. The run on gold was so serious that for the first time since 1866 the government was obliged to step in to guarantee the bank. On 2 August 1914, the normal Bank Holiday was extended for three days while the printing of Treasury Notes (Bradburys), to be accounted legal tender, was hurriedly undertaken. In the circumstances, of course, no blame

[15] Ashworth, p. 270; U. K. Hicks, *The Finance of British Government, 1920–36* (Oxford, 1938), p. 312; F. W. Hirst, *The Consequences of the War to Great Britain* (London, 1934), pp. 144–67; Morgan, chap. 1, pp. 91–108; Pigou, p. 149.

could be attached to the country's financiers, though it was not so certain that a system which *ex hypothesi* could never satisfy all the creditors at the same time was equally blameless, and on this point many who had previously taken the system for granted must have been made to think.

The later record of the financial authorities during the war was certainly not impressive, unless the ability to make money for one's clients by the use of methods of doubtful honesty can be considered praiseworthy. On the government side there was never an adequate grasp of the advisability of paying for the war as much as possible out of revenue; indeed the earlier war budgets amaze by their halfhearted attempts to tackle what, even on the most optimistic estimate of the duration of the war, was certain to be a pressing problem. The extra tax yield for 1914 was a paltry £ 15 million, and in a full year the income tax was not expected to produce more than £ 65 million. In May 1915, when the Peace by Christmas slogans had been finally stilled by the realities of Loos, no less than £ 865 million was borrowed against an ordinary revenue of £ 267 million. The first serious attempt to deal with the problem of war finance was not taken until September 1915, when Chancellor of the Exchequer McKenna brought in the third war budget, but even then it was only to establish the principle that taxation should be enough to service the debt charge only. In all, only 28 percent of war expenditure was financed out of revenue, and Britain in fact paid a lower rate of tax than she had done over a hundred years earlier against Napoleon. At the end of hostilities, then, Britain, thanks to an insufficiently stringent tax policy, was saddled with a debt charge which amounted to 38.7 percent of the national expenditure against a prewar figure of only 12.3 percent.

Far worse than these allegations of bad management was the accusation that the method of raising the war loans was dishonest or unduly favourable to certain classes. The terms, it was said, were unnecessarily generous; for instance, the 6 percent Exchequer Bonds issued in October 1916 and maturing in February 1920 could be converted at par in any subsequent war loan. More serious was the fact that certain fortunately placed institutions and individuals were able to arrange large future profits at no real cost to themselves. The method was the following: the banks lent the full issue price to those who wished to "buy" a war loan and in order to do this were allowed to borrow the necessary money from the Bank of England at 1 percent less than the Bank Rate; in return the borrowers deposited the loan certificates at the banks as security. Thus the process was essentially one of book entry which netted the adroit a 1 percent return on nonexistent capital at no risk. The way in which war finance was altering the normal pattern of security holding and laying the foundation for future recrimination was shown by the fact that securities in private hands rose from 2.5 percent of the total private property in 1913 to 25 percent in 1925.

The war, then, had exposed the tremendous gulf between the financial and the industrial-commercial spheres and had given the underworld useful material for future attacks. But the war had a second impact perhaps more important than this. From 1914 to 1918 certain developments had taken place which seemed to promise a better world —a world, in fact, fit for heroes. And at the end of the war it did seem as though the transition could be made smoothly and standards could continue to rise. Despite the draconian demobilization which Churchill sanctioned and which demanded the reabsorption into industry of over four million men within a year, and despite an almost indecent jettisoning of controls, which had been completed in 1920, the standard of living continued to improve as industrial activity began to soar. Between May 1919, when the boom got under way, and the summer of 1920, when it came to an end, the wholesale price index had gained no less than 43 percent. The cost of living had of course risen seriously, but it was matched by a rise in wages, a rise which continued longer than the rise in the cost of living index. Moreover, the unskilled workers were benefiting at the expense of the skilled, and in the short run this was contributing to the feeling of optimism.

Within months, however, the boom had turned into a slump. By late 1920 the wholesale price index was 49 percent down from its peak figure, or 30 percent below the level at the beginning of the boom. Wage rates and cost of living indexes both fell 33 percent below the April 1919 figure. For the next two years the country remained in a trough from which it began to emerge only slowly.[16]

Here was a cruel case of hopes being raised only to be dashed. Observers were quick to point out the contradictions and absurdities of the situation. During the war, when an unprecedented number of men had been taken from their jobs and sent to the front to destroy, when the country had been geared to waste rather than to gain, the standards of living had improved to a level never previously enjoyed

[16] Pigou, pp. 161–68.

by the great mass of those workers. Far from the nation as such having suffered, it had gained. There were writers to call attention to the fact, for example, that whereas Britain had begun the war with an annual capacity for eight million tons of steel, she had ended with one of twelve million tons.[17] It was noted that any scheme which the government decided upon could be put into effect with little or no regard for financial considerations, and nobody believed that the war would end because the money had run out. Moreover, about the end of the second decade of the twentieth century people were just beginning to grasp the fact that the Power Age had definitely arrived. Towards the close of the nineteenth century widespread use began to be made of electric power, and this in conjunction with other technical advances, especially the extension of mass production techniques, had opened up new possibilities for man's control over nature. Awareness of these changes had been communicated by such writers as Wells, and in a slightly different manner by Veblen. In America the technologists were groping their way to conclusions which would appear about 1930 and cause, for a while at least, intense excitement. Meanwhile, a most popular hint of what was to come was given by the American Stuart Chase in the book *The Tragedy of Waste*, in which the advantages to be derived from the efficient application of technology were put forward, backed by clearly presented statistics.

The tragedy of waste could also be seen in a slightly different way when summed up in the paradox "Poverty in the midst of plenty." Almost as soon as the war ended, plans were announced to curtail the production of goods. As the years passed, the sickening notices were encountered more and more frequently: of cocoa being allowed to rot, of coffee being used for fuel, of cotton being ploughed under, of oranges being thrown into the sea upon arrival at port, of wheat being burnt, of fish being dumped back into the harbour. The list could be extended by the page. Here were concrete instances of the truth that the Power Age had arrived and yet the parallel truth that man was not to enjoy the blessings. There was to be no security of employment, no satisfactory standard of living for the majority of the people. All the glories of technology and science, all the labours of the past generations, all the sufferings of the war, seemed to have been for nothing.

A full grasp of these questions was limited to a specialist readership

[17] G. C. Allen, *British Industries and Their Organization* (London, 1933), p. 96.

which was understandably restricted. There were, however, two ways in which the same lessons were taught with a brutal insistence which asked for little intellectual mediation. In the first place there was the unemployment problem. Already by 1921 no fewer than 17 percent were unemployed, and while the total fell during the remainder of the 1920s it rose to frightening levels in the aftermath of the Wall Street crash. From February 1931 to July 1935 there were never less than two million people looking for work. The peak was reached in August 1932 with 23 percent unemployed, and the improvement was so slow that in 1938, the last year of peace, 12.9 percent was still the figure. What was, if possible, worse was the existence of pockets of specially hard-hit industries, generally the older, heavier industries of South Wales, Clydeside, and most notorious of all, Jarrow, "the town that was murdered."[18] Here unemployment towered as high as 75 percent, and men grew up who had never known employment. Relief was minimal, and given grudgingly after a prying inquiry into means.

Secondly, the vulgarity and sordidness of wealth and finance were revealed. Perhaps the old absolute wealth had disappeared, but there was a new wealth about which could only flaunt itself.[19] There was also at this time a greater number than usual of financial rogues brought to book. The Farrow's Bank scandal took place in 1921. In the years which followed, the public was further shocked by the Lee Bevan and the Horatio Bottomly cases in 1922, the James White suicide in 1927, the Hatry fraud which was uncovered in 1930, and above all, the Krueger smash. Each of these unsavoury cases showed how fine was the line which divided the acceptable from the unacceptable.[20]

The most striking of such cases, however, was what became known in its English aspect as the Waterlows case.[21] In 1924 Artur Reis, a Portuguese, contacted the London printers, Waterlows, through intermediaries, purporting to have authority from the Portuguese government to have £ 1 million worth of Portuguese notes printed. Waterlows had already filled orders for the Portuguese government and so already had the plates for such an undertaking. Amazingly,

---

[18] This was the title of the book by Ellen Wilkinson, published in London in 1939. See Hicks, p. 182; and I. Svennilson, *Growth and Stagnation in the European Economy* (Geneva, 1954), p. 31.

[19] M. I. Postgate, *The Story of Fabian Socialism* (London, 1961), p. 135.

[20] These examples are conveniently summarized in T. Johnston, *The Financiers and the Nation* (London, 1934). Johnston will be met with later in chapter 9.

[21] M. T. Bloom, *The Man Who Stole Portugal* (London, 1967).

Reis managed to get Waterlows to go through with the arrangement and the "money" was invested in Portuguese and other concerns, incidentally leading to a modest upswing on Keynesian lines. But when the fraud was discovered (the serial numbers were duplicated), a civil suit in England resulted. Waterlows were called upon to make good a loss of £ 1 million. They pleaded, inter alia, that if liable the limit of their liability was the value of the paper involved; after all, if the "money" was not genuine then it could not be worth £ 1 million. Such a defence dramatized spectacularly the whole question of what constituted money and value. Given such a true story it is surprising that a fictitious one should have been so popular: it concerned a forged banknote which spent the day in a round of useful exchange, setting projects on foot and men to work, until its true parentage was accidentally discovered and the last passer committed to prison.

In such an unreal world, it is not surprising that industrial and social relations hardened further into warlike confrontation. If a new wave of amalgamations set in, raising up new giants like Imperial Chemical Industries—amalgamations which in some cases, such as shipping, steel, and cotton, received government backing—or if a new wave of restrictive agreements was entered into, cutting coal production in the midlands, for instance, then there was an equalizing regrouping of trade unions, which took place at the end of the war; at the same time a reorganized Trades Union Congress became available as an aid. The mood of confrontation was seen nakedly when the Triple Alliance and the recently formed Federation of British Industries faced up to each other, and of course even more dramatically when the coal crisis became the centre of a workers-versus-government constitutional battle. The prewar violence had not been dissipated by four years of carnage. The General Strike was preceded by years which ran 1912 close for the number of days' work lost; in 1919 it was 34 million. The Glasgow Riots of 1919, when the Red flag was raised, matched the disturbances in Liverpool in 1911; Lansbury's Poplarism was the equivalent of Parnellism transferred to the streets; Hannington's National Unemployed Workers movement was in its directness a form of syndicalism.

Such developments made the poverty of liberalism patent. Only one element was needed to complete the picture of rottenness. It was possible to argue that government measures had actually *caused* the postwar slumps. And it was easy to believe this. Not only the man in the street but the professional economist accused the government of bringing about disaster by a policy of extreme deflation. At a time when the economy needed a careful helping hand to guide the transition from war to peace, the authorities acted with unjustifiable rigour. As soon as the war came to an end orders were discontinued or even cancelled, leaving some manufacturers in an awkward position. That they recovered so soon was not thanks to the government's policy. During 1919–20 public expenditure was cut by £ 470 million, and in the following year a further £ 116 million was lopped off. In 1920 the return to normalcy was signalled by a budget which called for a surplus of no less than £ 234 million in a total revenue of £ 1,418 million. To raise such an amount the Excess Profits Duty was raised from 40 percent to 60 percent, stamp duty was raised too, and a corporate profit tax introduced. The Bank Rate went up to 6 percent in November 1919 and rose a further 1 percent in April 1920. To cap it all, in 1921 the Geddes committee removed still more money from circulation.

It does not matter that today the postwar economic history is written in a different light. For instance, Pigou claims that monetary deflation did not cause the slump, though it may have intensified it.[22] He points to the nature of the boom, during which the index of commodity prices rose ahead of that of capital goods, the reverse of the normal procedure, indicating that the boom was based on the satisfaction of wants, both real and psychological, which had been bottled up during the war. When this once-and-for-all demand had been satisfied, claims Pigou, the willingness to invest and produce slackened, and a slump inevitably took place. The important thing was that at the time the government's part in causing the slump by a deliberate deflationary policy was widely believed. Perhaps more important is the attitude which lies behind Pigou's writing, for he seems to believe that an artificial boom must and ought to collapse; he is arguing in effect that what was wrong in 1919–20 was not the slump, but the boom. Even at the time, however, there were those willing to maintain that no matter what caused the boom, no matter what its nature, it could be kept going with a little help from the authorities. At bottom they were arguing that boom is the normal condition, not the abnormal one to be paid for later. Reaction to the boom was significant, then, as marking a watershed between those who instinctively believed that full employment and plenty were

[22] Pigou, pp. 184–88; also see Morgan, p. 296.

somehow wrong or at least impossible and those who guessed, rather than knew, that these conditions could be made possible. For those willing to accept the latter view, the government's policy was grossly inept, if not criminally so. When the socialist chancellor, Snowden, showed himself in these matters more orthodox than his predecessors, a large body of opinion realized that not one of the three political parties was prepared to break with the existing creed. Disillusionment was complete.

In the half-century or so between the slump of the 1870s and the return of normalcy after the war, Britain had been through a period of tremendous stress. A prominent feature of the period was the revelation of what could be achieved by planning. Many, recognizing the part which the state had played in directing this exercise in efficiency, were content to see such developments carried further and looked with favour upon a strong state. Some, however, even while fascinated, had their misgivings. The following three chapters will trace such responses. The first will deal with those persons who held that a new kind of economics could avoid the shortcomings of classical liberalism without having recourse to leviathan. The second will deal with a less economically motivated but equally important tradition of antiliberal and antisocialist thought, one which expressed itself primarily in political terms and concentrated upon "liberty." The third will show the fusing of these two criticisms and describe how a brand of socialism, swept up in a growing repudiation of its past, moved towards a new philosophy and incidentally became the intellectual mother of early Social Credit.

chapter two

UNDER-CONSUMPTIONISM IN ENGLAND 1875-1925

When Keynes traced the fortunes of the underworld, he was not interested in its inhabitants for their own sakes. His treatment of underconsumptionism was not a thoroughgoing study, but rather a sidelong glance at a history which was of interest but not essential to his thesis. In choosing J. A. Hobson as his starting point for the modern development of the doctrine, Keynes was no doubt restricting himself to those underconsumptionists with claims to serious consideration, those who presented a more or less systematic account of boom and slump and who used the methods of the professional economists. If so, Keynes was right to ignore the underworld which surrounded Hobson, for although the period was dotted with monetary reformers few of them managed to rise to the level of sustained criticism and suggestion. And yet no study of that particular brand of underworld thinking, Social Credit, can afford to pass over these reformers. While in general their systems were not rewarding in themselves, their shared styles and patterns of thought are significant, and an understanding of them will eventually contribute to a fuller understanding of Social Credit itself. In this chapter such thinking will be traced, but Hobson himself, on whom adequate secondary material exists, will not be mentioned except incidentally.

By the time, about the end of the 1870s, that England had begun to face up to the fact of depression, critical minds had before them the germs of three quite different attacks upon orthodoxy from which to choose. The first was a sober and restrained analysis adopted by the thoroughgoing liberals, men principled enough to wish for general improvement but unwilling to sacrifice the basic beliefs of laissez-faire individualism. In this period the earliest writer on these lines was R. S. Moffat, who had attacked the "parsimony" of Smith, Mill, and the classical school and had hinted at an underconsumptionist critique, but who had not fully developed the implications of his thought. Perhaps for this reason, perhaps owing to the dullness of his writing, Moffat was ignored, and he had no disciples.[1] Thus the examination of this first brand of underconsumption may begin with O. E. Wesslau.

In 1887 Wesslau brought out *Rational Banking versus Bank Monopoly*, and although the writer himself did not use the term *underconsumption*, it was used quite unambiguously in the introduction to characterize the trouble facing Britain. The book was, in fact, an attack upon the Bank Act of 1844. This act had established the principle that one central bank should have the power of issuing notes, and then only against gold backing (the fiduciary issue was insignificantly small), and that the local banks were to be restricted in their note issue to the amounts they were then putting out. The effect of this centralism was that lending policy had to be governed by the criterion of real security and that the old localism, which could judge an individual's credit-worthiness by repute, was no longer operative. English banks, then, were money lenders to the rich. Wesslau contrasted such an undesirable state of affairs with the old Scottish system which had existed from c.1690 to 1845 and which had depended upon local banks enabled to make note issues to borrowers of established reputation. The result had been a period of economic growth which no other European country could match, a period in which very few bank failures had been noted.[2]

What Wesslau was doing was adding his mite to the once powerful but now waning influence of Herbert Spencer, the individualist par excellence. It was not surprising, then, when Wesslau's suggestion was

[1] R. S. Moffat, *The Economy of Consumption* (London, 1878), especially pp. 12–14, 19, 63. He was known to antisocialist circles, however: see *Jus*, 14.1.87 and 11.2.87, and Liberty and Property Defence League, *Annual Report, 1892–93*, bibliography.

[2] O. E. Wesslau, *Rational Banking versus Bank Monopoly* (London, 1887), pp. viii and 60.

taken up by people intent on resisting the creeping socialism which, it was alleged, both political parties were fostering.[3] In 1888 greater publicity for Wesslau's views was secured when A. E. Hake, an experienced writer, published in London *The Unemployment Problem Solved*. Here he accepted Wesslau's theory and applied it to the defeat of socialism, which he recognized as a valid system of wealth production but at the price of slavery. The idea of underconsumption was also accepted and the term used openly. Also insisted upon was the true function of credit, the link between capital and ability, and in this more general way the importance of local banks, about which Wesslau had been so concerned, was urged.[4]

The compatability of Hake and Wesslau bore fruit in the next year, when the Free Trade in Capital League was established with their backing and later when their joint work, *Free Trade in Capital*, was published in London in 1890. In this book the claims of individualism were insisted upon, and it was asserted that the business of economics was not to have anything to do with morals or aesthetics, but quite simply was to expand wealth.[5]

This Spencerian pose meant that Hake and Wesslau were welcomed by the recently reformed Liberty and Property Defence League, an organization explicitly antisocialistic. In turn they showed their agreement with the society's aims by attending the annual dinner.[6] The leading figure in the league was the Hon. Auberon Herbert, third son of the Earl of Carnarvon. Originally he had been a lecturer and Fellow of St. John's, Oxford, but he had resigned these posts in protest against the practice of restricted fellowships and the need to subscribe to the Thirty-nine Articles. At first a Conservative, he had subsequently moved over to the Liberals, representing Nottingham from 1870 to 1874. But a meeting in 1873 with Spencer had pushed him into the extreme Liberal camp. His antistatism made him persona non grata to the Nottingham Liberals, and he broke with political life. In 1887 he began *Jus*, a weekly devoted to what he liked to call "voluntaryism." At first *Jus* was the semiofficial organ of the Liberty and Property Defence League. However, the strength of the reactionary wing of the league very soon became evident, and Herbert resigned

[3] *Jus*, 7.1.87.

[4] A. E. Hake, *The Unemployment Problem Solved* (London [1888]), p. 11.

[5] A. E. Hake and O. E. Wesslau, *Free Trade in Capital* (London, 1890), p. 19.

[6] A short account of the society and its predecessors may be found in *Jus*, 11.2.87. Also see Liberty and Property Defence League, *Annual Report, 1889–90.*

from the organization, which he stigmatized as the "Harrassed Interest Defence League."[7] At the same time *Jus* was closed down.

Herbert is not significant for his views on the currency question. He did repudiate the National Thrift Society, towards which he confessed "a luke warm interest." "A cheese-paring and penurious attitude," he said, "is not always the most economical."[8] But this was the closest he came towards an underconsumptionist statement. He was, however, important in the tradition of economic criticism, and his importance was twofold. Under his wing the principled section of the Individualists was held together, and especially was Wordsworth Donisthorpe given a platform. Secondly, as will be explained later, he formed a bridge by which the Individualist school was linked with another, in many ways different, philosophy.

Donisthorpe, a coal owner and barrister-at-law, was an honest thinker who could command the respect of Shaw for his views. He was no reactionary, and his belief in the need to abolish the peerage and to replace the House of Lords by a House of Notables could not have endeared him to his fellow council members of the Liberty and Property Defence League. Donisthorpe was committed to resisting state interference, as his membership of the league indicated, but at the same time he was realistic enough to recognize that the bland individualism of Spencer, which had assumed that the workless were feckless or worse, was no longer tenable; if the concept of primary poverty had yet to be established by Rowntree and Booth, it did not mean that Donisthorpe was incapable of recognizing Spencer's error. A sincere and principled man, he thought to find a way out of the dilemma in the theory of *labour capitalization*. According to this theory the labourer, too, possessed capital (himself), and when he put himself into an enterprise he was sinking his capital and ought to receive a return upon it. What in fact happened was that the labourer, unable to support himself during the time necessary for a return to be shown, was obliged to forgo his right to interest in return for a weekly sum. However, beginning with the élite of the artisans, the system could be altered, and with the help of workingmen's banks, which might be set up to see them over the awkward times, the workers might come to share in the dividends—not the wages, it is to be noted—of their enterprise. Donisthorpe also accepted that such

[7] See S. H. Harris, *Auberon Herbert* (London, 1943); A. Herbert, *The Voluntaryist Creed* (London, 1908); *Jus*, 30.3.88.

[8] *Jus*, 7.1.87.

a scheme would and should lead to a workers' share in the direction of industry. The practical difficulty was that the capitalization of a worker could not be determined except by trial and error. But at least, Donisthorpe claimed, the scheme was based upon principle, whereas "wagedom" and its derivative, profit sharing, were unprincipled exploitation. The importance of this conception was that it opened the way to seeing capital in a nonmonetary light; now it could be seen as a measure of the real capacity of the person or community to produce in the future. Meanwhile, his scheme retained the liberal framework yet provided the promise of an escape from what were becoming intolerable conditions.[9]

The honesty which Shaw had noted in Donisthorpe was such that Donisthorpe was not afraid of confessing, in the final analysis, to a most thoroughgoing repudiation of principle—of abstract principle, that is. As time went on, the dogmatic Spencerian element faded further into the background. "We must give up all hope of deducing good laws from high general principles," he asserted, "and rest content with those middle principles which originate in expediency and are verified by experience." In enlarging upon this observation he added that "the only available method of discovering the true limits of liberty at any given period is the historic." This acceptance of the organic was qualified by the view that this was to be a negative aim, not a positive principle, and that what was necessary was "to find the Least Common Bond in politics." In holding to this negative conception Donisthorpe had put his finger on the weak spot of the anarchist case, to which in many ways he was attracted—that public opinion may turn out to be a worse tyranny than the state's, so that "a people might utterly abolish and extirpate the state and yet remain steeped to the lips in socialism of the most revolting type."[10]

The application of these principles to his own day was made clear in his book *True Money*, which he published in London in 1905. The point was made that under the present system it was possible to make socially undesirable profits from currency manipulation, though any idea of deliberate conspiracy on the part of the financiers was rejected. Prevention of such frauds would be possible, however, by declaring the mints open to all comers and to all substances—tin, iron, anything.

[9] W. Donisthorpe, *Individualism, A System of Politics* (London, 1889), preface; *Anarchist*, 8.86; *Commonweal*, 3.85; *Jus*, 27.1.88, 17.2.88, 23.3.88.

[10] W. Donisthorpe, "The Limits of Liberty," in T. Mackay, ed., *A Plea for Liberty* (London, 1891), pp. 63–106.

The thesis of *True Money* was the extremely simple one which could be "summarized in one word—freedom. From this would follow the remonetization of silver and the concurrency of silver and gold. The fixed ratio would come about of itself without state aid or political jugglery."[11] As a final broadside against the state, Donisthorpe noted that no private coiner had ever debased the coinage in the way that Henry VIII had done.

Donisthorpe had brought the Individualist school of monetary reform down through the 1890s and into the twentieth century. Here it was taken up by Henry Meulen, a writer who knew of Donisthorpe's ideas through the correspondence columns of papers willing to discuss this subject.[12] Four years after *True Money* appeared, Meulen put his ideas into book form. The debt which he owed to Hake and Wesslau was indicated perhaps by the praise which he gave to the Scottish banking system. From Donisthorpe he might have taken the idea that each producer should be free to "monetize his own personal credit."[13] But it was not until 1917 that he gave extended treatment to his views, a treatment encouraged by the commonsensical realization that "the able and willing worker was calling for bread, but present Anti-Socialism could offer him nothing but a philosophical principle."[14] What emerged from this later book was a brand of underconsumptionism on the Hobson pattern, and nothing further will be said here of Meulen.

The early twentieth century also saw the appearance of Oswald Stoll among the ranks of liberal currency reformers. Stoll was a self-made man who had built up a chain of theatres and who was best known for the Coliseum. In a firsthand way he had experienced the difficulties of raising money to finance his shows, and he, too, was led to the notion that credit belonged of right to the people. When he published his views upon these matters in the middle of the war, the Bank "failure" of August 1914 was fresh in people's minds, and it gave force to his declaration that "British credit, being based upon British property, belongs therefore to the British people and to them it should consequently be given for their own use." In addition, Stoll offered a practical scheme for the better use of the country's productive resources. Any producer should automatically be given credit to

[11] W. Donisthorpe, *True Money* (London, 1905), pp. 35, 65, 76.
[12] Notably in NA, especially 1908–12.
[13] H. Meulen, *Banking and the Social Problem* (London, 1909), pp. 3, 12.
[14] H. Meulen, *Industrial Justice through Banking Reform* (London, 1917), p. xi.

half the value of his existing fixed capital, and upon this loan no interest should be charged; only a 2/6 percent per annum charge on the outstanding balance should be levied to cover operating costs. The scheme was proof, he claimed, against inflation, for although it would add a large sum to the country's currency, it could not add too large an amount. "The justification of currency," he wrote, "is that it is based on value and that there is a need for it. Well, this currency will be based on value, and if no demand for it arises, will not be drawn upon. Should it be drawn upon that will provide the proof that a demand has arisen." Stoll was firmly in the tradition begun by Wesslau, in other words a thoroughgoing liberal. His scheme was directed solely against the "banks which virtually governed even the Government in the practical use of the National Credit." He was impelled by the belief that the aim of any social system was so to arrange matters that the ordinary man "may reasonably do what he likes with his own." On another occasion he proclaimed, "Individualism is the basic fact of mankind." So it was that Stoll, for all his air of novelty, could never bring himself to give up belief in that rock of the liberal system, the gold standard. His grounds for wanting to preserve it were muddled, but on the subject of gold he was unshakeable.[15]

This contradictory halfheartedness was certainly not true of Stoll's contemporary, Arthur Kitson. Kitson was the black sheep of a family prominent in the British iron and steel trade, but much of his formative experience was gained in North America, where he worked with Alexander Graham Bell and also engaged in engineering construction. He was a prolific inventor, with over 500 patents to his credit, of which he presented the most important, the Kitson Light, used in lighthouses the world over, to Trinity House. From his other patents and from his professional undertakings he made a sizable fortune, alleged at one time to be over £ 500,000. Much of this was lost in financial smashes, and of the remainder he spent some £ 20,000 in the cause of monetary reform. It was while in the United States that he came to realize the way in which the monetary system worked to defeat the possibilities of the machine age, and in the 1892 election he turned to agitation in favour of silver as a partial way out of growing crisis. It was in the aftermath of the election he wrote what

[15] See his *More Broadsheets on National Finance* (London, 1922), p. 153; *National Productive Credit* (London, 1933), pp. 20, 35; *The People's Credit* (London, 1916), pp. 154–70, 196; *The Right to Create Credit* (London [1916]), pp. 6–7.

turned out to be the first of a long series of writings on behalf of currency reform.[16]

A Scientific Solution of the Money Question was a thorough reappraisal of the subject. The book showed the influence of Proudhon's and Spencer's lines of thought—the former's in the claim that modern technology should have given far more blessings than in fact had been the case and in the complaint "Instead of labour employing capital . . . we find capital employing labour," the latter's in the statement "Benefits received should be proportional to merits, a theory as essential to a sound economic system . . . as to the development of species." And included in the book, in systematic manner, were the scattered observations of the former Individualists, expressed in a direct and forceful style. "Production is made possible only by consumption which . . . must necessarily precede production. . . . Abstinence never did and never can create wealth, it is absolutely unproductive; . . . a restricted currency means restricted commerce, restricted commerce means restricted production and restricted production means poverty, misery, disease and death." On the basis of such sentiments Kitson reached the conclusion that "credit should be based on the productive capacity of the whole of society." As a step in the right direction he urged that "the medium of exchange must necessarily . . . be free from the control of both governments and individuals," and he rubbed in his belief in the natural goodness of man by declaring that "the idea that governments must necessarily control the currency arises partly from a misconception of their powers and functions and partly from the erroneous but prevalent idea that governments are more trustworthy that their subjects."[17]

If an antigold-standard treatise were the only contribution which Kitson made to monetary reform, he would not deserve that reputation which rightly became his. The practical steps which Kitson took to preach his gospel in England and the significant change of emphasis which his later work took on are points which deserve closer attention. In 1905 he began the Credit Reform League to propagate his and similar views. The league, which became the Banking and Currency Reform League in 1909, had its own outlet in the *Open Review*; Kitson

[16] *National Review*, 1931, p. 685; L. Wise, *Arthur Kitson* (London [1946]); personal communication from T. M. Heron, 1967.

[17] A. Kitson, *A Scientific Solution of the Money Question* (Boston, 1894). The edition used here was the second—Boston, 1895, pp. x, 33, 47, 63, 280, 284, 301, 335.

was the editor and Meulen was the assistant editor. Unfortunately, the *Open Review* had but a short life and did not appear after November 1910, a comment upon the low state of interest in Britain at this time in monetary matters.[18]

Perhaps it was the failure of his *Review*, perhaps a more general disillusionment when as the years went by his ideas failed to take, but the beginnings of a conspiracy theory gradually began to emerge from his writings. The United States panics of 1893 and 1907 were said to have been engineered; before the end of the war he predicted that peace would be used by the conspiracy to initiate a deflationary trend (so adding another successful prophecy to his prewar judgement that in the event of hostilities Britain would go off the gold standard). As might have been expected, this conspiracy could be traced to the Jews. Sometimes the anti-Semitism took the form of anti-Jewish references. At times it took the odd form that if a German-Jewish conspiracy did exist, then credit control would be the ideal way of enslaving the world.[19]

This sourness was a great pity, for at the same time Kitson had developed his earlier ideas to the brink of an underconsumptionist theory which would have provided a solution without the need to call in conspiracy as an explanation. Reemphasizing the communal nature of credit and insisting upon the corollary, "The theory that trade and production can only be properly financed by the *surplus* idle wealth of individuals . . . will have to be scrapped," he advanced the new claim that the insufficiency of currency, the brake upon expansion, was "chronic." Having approved the notions of Stoll on public credit, Kitson underlined his claims by asking why, if war had brought prosperity, peace should not bring Britain "National Wealth in place of National Debt." But this position was as far as Kitson went, and he did not manage to suggest a positive scheme. He knew that his talents were for destructive criticism and for this reason later chose to remain outside all but the most general of the monetary reform groups.[20]

---

[18] Wise, p. 3. The *Open Review* was founded 3.09.

[19] A. Kitson, *A Fraudulent Standard* (London, 1917), pp. 2, 84, 219; idem, *Unemployment* (London, 1921), pp. 7, 12; Wise, p. 4.

[20] Kitson, *A Fraudulent Standard*, pp. 80, 213; idem, *Money Problems* (Stamford, 1920), p. 34; NA 7.10.37.

Kitson was the culmination of the Individualist school, a line of thought increasingly difficult to maintain in the changed conditions of the twentieth century. But meanwhile another line of criticism had been developing, which from uncertain beginnings became an impressive body of underworld thought.

In this instance it is not so easy to understand Keynes's silence. For the fountainhead of this brand of heterodoxy, John Ruskin, was a writer who exercised a great influence upon English thinking in the period immediately before Keynes's own. Perhaps it was the apparent lack of consistency in Ruskin which repelled Keynes, and certainly it is no easy matter to dig out the economic doctrines from the confused mass of ideas and asides. This economic side of Ruskin should not be ignored, however, and especially not in any discussion of Social Credit, for the kind of mind which could proclaim itself at once "Communist, reddest of the red" and "violent Tory of the old school" was, as will emerge in time, by no means uncommon in Social Credit and kindred circles.[21]

Ruskin's interest in social matters was a late development and grew, almost despite himself, from the observations which were essential to his vocation as the champion of art. Ruskin's approach was primarily aesthetic. It was triggered off as much by the realization that in classical terms the tattered Tintorettos he had seen in Venice were worth less than the crude, obscene lithographs sold in Paris, or that the sum just voted for the purchase of a Veronese was less than one season's dress bills, as it was by a disinterested concern to correct the economists.[22] In this he began a tradition of emotional humanitarian criticism which was to run on well into the twentieth century. He never lost this amateur approach, and the lectures which he gave at the Working Men's College called forth no extended examination of economics. But they lost nothing in effectiveness by this omission.

The first hints of his criticisms of the existing order came in 1857 when he braved the orthodox in their citadel and gave the address at Manchester which was later printed as the *Political Economy of Art*. At this stage the dissatisfaction was with a system which could ignore the artistic potentialities of so many people; there was no grasp of the principle which underlay this waste. The way was opened for a new

---

[21] J. Ruskin, *Fors Clavigera* (Orpington, 1896), letter vii, p. 188.

[22] J. Ruskin, *Munera Pulveris* (London, 1872), p. viii; idem, *The Political Economy of Art* (London, 1907), p. 245.

approach to the problem within a year, however, when Ruskin was "unconverted" in a Turin Protestant church from the narrow Evangelicalism in which he had been brought up and when he opened himself to a southern philosophy of enjoyment, not denial. The result was a series of articles which appeared in *Cornhill Magazine* in 1860 until a public outcry forced the editor, Thackeray, to discontinue them; it was these articles which were subsequently published as *Unto This Last*. Other similar works followed, notably *Munera Pulveris*, *Time and Tide*, and *Fors Clavigera*.

Here many fascinating insights were touched upon, though too often they were not developed or defended in any detail. But the theme was clear enough. It was an attack upon the classicists (and especially upon Mill, who was named) for their failure to base their so-called science upon any firm foundation. Their fault was a refusal to recognize the existence of absolute wealth as such, talking about only value or riches. This approach had led them to take as their yardstick the bare accumulation of value, regardless of the ends to which this accumulation was directed. Such an attitude was summed up in what has become a famous condemnation. "Capital . . . is a root, which does not enter into vital function till it produces something else than a root; namely fruit. That fruit will in time again produce roots; and so all living capital issues in reproduction of capital; but capital which produces nothing but capital is only root producing root; bulb issuing in bulb, never in tulip; seed issuing in seed, never in bread. The Political Economy of Europe has hitherto devoted itself wholly to the multiplication . . . of bulbs. It never saw, nor conceived such a thing as a tulip." For Ruskin the definition of economics was simple and completely opposed to the prevailing abstractions; it was "the multiplication of human life at the highest standard," or as he put it still more plainly, "There is no wealth but life."[23]

This was not underconsumption, for that title should be reserved for those systems which hold that slumps or stagnation are caused by blocks to consumption, and not to those which suggest that a more rational pattern of production would solve material problems. But by repudiating the classical overemphasis on the need to produce, Ruskin had shown an incipient underconsumptionism. And the tendency to move in this direction was reinforced by his treatment of other economic matters, notably the currency. He observed, "The use of sub-

[23] J. Ruskin, *Unto This Last* (London, 1907), preface, pp. 164, 184, 190; idem, *Munera Pulveris*, p. 5.

stances of intrinsic value as the materials of a currency is a barbarism," and "The currency of any country consists of every document acknowledging debt which is transferable in the country." He believed, too, that the disadvantage of gold for a currency was that its scarcity made it "opaque, . . . half currency and half commodity." As a better basis for the currency he suggested the use of "several substances instead of one."[24] Like so much else of Ruskin, these observations were unsystematic, but they were again enough to show the broad direction of his thought. The real basis of wealth, as opposed to its financial reflection, was being insisted upon, and while this in itself is not underconsumption, it very frequently accompanies underconsumptionist thought. For once it is recognized that it is the business of the economist to examine wealth and not value and that it is the business of the currency system to measure this wealth and not value, then it follows that the pressing need is an examination of distribution (consumption) and not manufacture (production).

It was a broad tradition, not an exact school, which Ruskin founded, for he cannot be said to have had any disciples in economic matters. It is true that William Smart, Adam Smith Professor of Political Economy at Glasgow University, had been attracted by Ruskin's teaching, becoming first president of the Glasgow Ruskin Club and publishing a book upon him. But this was in his youth and before his professional appointment, and when that came he turned away from Ruskin, though a memory of his influence showed in the eagerness with which he turned to the Austrian economists whose works on marginal utility he translated.[25] And there was, too, C. S. Devas, a Catholic and examiner in economics at the Royal University of Ireland, who contributed an appreciative article on Ruskin to the *Economic Journal* (1898) and mentioned him sympathetically in his book.[26] But Devas, too, was not an uncompromising supporter of Ruskin. Rather, Ruskin's importance was in his beginning a tradition of ethical concern with economics. Among those who took up this tradition were the anarchists. Indeed, at one point there was direct influence, for William Morris, who came very close to being an anarchist, acknowledged himself a disciple of Ruskin.

Oddly enough, however, the main link between the anarchists and

[24] J. Ruskin, *Munera Pulveris,* pp. 18, 66, 71, 74.

[25] W. Smart, *Second Thoughts of an Economist* (London, 1916), pp. xvi, 4; idem, *A Disciple of Plato* (Glasgow, 1883).

[26] C. S. Devas, *Political Economy* (London, 1892).

underconsumption and monetary reform was not so much through Ruskin as through the Liberty and Property Defence League. The connection was provided by Herbert and by Donisthorpe, who, alarmed by the reactionary posture of that body, had begun to consider the anarchist case. Herbert's "voluntaryism" had been close to this position, and he had gone so far as to write that "the society of the remote future will be held together on the principle of absolute philosophic anarchy."[27]

The linkup of the league and anarchism was facilitated by the traditional English distrust of the violent continental anarchism of the deed and by the factional nature of English anarchism, which opened the way for wide divergences of belief. At this period there were three anarchist groupings. The best known, the one which included Kropotkin, Malatesta, and the others of the anarchist élite, was the Freedom group, which revolved round the paper of that name; it stood for anarchism in the traditional sense and defiantly subtitled its weekly *A Journal of Anarchist Socialism* (later changed to *A Journal of Anarchist Communism*). This was to distinguish it from the rival brand of anarchism, that of the Individualist-Anarchists, centred on Henry Seymour and the journal *Anarchist*. The inspiration of the Individualist-Anarchists was Proudhon rather than Bakunin, and close links were maintained with Benjamin Tucker of Boston, the translator of Proudhon and editor of *Liberty*. But it should not be thought that the gulf between the two schools was a wide one. Although *Freedom* scorned the *Anarchist* group as "disciples of Proudhon who . . . accepted the master's views unmodified by the experience of the last thirty years of the labour movement" and castigated their very name as "a round square," they were willing to work together more closely than this language would suggest; indeed, at one time Seymour recanted his individualism and professed communism before lapsing once again, and he and Kropotkin were always friendly. Their journals were open to the advocates of the rival brand of anarchism, and the discussion was generally on an amicable footing, for each was secure in the knowledge that together they represented the pure truth in opposition to the despised Social Democrats, for whom their most bitter invective was reserved. On the fringe hovered the third group, the Socialist League, and its weekly, *Commonweal*, the message of William Morris, who had broken away from his original social

[27] *Jus*, 25.2.87, 26.8.87, 30.3.88.

democracy. When the Socialist League split up, the anarchists in it drifted into the Freedom camp.[28]

As might have been expected, it was the Seymour faction which was most forthcoming in response to the overtures of the Individualists. As one of the early issues of the *Anarchist* acknowledged, "Herbert's views . . . do not differ materially from those advocated by *The Anarchist*." Later, it reprinted Donisthorpe's paper given to the Fabians. The attraction for the anarchists of Donisthorpe's ideas on currency was understandable, for as Seymour pointed out, "Free money kills capitalism [as] no rent kills landlordism and no taxes kill the State." He saw, too, that capitalism treated money as a commodity, subjecting the currency to unnecessary contraction, and that "coinage currency . . . produced an absolute obstruction to trade." Even so, he wrote: "Capital, or accumulated wealth, is not necessarily an evil for Socialists to attack. In an equitable social system the labourer would always be able to produce more than he can consume. The surplus he has a right to; and it is his duty to Society to save. It is the power created and supported by government which prevents everyone producing to the fullest extent of his capacity, and the power to compel one man or one class to labour at the bidding of another man or class by virtue of monopoly, that really is the only evil in our industrial system necessary to be attacked and remedied."[29]

Where the anarchists could not agree with the Individualists was the latter's unwillingness to go to the logical conclusion. Thus when the Individualists set up the Free Trade in Capital League the anarchists countered with the Free Currency League. However, although there was disagreement on this point, the analysis agreed on the hints of underconsumption. As an official publication noted: "Abnormal and congested states of the market, misnamed over-production but which in reality is enforced underconsumption, is due . . . to the power of *money* to command a revenue. . . . It is highly probable that with an adequate currency, the production of wealth would increase a thousand fold . . . it only being necessary . . . to absolutely ensure an effective demand for all the wealth produced." But the solution, like the analysis, was sketchy. Cooperative mutual banks would issue

[28] *Anarchist*, 20.4.86, 12.86, 5.87; *Freedom*, 10.86, 2.87, 2.88, 12.89, 2.20; G. Woodcock, *Anarchism* (Harmondsworth: Penguin, 1963), p. 420.
[29] *Anarchist*, 4.85, 8.86, 1.87, 6.87.

the required currency, and by pegging the issue to production, all danger of inflation would be avoided.[30] There was a tendency for the communist wing to dismiss any talk of currency or monetary reform as unnecessary. As *Freedom* pointed out in reviewing *Money*, a pamphlet by the Australian anarchist D. A. Andrade published in Melbourne in 1887, "Communism will need no currency." But this was anarchism in its "impossibilist" mood. At other times it was prepared to compromise more with the world as it was, recognizing that "the property idea is so deeply rooted in the nature of modern man that at least three generations must come and go before one can hope to transform this fixed idea into something socialistic." Such an acceptance of human nature was, in fact, close to the *Anarchist*'s philosophy, and it was a further reason why even the communist-anarchist should have had links with the Individualists. For it would be wrong to think that this brand of communism postulated a perfect world where all would give of their best without sanctions of a public kind. Even Kropotkin, the saintliest of the anarchists, was insistent upon this point. When citing the examples of practical anarchism which he alleged existed in the Europe of his day, Kropotkin made a point of upholding the value of alternatives in bringing about acceptable service. He noted with satisfaction that "when a railway company, federated with other companies, fails to fill its engagements, when its trains are late and goods lie neglected at the stations, the other companies threaten to cancel the contract, and that threat usually suffices."[31] There was in anarchism no belief in the natural goodness of man. Thus it was not so surprising to find Kropotkin holding views akin to those of Seymour and Wesslau.

It was Kropotkin, in fact, who provided the fullest treatment of communist-anarchist economics, tackled on this pragmatic basis. And in this treatment he added to a nascent underconsumptionism a new emphasis. Having insisted that "overproduction means merely and simply a want of purchasing power amidst the workers," he went on to probe the origin of the fallacy that the cause of crisis was overproduction. More than any other writer so far mentioned, Kropotkin recognized the power of the machine. "Truly we are rich, far richer than we think, rich in what we already possess; richer still in

---

[30] *Free Currency Propaganda Leaflet No. 2* ([London, 1895]); *Freedom*, 8.90; *Revolutionary Review*, 5.89 (edited by Seymour).

[31] *Freedom*, 2.88, 9.90; P. Kropotkin, *Fields, Factories and Workshops* (London, 1909), pp. 31, 34.

the possibilities of production of our actual mechanical outfit; richest of all in what we might win from our soil, from our manufactures, from our science, from technical knowledge were they but applied to bringing about the well-being of all." From this belief Kropotkin was led to conclude that the root fallacy of previous economics had been its refusal to "rise above the hypothesis of a limited and insufficient supply of the necessities of life." What was needed now was a totally new way of looking at economics. "If you open the works of any economist," he wrote, "you will find that he begins with PRODUCTION . . . but it would . . . be quite as logical to begin by considering needs and afterwards to discuss the means of production. . . . But as soon as we look at it from this point of view Political Economy entirely changes its aspect. It ceases to be a simple description of facts and becomes a *science*. We can define it as *The Study of the needs of humanity and the means of satisfying them with the least possible waste of human energy*." As a corollary of this last point Kropotkin repudiated that preoccupation of contemporary Labour politicians, the right to work; far more important for him was the right to well-being.[32]

In all this there was much which would later appear in Social Credit. The parallel is strengthened by further elements of Kropotkin's analysis. Included there was a hint of the argument, associated with J. A. Hobson and implicit in Douglas, that imperialism was the outcome of underconsumption at home. Kropotkin put it thus: "We export the necessary commodities. And we do so because the working men cannot buy with their wages what they have produced, and pay besides the rent and interest to the capitalist and the banker."[33] It was a bold statement of the case, but that such a claim should have been presented without any explanation was not so surprising. For the idea, while not yet generally current, seems to have been an accepted part of anarchist thinking. E. Belfort Bax, a member of the Socialist League, had hinted at such a view as far back as the mid-1880s.[34] And finally Kropotkin added this fascinating observation, which may have signified a grasp of the outline, at least, of Social Credit: "The evil of the present system is therefore not that the surplus value of production goes to the capitalist . . . the surplus value itself is but a consequence of deeper causes. The evil lies *in the possibility of a*

[32] P. Kropotkin, *The Conquest of Bread* (London, 1906), pp. 3–4, 30, 236.
[33] Ibid., p. 243.
[34] In *Commonweal*, 2.85.

surplus value existing instead of a simple surplus not consumed by each generation; for that a surplus value should exist means that men, women and children are compelled by hunger to sell their labour for a small part of what this labour produces, and above all, of what their labour is capable of producing."[35] Unfortunately, this point, like so many others, was not followed up nor elaborated.

The third strand in this pattern of underworld thinking was provided by a body of doctrine the importance of which is only now being established. Positivism had little success as an organized movement in England, despite its wide dissemination there from the 1860s on by influential people, notably Frederic Harrison, who used his journal *Fortnightly Review* to put forward the doctrine. But positivism's influence was extensively felt, if often in an attenuated form, and it has been claimed that it was "the most distinctive intellectual movement . . . between 1860 and 1880."[36] Several groups traced their descent from the original impulse; for instance, the South Place Ethical Institute and the Ethical Church were very much imbued with the spirit of positivism.[37] Hobson himself was one who was connected with the Ethical movement, and Ruskin, despite his attack upon positivism, was close to the doctrine, a fact which Positivists at the time recognized.[38]

Comte's thinking sprang from the fact that he could not give up his allegiance to either of the two ideas which dominated his early life in particular and the whole outlook of his beloved France in general, Catholicism and the Revolution, considered at the time to be diametrically opposed. Not, however, that Comte was a doctrinal Catholic; rather, like that later Frenchman, Maurras, whose Action Française was to receive many a renegade Positivist at the turn of the century, he valued the church for the social benefits which it conferred.[39] The mediaevalism which, as an almost inevitable consequence, ran

[35] Kropotkin, *The Conquest of Bread*, p. 126.
[36] R. Harrison, *Before the Socialists* (London, 1965), p. 251.
[37] W. M. Simon, *European Positivism in the Nineteenth Century* (Ithaca, 1963), p. 230.
[38] J. A. Hobson, *Confessions of an Economic Heretic* (London, 1938), p. 57. He had addressed the Ethical Society on the problem of interest as long ago as 1896; see G. Spiller, *The Ethical Movement in Great Britain* (London, 1934), pp. 17–18. R. Harrison, p. 252; J. T. Fain, *Ruskin and the Economists* (Nashville, 1956), p. 17.
[39] Simon, p. 68.

through Comte's thinking was yet offset by an equally sincere attachment to the Revolution, though again not so much for its own sake, which he considered negative, as for its essential lesson. For Comte these two phenomena were to be reconciled in the motto "Order and Progress": "Order is the condition of all Progress; Progress is always the object of Order." The concept of order was based on the realization that the triumphs of the present were rooted in the past. The statements "Positivism . . . is the slow result of a vast process carried out in separate departments" and "Every Social innovation has its roots in the past" carried with them the corollary that the "positive" included the "organic"; for this reason Aristotle was preferred to Plato.[40] Such an outlook had led the English disciple Harrison to declare, "Every true Positivist is a real Conservative . . . our turn will come to defend the immortal institutions of man against sentimental sophists."[41] When it is remembered that at this time the English Positivists were working closely with the trade unions and with Marx,[42] the paradoxical nature of their commitment becomes plain, and one is reminded of Ruskin; nor was it surprising that Harrison should choose to write a study of Ruskin.[43]

Given such an outlook, the concept of the sovereignty of the people was, for Comte as for Ruskin, an impossible one. "Positivism rejects the metaphysical doctrine of the sovereignty of the people. But it appropriates all that is really sound in the doctrine." In Comte's opinion the soundness applied only when there was some large, fundamental decision to be made—the declaration of war would be an instance—when the people should be consulted; but in all other matters, and above all in the technical aspects of any question, the rulers would have to decide. As a further blow to the principle of the sovereign people, in Comte's view the wrongly identified heirs of the Revolution, he rejected the belief in rights, for "no one has . . . any Right but that of doing his Duty." To round off the attack, liberty and equality were declared to be incompatible.

What part could progress play in a system so circumscribed by order? Progress was no mere bow in the direction of the Revolution, but the very essence of the Comtean scheme; Comte always claimed

[40] A. Comte, *A General View of Positivism*, trans. J. H. Bridges (New York, 1857), pp. 27, 116, 174.

[41] R. Harrison, p. 332.

[42] R. Harrison, p. 269.

[43] F. Harrison, *John Ruskin* (London, 1902).

that his age was superior to any other because it was a "progressive" one. This belief in progress was revealed in the Law of the Three Stages, in which the positivist stage was seen as the crown to the earlier gropings of the theological and metaphysical stages. Positive meant scientific, and so Comte was eager to welcome the discoveries of science and technology and large-scale production. (But like the anarchists, he maintained that this would be compatible with localism; France itself was to be broken up into seventeen units.) But science was not to be seen as a sovereign, autonomous, concept. The Baconian philosophy, which was interpreted as the preference for "how" questions above "why" questions, was taken to be the *method* to be used. At the same time, however, this method was to be put at the service of the heart, for "Heart preponderates over the Intellect."

If the bases of the Comtean synthesis were order and progress, the principle which animated them was "love." More precisely, this principle was identified with "social sympathy." Like the anarchists' conception, this was not a belief in the naturally pure social impulse, for Comte was aware that antisocial impulses existed. He was sufficiently soaked in his Catholicism to go so far as to insist that these evil impulses could not, and should not, be eradicated, but turned into socially acceptable directions. It was for this reason that education played such an important part in the Positivist scheme of things, an education which contained the germ of the recapitulation theory of child development. And it was the dynamic of social sympathy which marked off the Positivists from their rivals, the Marxists. As Comte himself noted, "The chief difference between our own solution and theirs is that we substitute moral agencies for political."[44] It was a hint of the later anarchist-Positivist sympathy.

Because of the relative failure of positivism in England, an examination of more specifically economic elements of the doctrine cannot be extensive. Unless E. Belfort Bax be considered a Positivist,[45] only three Positivists wrote on economics, and even then in no case was the Positivist line made explicit. John Kells Ingram, geometer, poet, and professor of Greek at Trinity College, Dublin, was certainly a Positivist, though he did not avow this allegiance until after he had retired from teaching. John Beattie Crozier, an Ontario physician,

---

[44] Comte, pp. 7, 18, 103, 115, 147–53, 173, 192–95, 401, 420; J. E. McGee, *A Crusade for Humanity* (London, 1931), pp. 11, 27, 37, 50.

[45] R. Harrison, p. 336; Simon, p. 225.

philosophical writer, and historian, long resident in London and a prolific writer, made use of Comtean concepts and accepted some of Comte's conclusions, though he differed on many points. David Syme was an Englishman who made his money and reputation in Australia in the mid-nineteenth century but who published his *Outlines of an Industrial Science* in England. He did not acknowledge positivism, but that he accepted the system shines through his argument.[46]

Of these three writers, Crozier, the least committed of the Positivists, was the most advanced in his critique. The reason was that Crozier was writing some twenty years later than the others and had been influenced by the views of a neo-Positivist current which had taken root in England at the end of the century. This was the sociological thought of Frédéric Le Play, transmitted to Crozier via J. A. Hobson and Victor Branford, whose thought Crozier admired.

Le Play was not directly linked with the Comtean movement. In fact, his attitude towards the Revolution was one of explicit rejection, and it had been the shock produced in him by the events of 1830 which started him on his lifelong examination of society. Like Comte, and especially in tune with Harrisonian conservatism, he wanted to retain the organic truth of the past as the framework of the future. Thus he was led to value highly the family and also the regionalism of former days before the centralizing deadness of Bonapartism blighted France. And yet the foremost mining engineer in France could not be dismissed simply as a reactionary. He was a forward-looking thinker and shared many of the progressive ideas of the Comteans. Early Sociologists were right in placing him alongside Comte.

In the 1890s Le Play's style was taken up by Patrick Geddes and Victor Branford. Geddes was a many-faceted and unorthodox thinker, practical man, and academic. Much influenced by Ruskin, on whom he wrote a book, he had been encouraged to organize a series of sociological conferences at Edinburgh in the summers of the closing years of the century.[47] To these conferences Kropotkin and the anarchist brothers Reclus had been attracted, no doubt by the regionalism of Le Play and by the anticlassicism of Ruskin. From these

[46] McGee, p. 113, n. 2; J. B. Crozier, *History of Intellectual Development*, vol. 3 (London, 1901), pp. 10 ff.; for Syme's positivism see especially chapter 10 of his book (London, 1876), pp. 157–65.

[47] P. Mairet, *Pioneer of Sociology* (London, 1957); P. Geddes, *John Ruskin, Economist* (n.p., 1884).

beginnings had later developed the Sociological Society, founded in 1903. Branford was the organizer behind the venture. A chartered accountant by profession, he too was a man of wide and overlapping interests.[48] These two leaders gave the society a pronounced Le Play tinge (later the headquarters of the society was to be called Le Play House), but the broader Comtean style was never wholly forgotten. The election of Frederic Harrison as president in 1910 was an indication of this background.[49]

Sociological Society thinking before the war on the subject of monetary reform had been evident in scattered observations in the society's journal, the *Sociological Review*. Inevitably the war itself gave a new impetus to these searchings. On 10 December 1914 a conference was held by the society on the subject "The Mobilization of National Credit"; J. A. Hobson was in the chair. From this impulse there resulted a series of pamphlets and books directed towards the inevitable problem of reconstruction, and in this work Geddes and Branford played the dominant role.

The undertaking was introduced by an article in the *Review*. Naturally the starting point was the war. And to the authors, Geddes and Branford, this war was "a war of ideas." The Allies were fighting against the twin ideas of the state based on force, as perfected in Prussia, and of profiteering in business—notions which were closely connected as "aspects of one pervasive tendency" and which had "historically risen together." The situation was a hopeful one, however, since the spirit of self-sacrifice engendered by the war could give rise to a new determination to build a better world. Traces of this renewal had been noticeable before the war began. Three elements could be identified: the first was the regionalism of Le Play; the second was an outlook which saw "the progress of mankind as an unfolding of ideas and ideals . . . a view of life . . . inimical to the Prussian cult of force" (included in this tradition were Comte, de Maistre, and Kropotkin); and finally civism, the movement to turn cities into garden cities. The significance of this article was that it brought out very clearly the style of the authors. They had a tendency to make their points in a shortened form, almost reducing arguments to slogans, and indeed at times drifting into ellipsis. Their own summing up of their outlook as a fusion of "the Hebraic ideal of adjusting city life to the

[48] An obituary appeared in the *Sociological Review*, 1931, pp. 2–14.
[49] His presidential address appeared in the *Sociological Review*, 1910, pp. 97–104.

care and culture of child life and the Hellenic ideal of seeking the Good, the True, the Beautiful, through a citizenship, active and contemplative" was typical of them.[50] In judging their writings allowance should always be made for their style.

The pamphlets themselves contained identical prefaces which echoed the Ruskin-anarchist demand, "For our money economy must be substituted a life economy." The main insistence, however, was on the statement demanding "free use of the public credit for . . . social investments," with the admonition: "But don't pay the tribute called market rate of interest; create the credit against the new social assets. . . . The present unacknowledged use of the public credit by bankers must be recognized and regulated, and being for private profit must be subordinated to the new community uses."[51] As the title, *The Modern Midas*, suggested, the first pamphlet was an attack on the gold bugs and the fact that in the war manpower but not moneypower had been conscripted. The positive proposals were vague. The second pamphlet, *The Bankers' Part in Reconstruction*, was little better in this respect, but it was significant in that the attack on finance included adverse references to cosmopolitan and Jewish elements. The significance lies in the fact that the people and the society using them had no anti-Semitic or racial feeling at all; the work of Geddes in designing the buildings for the Hebrew University and his sterling work on behalf of India are sufficient testimony of this.[52]

For positive measures it was necessary to wait for the appearance of the Geddes-Branford publication *Our Social Inheritance*, the economic chapters of which had been submitted to Hobson before publication. Now that the lessons of the war had been noted, it was possible to conclude, "If [the credit system], this master piece of the industrial era, is so well adapted to the kakotopian finance of war may it not now be adapted to the eutopian finance of a militant peace?" For it could not be denied that "this war, by filling labour's pockets with 'Bradburys' brought the people within sight of their full social inheritance from the Industrial Revolution." The only step which was necessary to put the community on the right lines for a splendid new advance was the realization, "In goods and services reside the real and true

---

[50] "The Making of the Future," *Sociological Review*, 1917.

[51] Sociological Society, *Papers for the Present, 1, The Modern Midas* (London [1918]), p. iii.

[52] Sociological Society, *The Bankers' Part in Reconstruction* (London, 1918), p. 11. Geddes was appointed to the International Zionist Committee in 1919; see *Sociological Review*, 1919, 1925. Also Mairet, *Pioneer of Sociology*.

assets of the banking business and its subsidiary trades. It is this flow of energies which the Cheque fund registers and measures."[53] For critics who were not primarily economists this was a striking position to have reached.

So stood underconsumptionist thinking on the eve of Social Credit. The first point to emerge from this examination of the underworld is the relative poverty of the tradition and its ineffectualness. It could not be said that any school existed, and even those who looked ultimately to Proudhon did not write from the strength of the "master." Despite Kitson's background, the lessons of the well-developed United States tradition were not discussed or applied. Almost all the critics were content to attack upon isolated points, accepting too much of the remainder on trust; only Kitson can be freed from this charge, and then only partially. Even more crucial was the failure to face up to the potentialities of the machine age, and even when these were recognized as, for instance, by Kitson, Kropotkin, and the Sociologists, there was too great a tendency to take refuge in vague utopias. It is a fair comment upon the weakness of the English monetary reform tradition that the only periodical established specifically for this end collapsed after little more than a year. Moreover, during this period, with the exception of Stoll's restricted scheme, only one concrete plan of reform was advanced, and that from a source which had nothing to do with the tradition itself.

At the very end of the war proposals of a radical kind were put forward in a pamphlet entitled *Scheme for a State Bonus*. Seizing upon the ever-increasing acceptance of welfare payments, the authors called for "a frank recognition that there is an element of communism underlying many of our social arrangements."[54] It was suggested, therefore, that everybody be eligible for an inalienable dole sufficient to maintain bare existence, to be provided from a fund to which all would contribute in proportion to capability. But despite the existence of a State Bonus League to foster the plan, the proposal sank almost without trace. It was canvassed at Labour party conferences, but it was so out of touch with contemporary Labour thinking that it could be shuffled away with little trouble. Within a few years the league was but a memory and the field was wide open for Social Credit.

But, however ineffectual, this threefold tradition of monetary reform does have a significance for an understanding of Social Credit.

[53] P. Geddes and V. Branford, *Our Social Inheritance* (London, 1919), p. xxvii, pp. 100–02.
[54] E. M. and D. Milner, *Scheme for a State Bonus* (n.p., 1918), pp. 5–10.

For the three critiques were not wholly self-contained; as has been seen, they overlapped. It will help the analysis to draw out some of the common elements in this background and to distinguish those with a future from those which were out of date.

One begins by noting the close connection of the Individualist and anarchist critiques, especially Herbert's belief that "the society of the remote future will be held together on the principle of absolute philosophical anarchy."[55] It may, in fact, be objected that any line of division between them was artificial. However, this was not how the participants felt; when Herbert and Donisthorpe showed their willingness to treat with the anarchists, the Liberty and Property Defence League was deeply affronted; Seymour and his allies were conspicuously absent from the league functions and expressly set up the Free Capital League in opposition. So fundamentally different was the thinking of the two schools that even the individualist wing of the anarchists was far removed from the true Individualists. These latter, as befitted the logical inheritors of the liberal tradition, placed their faith in the value of competition, that is, competition in the sense of individual competing against individual for sales, ultimately for wealth. The anarchists, however, began from a position instinctively organic, and when Kropotkin put his faith in competition he meant something quite different; he meant competition as to excellence of product or service. It was a distinction to be made much of by subsequent critics of liberalism.

There was a further difference between these two schools, a corollary of the first. The Individualists were satisfied with a call for the easing of credit, for the granting of further benefits to those who already had something, for help to *producers*. This orientation came out very clearly in the case of Stoll. The anarchists, on the other hand, always saw man in his social aspect, and hence demanded not producer credit, but *consumer* credit in some form or other. In this they more nearly represented the organization of the future. At a time when industry was swinging away from the small scale to the large, when individual buyers and sellers were being replaced by groups, when industrial federations and labouring unions were increasingly dividing up the control of economic life, the producer orientation was bound to succumb to the consumer. The progressive bankruptcy of the Individualist school was striking. Hake and Wesslau showed every sign of being content with their position. But Herbert had to throw

[55] *Jus*, 30.3.88.

over his former allies; Donisthorpe became isolated; Meulen drifted closer and closer to the anarchist camp, so much so that his last book was entitled *Individualist Anarchism*;[56] and Hobson moved from his original liberalism towards the Independent Labour party. But the most interesting conversion was that of Kitson.

Under the impact of the war Kitson jettisoned his liberal belief in the natural goodness of mankind and in free trade. He began to remember his experiences as "one of four men who bought under the hammer an entire railway system which had been previously ruined by a financial group to prevent competition with the system they owned," but now he saw his action in a different light. In his repudiation of liberalism he upbraided Britain for her "unenlightened, selfish, individualistic philosophy." In 1910 a Liberal candidate, he was in 1918 a National party candidate. Significantly, he began to express the belief, towards the end of the war, that "Ruskin was one of the greatest economic writers that this country has produced" and, slightly later, that Kropotkin would repay study.[57] At a time when no one resurrected Moffat but an increasing number appealed to Ruskin, poor Stoll had all the air of a dinosaur.

The Positivists were evidently in the anarchist tradition rather than the Individualist; indeed, with the Positivists the social element went so far as to become caught up in the organic. But there was also a deeper identity between them, which again serves to point up the contrast between these two schools and the Individualists. Anarchists and Positivists united in their claim that economics should be subordinate to other aspects of life. The Individualists, by treating economics without reference to the rest of living, had implicitly stated that the good life flowed naturally from an efficient system of production and exchange. Release man economically, they claimed, and man is released spiritually too; Hake and Wesslau, of course, had made this belief explicit. Ruskin had denied such a view repeatedly, above all in the "tulip" quotation given above (page 27). In this tradition Ingram could urge that "a separate economic science is, strictly speaking, an impossibility" and Syme that "Ethics, Sociology and Industrial Science are not separate and independent, but inseparable and interdependent sciences, each being necessary to the other, and

[56] H. Meulen, *Individualist Anarchism* (Glasgow, 1949), and his articles in *Freedom*, 1931.
[57] Kitson, *A Fraudulent Standard*, pp. xi, 22; *Money Problems*, p. 11; *Trade Fallacies* (London, 1917), p. viii; *Unemployment*, p. 87.

forming a part of one whole Science of Man."[58] The "total" claims of the Sociological Society were even more pronounced and were the basis of the Geddes-Branford manifesto already quoted. The anarchists were never so outspoken on this point, but it ran clearly through Kropotkin's works, especially in *The Conquest of Bread*: "Might it not be that production, having lost sight of the needs of man, has strayed into an absolutely wrong direction . . . ?"[59] Even the erstwhile Individualist Kitson came round to a belief in the unity of science: "I cannot imagine one branch of human knowledge in its development deliberately contradicting another branch."[60]

If on these points the anarchists and Positivists formed a bloc against the Individualists, there was one point on which all three agreed. All three felt the need for some absolute standard by which social action might be judged. .

Ruskin's "There is no wealth but life" was a tremendous emotional insistence upon an absolute standard, and it was basically this which led almost all underconsumptionists, at some time or other, to look up to him. But on a practical level such a statement had its limitation, and indeed this lack of contact with the world as it was had been responsible for causing Smart to break his allegiance. Some sought to bring the concept down to earth by reintroducing the idea of natural law. This starting point had been the crux of the Spencerian position, and traces of it could be found in the early Kitsonian system. One Individualist-Anarchist noted his agreement with the Spencerian faith "in the superiority of Natural over Human Law," and Seymour himself proclaimed that "Nature . . . is a complete expression of Anarchy."[61] The true anarchists shared this belief, for Kropotkin's *Mutual Aid,* published in London in 1902, was also a claim that human law was natural law. But this form of the absolute was in one way a regression from the Ruskinian position. Ruskin had at least emphasized a concrete, not an abstract, test, and in this connection Meulen's complaint, that anti-Socialist writers were out of touch with reality, was telling. Accordingly, the idea of natural law, though never rejected, was replaced by other formulations.

A redefining of value was an avenue which many decided to

[58] J. K. Ingram, *A History of Political Economy* (London, 1907), p. 199; D. Syme, *Outlines of an Industrial Science* (London, 1876), p. 175.

[59] Kropotkin, *The Conquest of Bread*, p. 240.

[60] Kitson, *Trade Fallacies*, p. ix.

[61] *Anarchist*, 1.87; *Freedom*, 8.90.

explore. J. Armsden, an Individualist-Anarchist, devoted an entire study to its determination, contrasting Proudhon favourably with Marx in this respect.[62] Another anarchist, D. A. Andrade, fell back upon that old standby, the labour note.[63] Kitson's preferred solution, one shared with Donisthorpe, was a price index to replace the fluctuating gold standard.[64] Kropotkin implied, by the attention which he gave to agriculture and basic production, that once this absolute need had been provided for, people could be left to arrange their luxuries any way they pleased. And while Le Play did not suggest any absolute, his Sociological Society descendants praised his "search for a factual basis of economic observation."[65] But the most important method of drawing attention to an absolute standard was by stressing the distinction between real and nominal capital, real and financial credit. This approach was central to Ruskin, to Hobson, and to the Sociological Society. Even Stoll had grasped the notion that capital was real only when it reflected productive capacity which consumers wished to set in motion.

There seems to be a contradiction here. A world of totality should be one inherently hostile to absolutes. And the seeming contradiction is heightened when it is noted that the system with which the underworld was in conflict, liberalism, was a relative world, in which reigned the most tyrannous absolute of all—gold. But the contradiction is more apparent than real—a paradox, in fact. It is only a relative system which needs an artificial standard endowed with absolute significance, and only a system containing an absolute standard can tolerate relativism in other spheres. For a true absolute can open the way to a truly total world, confident that meaning can never be lost while orientation, against the background of that absolute, remains possible. And it was such a structuring which the underworld wanted. Interestingly enough, Comte had foreshadowed this situation when he noted, "Positivism, by rejecting the absolute, and yet not introducing the arbitrary, represents Order in a totally new light, and adapts it to our progressive civilization."[66] As will be seen, this problem was to be as crucial to Social Credit as it was to the wider context of the modern period itself.

[62] J. Armsden, *Value* (London, 1892).
[63] D. A. Andrade, *An Anarchist Plan of Campaign* (Melbourne [1888]).
[64] Donisthorpe, *True Money*, p. 5; for Kitson see NA 13.9.23.
[65] P. Geddes and V. Branford, *The Coming Polity* (London, 1919), p. 184.
[66] Comte, p. 115.

chapter three

DISTRIBUTISM

The last chapter surveyed the nature and extent of an attack on liberalism which was economic. In this chapter the attack on the more political front will be considered, an attack which went under the name of *distributism*. At first sight, however, it must appear strange, if not impossible, for any connection to have existed between this doctrine and Social Credit, for the gulf between the engineer's age of plenty and the neomediaevalism associated with the Distributists seems too wide to be bridged. But while the solutions which each school advocated may have been very different (in the popular estimation the one pointing forward, the other backward) there was a great deal in common in their points of departure, and both shared many of the same general hopes and fears.

To begin with, links between the two critiques were indicated by the overlap of adherents. A leading Social Crediter, M. B. Reckitt, was a member of the Distributist League executive; Philip Mairet, the compiler of the *Douglas Manual* and another leading Social Crediter, had contacts with the Distributists through the Arts and Crafts movement; Geoffrey Davies, a member of the Social Credit intellectual circle, came to Social Credit from distributism, as did the Catholic priest, Father F. H. Drinkwater.[1] And as the years passed, both Social Crediters and Distributists began to acknowledge the element of truth which the other contained. Hilaire Belloc, the coleader of the Distributists, allowed, "The partial objection which I and some others who think like me offer to the full policy of socializing credit for consumption is not an economic attitude but a moral and political one."[2] On his side Douglas acknowledged that the "Distributists, in common with the Catholic Church, were fundamentally right in

---

[1] For these and other facts on distributism I am most grateful to M. B. Reckitt and P. Mairet, who communicated to me their personal knowledge of the movement.

[2] NEW 1.11.34, 28.6.34.

recognizing stable property tenure as essential to liberty."[3] Indeed Douglas's attitudes probably owed more to Belloc than he would have liked to admit, and his frequent use of Bellocian terms of abuse would indicate this; a later Social Credit publication, closely connected with Douglas, chose to serialize a Belloc book.[4]

In the growth of distributism, three immediate sources may be identified. The earliest in time, and easily the most interesting, was that which flowed from the writings of Arthur James Penty. Maurice Reckitt, a close friend of Penty, has described the different phases of Penty's outlook as follows: "Penty's method was to discover an evil and attribute to it every social disaster he could think of at the moment. . . . Machinery, the sub-division of labour, Roman Law, Social Credit, Free Trade, and finally and more conventionally, Communism, were successive objects of his castigation."[5] And indeed Penty did hit out violently against these "evils." Yet the summary is unfair to Penty, suggesting as it does a weathercock attitude, whereas the truth was that to Penty the evils were but aspects of a single general malaise, which, be it admitted, he never completely identified, but which he sensed well enough. Not that his inability to show every step of the argument bothered Penty. "Feeling comes nearer to truth than logic," he had written in his first book. But then Penty's thinking was that of a practical man, academically untrained, who had felt obliged to turn to social considerations only when disillusioned. The way in which he came to writing is important.[6]

Penty, born in 1875, had entered his father's drawing office at the age of thirteen and had been trained as an architect. By 1897, greatly influenced by Ruskin and Morris, he was calling himself a socialist, and in the following year, he joined the York Fabians and the Independent Labour party. In 1902, he moved to London, where he at first felt successful. After a while, however, his designs began to be

[3] *Fig Tree*, 6.38.

[4] *Social Credit*, 13.11.36, 11.12.36 ff.

[5] M. B. Reckitt, *As It Happened* (London, 1940), p. 116.

[6] Details of Penty's life may be found in *American Review* 3–4.37 and in E. J. Kiernan, *Arthur J. Penty: His Contribution to Social Thought* (Washington, D.C., 1941). Kiernan was more interested in discussing the validity of Penty's thought on the Just Price from a Roman Catholic standpoint than in placing him in his wider context. There exists a study by K. Munkes, *Arthur Penty und der Nationalsozialismus* (n.p., 1937), a thesis done at Bonn. It contains some biographical material but is vitiated by the attempt to show parallels with the life of Hitler.

passed over. He did not make too much of this until he experienced such an example of tastelessness that he felt compelled to reexamine his system of artistic belief. The Fabian Society had organized a competition for the design of the proposed new London School of Economics buildings. Penty discussed the competition with E. R. Pease, the Fabian secretary, and when he asked on what grounds it was proposed to judge the entries, was appalled to hear that Pease, in a travesty of Fabianism and in all seriousness, intended to measure the total room area in each design and award the prize to whichever entry packed the most room space into the given area. Penty may not have broken formally with the Fabians until 1916, but spiritually the break must have taken place at this point.

In so reacting, Penty's point of departure was the necessity of protecting the artist-craftsman. Inevitably this concern led him to repudiate capitalism, a system whose driving force, profit, confused commercialism and competition. Here was a distinction vital to Penty. "Commercialism," he noted, "means the control of industry by the financier (as opposed to the master craftsman) while competition means the rivalry of producers." But at the same time his analysis also meant a repudiation of the prevailing socialist alternatives, especially Fabianism. To Penty, Fabianism was a variant of collectivism, a doctrine whose "great political fallacy . . . was the assumption that government should be conducted solely in the interests of Man in his capacity as consumer." Since artistic endeavour was always a feature of production, but less frequently so of consumption, Penty felt that the Fabian solution missed the point.

Capitalism and collectivism alike repudiated, there remained the remedy of mediaevalism. In that system the otherworldly ordering of society prevented the emergence of the profit motive. Furthermore, the economic system, controlled by the all-embracing guilds, which were associations of producers, allowed man to compete only in terms of excellence. This framework thereby prevented exploitation of the consumer and so at one stroke cut the ground from under the collectivist argument.

Once committed to mediaevalism, Penty found himself fully at home there, even to the extent of emphasizing and defending those other facets of mediaevalism not so essential to an aesthetic study. Thus he advocated a return-to-the-land policy, quoting with approval Kropotkin's *Fields, Factories and Workshops*, in which the anarchist showed the possibilities of intensive agriculture. The local character of mediaevalism Penty accepted too; and of the Renaissance, he could write, "It would not be too much to say that it failed because its ideas were international." Such localism, and the suggestion made earlier that the financier was the enemy of the craftsman, combined to produce conclusions startling to Edwardian complacency. "The capital we account for in the columns of the ledger is indeed only of a very theoretical character . . . our system of finance . . . not studying things, but only the profit and loss account of them, fails to distinguish between what are assets and what are liabilities. A tramway is a liability because it is not one of the ultimate needs of human society but an artificial one arising through the abnormal growth of big towns and cross distribution."[7]

These ideas appeared in a book published in 1906 under the title *The Restoration of the Gild System*. It was a slight book of a hundred pages and the ideas could not be developed adequately but only hinted at, and in this form could not be expected to gain many adherents. It was only on the eve of the war, when Guild Socialist ideas, which Penty had helped to inspire, became a viable alternative to collectivism, that Penty again began to develop his views.

Two notions came to preoccupy him. His financial views began to develop along underconsumptionist lines, but with a slant of their own. Accepting that Germany had been forced into war because she had lacked an outlet for her overproduction, he called for an end to the senseless reinvestment in capital resources. He advocated the mediaeval solution, the spending of surplus wealth on art. "Building," he wrote, "should be looked upon as a means of spending money, not as an investment." Secondly, Penty extended the attack upon the Renaissance. One target was its outcome, puritanism, which he characterized as "hard and mechanical, devoid alike of any love of beauty or of human sympathy." This was not too surprising; what did appear odd was the simultaneous claim that the Renaissance had also been responsible for the Rousseauesque notion of the naturally good man. Applying this insight to the politics of the day led to the conclusion that "the modern parliamentary system [is] the practical expression of the doctrine of the natural perfection of mankind." Naturally Penty preferred the guild system, the "political expression of the doctrine of original sin."

[7] A. J. Penty, *The Restoration of the Gild System* (London: Swan Sonnenschein & Co., 1906), p. 27.

Armed with a profound belief in the certainty of original sin and of the evil of machinery, Penty was able to identify and castigate, long before technology was in the public eye, what he called the Leisure State, that is, a state of society where work was considered as something to be reduced to a minimum. He warned that "the Leisure State in practice would turn out to be the State of Boredom." Although these notions were never defined or explained, it is clear what Penty had in mind; he came nearest to carrying conviction, perhaps, when he stated that "the pursuit of pleasure defeats its own purpose."

Bearing in mind Reckitt's summing up of Penty, it is perhaps understandable that Penty passed through a bewildering variety of political allegiances. Guild socialism and Tory democracy were tried before he turned to distributism. Then, however, he worried about its residual laissez-faire, and the closest he came to accepting that doctrine was an anguished series entitled "Am I a Distributist?" His last outlook showed him all but in the fascist camp, though he recoiled from the totalitarian aspects of that creed. His position was, in fact, that the Italian syndicates were the best examples of an industrial democracy which could be hoped for at that time.[8]

This kind of philosophy was too uncompromising to attract many, and there was never a Penty school. He did, however, exert some influence over a few thinkers. For many whom he impressed but did not convert, a natural home was distributism.

Another who was a channel to that philosophy was Montague Fordham, himself influenced by Penty. Fordham was in some ways the most genuine of the Distributists. Although a Senior Wrangler of Cambridge and later a member of the bar, he retained his intimate links with the countryside of his youth and in the early years of the twentieth century was a pioneer in the founding of the Land Club Union, later the Rural Reconstruction Association. What gave him his standing as a spokesman for agriculture was the part he had played after the war in helping to reconstruct the devastated areas of Russia recently annexed by Poland. There he had been brought into contact with a peasantry which still believed in peasant ways, and fortified by this experience, he returned to write his main book, *The Rebuilding of Rural England*.

[8] These views may be found in the following of Penty's writings, all published in London: *Old Worlds for New*, 1917; *Guilds and the Social Crisis*, 1919; *A Guildsman's Interpretation of History*, 1920; *Agriculture and the Unemployed*, 1925; *Means and Ends*, 1932; *Tradition and Modernism in Politics*, 1937; *Distributism: A Manifesto*, 1937; *G.K.'s Weekly*, 22.5.26.

What had impressed Fordham in Poland was the realism of the peasants, which he contrasted with the distorted outlook of England, where "a field of corn is not food . . . it is an item in an account." He was convinced that "what we want . . . is to get rid of theories and come down to facts and common sense and to a simple outlook." This, he was convinced, meant a return to the mediaeval outlook. In the Middle Ages the pernicious doctrines of Adam Smith did not hold sway, and the middleman was kept in check by the law so that the "Jew higglers" were not allowed to destroy the security of the small man. With such inspiration Fordham suggested ways by which prosperity could be returned to the land. The first necessity was fixed or just prices; the second was control of the middleman. Thirdly, each industry should be controlled by those employed in it, a point indicative of Fordham's links with Penty and the National Guilds movement. Finally, the surplus wealth of any community was to be used for communal amusements, building, and so on, and here perhaps Penty's ideas on overproduction may be detected.

Fordham knew that such a programme stood no chance of success unless the money was forthcoming to repair the damage done to the countryside since the 1870s. And by the 1920s Fordham was convinced that he had the solution to the money problem. Recalling the practice of his Quaker banking ancestors who, in the days of the local bank, had been accustomed to giving their trusted customers credit on the strength of their word, he concluded, "The true source of a nation's credit is . . . not gold or silver but the accumulated wealth and future productive power of the nation controlled by the State as represented by the Treasury." Once control of this credit was taken from private hands and placed where it belonged, all would be well, for the countryside would get its fair share of a vastly increased amount of credit. The source of these ideas on credit would seem to have been Branford's *The Bankers' Part in Reconstruction*, for this work was referred to in *The Rebuilding of Rural England*.[9]

The two streams, the aesthetic and the rural, flowed naturally into the mainstream of distributism. To see how this could be so, when the initial and main interest of that school was with liberty, it is necessary to examine the writings of the Chestertons and of Belloc.

[9] Fordham's views may be seen in his *Mother Earth*, 1908; *The Rebuilding of Rural England*, 1924; *Christianity and the Countryside*, 1938 (all published in London). See, too, *American Review*, 4.37 and *New Order*, 10.37.

Cecil Chesterton, the first into the field, was a polemicist, not a theorist. Indeed, he was so interested in the immediate issues of the day that he never seemed to have probed at all adequately his own political philosophy. He himself suspected his Tory radicalism and embraced socialism under the impression that such a creed would be an antidote to the atomizing individualism of liberalism. Had he not died in 1919 as a result of the war, he might have followed his conversion to Catholicism by a repudiation of socialism. The first fruit of his antiwhiggism was his book, *Party and People*, which appeared in 1910 and made use of the thesis that Graham Wallas had put forward, that politics was not the intellectual matter it pretended to be but a sham which took advantage of the alogical element in man. Chesterton noted that many people gave allegiance to the Conservatives or the Liberals for much the same reasons that they took sides in the Oxford-Cambridge boat race—it was the done thing, and enjoyment could be got out of it—and went on to show how the people were being duped. But Chesterton, while a good polemicist, was not capable of sustaining the attack to the length of a book. *Party and People* was a poorly organized piece of work in which free trade and a citizen army to defend France and civilization against Germany somehow became involved.

The book was soon eclipsed when, in the following year, Chesterton collaborated with Belloc. Belloc, whose Catholicism made him recoil from the orthodox whig interpretation of post-1688 history, was himself a disillusioned Liberal member of Parliament. This background, together with outstanding literary skills, he brought to the help of Chesterton, and the outcome was *The Party System*. The same starting point, the boat race, was used, and the development was along the same lines. But the detail was sharper and the targets more clearly defined. The recently failed Liberal-Conservative conference on the Lords was seized upon to confirm the earlier interpretation of Chesterton, that it was all a fraud upon the public. In the Belloc-Chesterton version, "the Conference did not fail. It did exactly what it was intended to do. It saved for the moment the life of the moribund Party System," because the agitation over the Lords was deliberately designed to take attention away from incompetence in the Commons. That Parliament was now a façade was indicated by comparing the last forty-year period with the similar period immediately before it: from 1830 to 1870, ministries fell following adverse votes in the Commons no less than nine times; for the next forty-year period, to

1910, this had happened but once. The following explanation was given for this state of affairs: "Power has passed to a political committee for which no official name exists (for it works in secret) but which may be roughly called 'the Front Benches'." A detailed description followed of the family ties which bound the two Front Benches together.

Thus was the negative aspect of distributism established, a claim that the trend of thought over the last two centuries had culminated in a deliberate, conspiratorial, and cynical attack upon the liberty of the people. But what of the positive side? The earlier Chesterton, the socialist, had typically put his faith in changes in the machinery of politics—for instance, in the initiative, in the referendum, in state payment of election expenses. But as Belloc became more involved this emphasis weakened, and when, soon afterwards, Belloc brought out his own book, *The Servile State*, the completeness of the volte-face was revealed.

In this little book Belloc, whose sympathies with the broad aims of socialism were patent, as was his readiness to praise the sincerity of socialists, argued the case against socialism in an entirely new and striking way. His objection was that the attempt to introduce socialism, given the assumption of the day, was bound to lead to something neither intended nor wanted by the socialists. Since the Labour party had not the courage to confiscate the capitalists' possessions, a policy of purchase would have to be used. This, however, would give the capitalist the added security of the state in place of a perhaps vulnerable company one, and it could only strengthen capitalist power. At the same time the working class's position was being improved in the wrong way. The workers were not being offered a position where they would be free to make equitable bargains; rather they were being offered security in the place of freedom. And what was even worse, legislation was using the capitalists as watchdogs to ensure that the workers had this security—a return to paternalism, in fact. As the first step in this direction Belloc cited the Employer's Liability Acts, which put responsibility upon an employer *qua* employer in relation to an employee *qua* employee and not upon man as man towards man as man. The mining legislation was also on these lines of guaranteeing too much security and not enough dignity. In this respect there was, above all, the National Insurance Bill, which to Belloc was a blatant example of class distinction, where employers and employees contributed at different rates and where—supreme indignity, though for reasons the opposite of the duchess's—the employers were responsible for affixing the stamps. What was happening was that by offering palliatives, the employing classes were freezing the relations of employers and employees forever and removing the possibility of a working-class child's climbing into the ranks of the middle and upper classes.

The appearance of *The Servile State* marked not only a hardening of Belloc's opposition to socialism but also the recognition that his thoughts were turning to a means wholly at odds with the prevailing conceptions. Completely gone was the concentration upon reforming the machinery of politics. Instead, predictably enough perhaps, a return to the inspiration of the Middle Ages was advocated. Belloc argued for this with an assurance made easier by the use of rigid alternatives. Capitalism would have to be modified; that much was conceded by the great mass of competent opinion. Only three possible schemes could take its place: slavery, socialism, or property. Slavery was immediately placed out of court on the ground that it ran so counter to the traditions of Western Europe that no sane man could be found to support it. Socialism he had rejected already, since the attempt to introduce socialism in a country solidly capitalist at heart produced a third thing, servility, which had all the marks of slavery. Property was thus the only viable alternative. This could be of two kinds, and two kinds only, if the gross inequalities characteristic of capitalism were not to reappear: it could be vested in the many or in none. And since the latter meant in effect the state, the evils of socialism returned once more. The acceptable solution, then, was to vest property in the many (distributism), which would mirror the Middle Ages, when widely held peasant property was the distinctive form of landholding.

Belloc's gifts were not those of a systematic constructor, but rather those of a gifted intuitive critic. It cannot be maintained that in *The Servile State* distributism received an adequate presentation. Even the founding of the Rota Club at Oxford just before the war (the inspiration was the philosophy of James Harrington) and the publishing of its sole product, *The Real Democracy*, helped little.[10] A few measures designed to encourage widespread landholding were included, it must be admitted, but the later complaint of Reckitt, himself a Distributist, remained true. Distributism, he wrote, "is right in almost all

[10] J. E. F. Mann, ed., *The Real Democracy* (London, 1913).

that it condemns and in much of what it affirms but there is far too much which it evades."[11]

The more formal organization of this movement had to wait until after the war. Then G. K. Chesterton, editing the *New Witness* while Cecil fought in the war, took the lead. An effective start came only later, however, in 1924, when *G.K.'s Weekly* was established. GK himself made the following acknowledgement: "I had assumed that the paper would be called The Distributist, or Distribution or something of that sort but since modern England . . . must be made to hear of Distributism and if it can only be done by using the name of some buffoon who [is] known to the public . . . it is clear that the buffoon must not complain"; and there was always difficulty with the name. The suggested names for the movement show its aims as well, perhaps, as any manifesto. "Cobbett Club" was a popular choice, and the Oxford University branch did take this name. "League of the Little People" was seriously considered, but fortunately never adopted. In the end the society remained the League for the Restoration of Liberty by the Distribution of Property, again expressive but unwieldly, and Distributist was generally employed. Initially at least, the league did well. Within a year, twenty-six branches were in existence and meetings were held, addressed chiefly by Chesterton himself. On one occasion a joint meeting with the Rural Reconstruction Association took place.

Slowly a Distributist philosophy was put out by a small group. In addition to the Belloc and Chesterton writings already mentioned were the former's *Economics for Helen* and *An Essay on the Restoration of Property* and the latter's *Outline of Sanity*. Minor figures also contributed.[12] At last, in 1934, *The Distributist Programme* appeared. Unfortunately its claim, "Distributism as a social system combines the *principle* that every human being has the right to liberty with the *application* of that principle that liberty can only be maintained through the ownership of property," was neither new nor forceful. The conclusion was similarly lame: "Distributism is equally opposed to modern monopolistic capitalism and to socialism." The positive measures to reverse the drift to servility were as vague as they had been in *The Real Democracy*: simple enactment would break up the rings, trusts, and cartels (though what constituted a trust was never defined); a stamp duty could be brought in to operate against

[11] Reckitt, p. 182.

[12] H. E. Humphries, *Liberty and Property* (London, 1934); H. W. Shove, *The Fairy Ring of Commerce* (Birmingham, 1930).

amalgamations; differential taxation was another possibility. The only novelty was the demand for better credit.[13] In fact, the appeal of distributism had come to be identified almost completely with GK, as shown, for instance, in the dramatically reduced attendance at the annual dinner when it became known that he would not be able to attend. And when he died in 1936 the movement received a blow from which it never recovered. But even had he lived, it is doubtful whether anything would have come of the philosophy, for its shortcomings were only too patent.

In summarizing the Distributist philosophy one begins by noting that the link which brought together Penty, Fordham, and the Chestertons and Belloc was not so much proposals, nor even the analysis, as the methods by which they worked. Their reliance upon what they took pride in claiming was a realistic or commonsensical outlook was very evident. In the case of Penty and of Fordham this could easily be connected with their practical interests, the one an artist-craftsman, the other a farmer. If the latter's call for "common sense" was an unequivocal statement of method, the former's denunciation of Roman law and the attack upon "abstractionism" were implicitly so. In the case of the Chestertons and Belloc, the realism is not to be accounted for so straightforwardly, but beneath the extravagances, it was recognizable all the same.

Along with such a realism went a way of looking at things which tended to set out problems in uncompromising antitheses and which bordered on the naive. If Chesterton would remark, "Either Private Property is good for Man or it is bad for Man. If it is bad let us all immediately become honest and courageous Communists,"[14] then Belloc would show that in replacing capitalism there was the choice of slavery, socialism, or property, these and no others. Indeed, he and Cecil Chesterton had regretted the passing of the days when political divisions were sufficiently meaningful for Pitt and Fox not to speak to one another.[15] Penty justified fascism for Italy partly on the ground that the choice was simply fascism or communism, and his whole system revolved around the implicit distinction between believers in and deniers of original sin. The very single-mindedness of his attacks which Reckitt had noted was symptomatic of a black-white, almost intolerant, attitude. Fordham alone seemed to have been free of this trait.

[13] *The Distributist Programme* (London, 1934), pp. 2, 17.
[14] G. K. Chesterton, ed., *G.K.'s: A Miscellany* (London, 1934), p. 15.
[15] H. Belloc and C. Chesterton, *The Party System* (London, 1911), p. 28.

Yet, if all agreed upon these methods of approaching problems, there was disagreement upon the remedies. On the one hand stood Penty and Fordham. They inclined, especially Penty, to a static society where any surplus was to be spent on art or in outright amusement. Penty had no use for many of the products of the scientific age, and he sneered at a civilization in which "the majority . . . would spend their time rushing about in automobiles, going to cinemas, dance halls, etc. . . . and as a consequence life would become still more externalized."[16] As an architect he was horrified by the building of houses to put cars in. Because of this static quality Penty and Fordham put great faith in the Just Price, the means whereby competition —or commercialism, as Penty would have insisted—would have been outlawed. And here it was that they parted company with the main body of Distributists—rather oddly, in fact, since Belloc and Chesterton, the Catholics, did not put the value upon the mediaeval economics that Penty and Fordham, the non-Catholics, did. The Belloc-Chesterton wing would have nothing to do with this primitive mediaevalism. For instance, they welcomed the motor car as a means of enabling the small man to combat the railway monopoly. To the Bellocian branch of distributism it was competition which was so important. Their aim was to break with capitalism, but not with the doctrine itself so much as with its logical culmination, monopolistic capitalism. The restoration of the small man to a position of making valid bargains, the restoration of the party system in place of the sham Front Benches, *that* was their aim: a return not to the fifteenth century, but to the eighteenth. Therefore, what at first sight appears strange, that the Catholic Social Guild, which might have been expected to support such prominent Catholics, was in fact lukewarm, becomes rather more understandable.[17] Had the Penty-Fordham variety been the Catholic one, a more effective movement might have resulted.

This split need not have been so significant, for the way should still have been open for the message of the forward-looking mediaevalists to be taken up by other groups. This could not happen, however, since the Distributist philosophy à la Belloc contained a fatal flaw. At one moment, distributism was calling for the restoration of property in order to give the ordinary man the means of security, to give him the freedom to resist the pressure to take employment at unjust rates. It

[16] Penty, *Tradition and Modernism in Politics*, p. 163.
[17] *Clergy Review*, 4.32.

differed from socialism in being an argument directed against the state; it was, in essence, anarchist, a truth recognized by at least one supporter, though understandably he balked at using the term.[18] Yet at the same time it was recognized that if matters were left to themselves, monopolistic capitalism would triumph once again. Belloc himself admitted that "a deliberate reversal of natural economic tendencies" would be necessary and, what was more troublesome for a philosophy basically anarchist, the state would need to be intervening constantly to prevent the capitalists' coming to the surface again.[19] This confusion meant that the Distributist position was continually being assailed from the flanks. If it was true, as Belloc claimed, that the "Distributist state [was] the natural state of mankind,"[20] then the need for direction would seem to be minimal, and the conclusion would be a step to the left. If, however, it was true that men were not to be trusted with the management of their own affairs, but that some organization would have to manage for man's own good, then the conclusion was a drift to the right, and Penty's final position was at least logical.

Moreover, on another level the Distributists were open to attack, this time to the jibes of the Leisure State advocates, those New Economists, including Social Crediters, who proclaimed the age of plenty. What, they argued, was distributism offering but security? But how old-fashioned to think of security in terms of land! In the modern world, a cash grant, the National Dividend, belonging by right to an individual and inalienable, gave every bit as much security as the Distributist could desire and did away with the absurdity of speaking of distributing factories, machines, processes, and the like. Distributists found such arguments very awkward. Penty marshalled all manner of arguments in an attempt to stem the drift towards Social Credit, but eventually his innate honesty obliged him to recognize that the logic of the world as it was demanded a solution along Douglas's lines. He still protested, however, and his final belief was that Social Credit merely embodied the artificialities of the liberal creed in a higher efficiency and that only a return to a Distributist position rooted in the soil would mark a return to fundamentals.[21]

This confusion undoubtedly weakened the appeal of distributism,

[18] K. L. Kenwick, "The Great Refusal," *Distributist*, 8.34.

[19] H. Belloc, *An Essay on the Restoration of Property* (London, 1936), p. 22.

[20] H. Belloc, *Economics for Helen* (London, 1924), p. 106.

[21] Penty, *Distributism: A Manifesto*, p. 44.

but that was not the worst of it. The problem of reconciling the natural state of man with the present perverted state of mankind was an ever-present one. As far back as 1911, Belloc and Cecil Chesterton had begun feeling their way to a conspiracy theory which would explain the paradox. In that year the *Eye Witness* was founded, with Belloc as editor and Chesterton as his assistant. This journal and its successor, the *New Witness*, were established in the flush of the success of *The Party System*, and its controllers were encouraged to extend the conspiracy by identifying it with Jewish financial interests. The bursting of the Marconi scandal about this time gave scope for this line of attack. The spectacle of a previously unsuccessful Jewish director, Godfrey Isaacs, making his killing at a time when his brother, Sir Rufus Isaacs, was attorney general, and another Jew, Sir Herbert Samuel, was in charge of the government department awarding the vital contract was a godsend to Chesterton. His abuse of the facts resulted in his being tried and sentenced for criminal libel, but his misrepresentation of the sentence encouraged him to go on with his crusade: a Clean Government League was sponsored by the *New Witness* and on one occasion debated "the Party System, the Money Power and the Jewish Problem."[22]

In fairness to Chesterton and to Belloc, the extenuating circumstances should be pointed out. At this date anti-Semitism had not acquired the same hateful and sinister ring which it later acquired. Belloc himself had a Jewish secretary, and to her he dedicated his book, *The Jews*. The *New Witness* protested, "It will be abominably unjust if Jewish artists and scholars suffer from our own reaction of our own servility to Jewish money lenders," and it also protested against the expulsion from Britain of the Jewish writer, Oscar Levy.[23] It was always *jewishness* to which they objected.

It will be appreciated from this summary that distributism's greatest problem was in knowing to what public and on what terms it was appealing. The nature of its complaint was essentially an intellectual one: while concern for the welfare of mankind included the material, the main interest was in the metaphysical problem of freedom, and freedom presented in an unusual way. However, to expect intellectuals to give sympathetic hearing to writers who took a perverse delight in being "realistic" and in defying the rules of the intellectual game (Belloc's method of writing history without any adequate

[22] Mrs. C. Chesterton, *The Chestertons* (London, 1941), pp. 113, 127.
[23] *New Witness*, 18.6.21.

documentation was a case in point) and who, in addition, indulged in anti-Semitic jibes was not reasonable. The result was that distributism tended to be a luxury interest, engaged in by a middle class when it had the leeway to be moved by, say, the plight of a Ramsgate hawker threatened by bureaucracy.[24] Significantly, the league did poorly in the postwar depression from 1929 to 1933; it did best in the mid-twenties and mid-thirties, when the middle classes enjoyed a comparative well-being and were not distracted by the spectacle of an overly widespread suffering among the working class. It may be doing a great injustice to the commitment of the leading figures, but an examination of distributism leaves one with the notion of having to deal with charming but ineffectual dilettantes.

[24] *G.K.'s Weekly,* 21.1.28.

chapter four

THE NEW AGE BACKGROUND TO SOCIAL CREDIT

Two criticisms of existing liberal-socialist thinking have been traced, the one an economic attack, the other directed more to politics and to liberty. They had almost no contact with each other. Yet they were not completely self-contained critiques, thanks to the existence of a third body of opinion which took note of both contributions and incorporated something of their message in its own, quite distinctive, set of beliefs. This third criticism was that of the *New Age*. Now its full importance as a synthesizer and herald of Social Credit must be examined. For it was through the *New Age* that Social Credit received, if not its first public hearing, at least its first sustained exposition. The nature of this exposition was to be crucial.

If Social Credit was to be anything more than an intriguing but sterile contribution to thought, it was essential that Major Douglas find an influential journal of opinion in which to state his beliefs. To publish a book would not be enough; the doctrine was too heterodox for the general public to bother with. In addition, Douglas was greatly handicapped by his awkward style, a mixture of technical brevity and pedantic qualification such that even his friends and admirers were forced to admit heavy going. What Douglas needed was the sympathetic interest of an editor who was prepared to open his pages to

Social Credit for that considerable period which would be required for an understanding of the doctrine. The editor would also have to be prepared to comment upon Douglas's writings in a way which would attract and not repel those inclined to consider the scheme.

Douglas's first attempts to find an outlet were not wholly successful. The earliest printed presentation of Social Credit was an article in the *Organizer* of 1917. This was a tiny, obscure journal devoted in the main to matters of importance to engineers. While its significance as a vehicle for revolutionary social ideas was severely limited, there was the conpensation, however, that the editor, improbably enough, was Holbrook Jackson, an important figure in the literary world and one who was able to introduce Douglas to perhaps the one man prepared to give Social Credit a hearing. This was Alfred Richard Orage, the editor of the *New Age*. Although Douglas published two articles in the *English Review* in 1918 and again two more in the following year, he was giving his main attention to the task of convincing Orage; this, Orage was later to acknowledge, occupied a whole year.[1] At length, at the end of 1918, a *New Age* editorial drew attention to "an ingenious and convincing article"[2] by Major Douglas appearing in the *English Review* of December of that year. The article itself was reprinted in the *New Age*'s first issue of the new year, and Orage and his paper were launched upon a championing of Social Credit to which both were to remain loyal to the death—that of Orage dramatically on the evening after his BBC talk on Social Credit, that of the *New Age* in 1938, when it faded out, unable to pay its way. Probably without realizing it, for he does not seem to have been a literary man at all, and quite by accident, Douglas had discovered the ideal medium for disseminating the new gospel.

At the same time it should be borne in mind that the importance of the *New Age* was more than that of a mere carrier of the Douglas message. For in its beginning Social Credit was above all a monetary technique and therefore not essentially connected with, or committed to, any specific political, ethical, or indeed any other values. In its close association with the *New Age*, Social Credit underwent a counterinfluence which shaped the later developments of the doctrine itself and filled out its bare skeleton. The nature of the paper, of the editor, and of his policy, therefore deserve examination.

[1] NA 1.4.26.
[2] NA 12.12.18.

It is frequently thought that the *New Age* was founded by Orage in 1907. This is a mistake, but as will be seen, a quite understandable one. In fact, the *New Age* had a history going back to 1894, when it first appeared, bearing the subtitle *A Weekly Record of Christian Culture, Social Service and Literary Life*. It stood for sweet reasonableness and a slightly dated muscular Christianity, and it claimed a circulation of 56,000. In 1898 Joseph Clayton, "a fierce and aggressive socialist," took over the editorship.[3] Despite his socialism, Clayton was a believer in working through the Liberal party, although he realized that there would have to be "a definite declaration of political policy on the part of Liberalism" if that party was to continue to receive his support.[4] His specific demands were typical of a certain brand of woolly socialism: anti-imperialism, a land tax, temperance, votes for women, and a nonhereditary second chamber.

The circulation of the *New Age* continued to fall during Clayton's editorship, and by 1907 he was obliged to sell out. In a farewell message he summed up the policy of the paper and at the same time unknowingly explained the cause of the failure. "We have stood up for the oppressed in India, Egypt and South Africa. We have fought for democracy the whole world over. The cause of Ireland, the cause of the disinherited labouring people in Great Britain and in all lands has been ours. For women struggling to be free at home and for the Revolution in Russia *The New Age* has said its word. For all the unfortunates in prison and workhouses we have pleaded for justice and mercy. And not human beings only but the wider kinship of the animal world has claimed our kinship."[5] This kind of diffused do-goodism was quite out of place. Progressive thought at this time looked either to a patient, methodical, well-thought-out Fabianism or, tired of a Labour party showing signs of subservience to the Liberals, turned to increasingly dogmatic parties of the extreme left. As was noted in the opening chapter, the Social Democratic Federation was enjoying a boom about this time, and the Colne Valley by-election was soon to return Grayson to Westminster, there to become the centre of violent and unparliamentary unrest which forced the question of socialism rather than labourism to the fore. And of course a few years later the syndicalists were to sweep over England—novel, uncompromising, and outlandish. If any advanced journal was to succeed in

[3] S. G. Hobson, *Pilgrim to the Left* (London, 1938), p. 139.
[4] NA 4.1.00.
[5] NA 28.3.07.

such an atmosphere it would have to be at once exciting, different, and yet soundly based in its fundamental attitudes. The advent of Alfred Richard Orage into weekly journalism meant that all three qualifications would be brilliantly fulfilled. On 2 May 1907 there appeared the first copy of what may be described as the new *New Age*.

To those who were active in journalism and politics at this time, the *New Age* became something of a legend. Yet the paper never built up a wide circulation and never placed itself upon a firm financial footing. Indeed, for almost the whole time that it was a force to be reckoned with it was, from the point of view of readership, in decline. The peak circulation had been 23,500 copies a week, when its championing of Grayson, recently expelled from the House of Commons, had brought it readers. But even at this stage a weekly loss of twenty pounds was being incurred, and from the beginning of 1909 almost regular exhortations for wider readership and threats of price rises or of page cuts appeared in the paper; by 1918 only 2,250 copies were being printed a week.[6] What, then, was the secret which gave the *New Age* such a standing in the eyes of the progressives?

The secret was the personality and the editorship of Orage. Born in 1873, the son of a none-too-successfull East Anglian farmer and private school teacher, but brought up by his mother and the elder children, he was able to prolong his schooling beyond the age of fourteen only because of the old-fashioned paternalism of the squire.[7] Orage's independent outlook made this patron think better of the idea of sending him to Cambridge, and Orage went instead to Culham Training College, Oxford. The outcome was elementary school teaching in Leeds. A little later, after a meeting with Tom Mann, the dockers' leader, he became a socialist.

While at Leeds he made two friendships of crucial importance. The first was with Arthur Penty, whose thinking has already been outlined. The second was with Holbrook Jackson. The importance of Jackson was that he always seemed to be in touch with the influential people, always knew the right person to see. His sending of Douglas to Orage has already been noted, and in addition, it was he who first introduced Orage to some of the important literary figures of the day. Edward Carpenter, the editor of the *Clarion*, G. K. Chesterton, and G. B. Shaw had been persuaded by Jackson to visit Leeds and lecture there, and it was in this way that Orage first made their acquaintance.

[6] NA 24.10.08, 7.1.09, 10.10.18.
[7] P. Mairet, *A. R. Orage: A Memoir* (London, 1936).

Possibly of greater importance, however, was Jackson's introducing Orage to the works of Nietzsche. No doubt Orage would have found his way to these writings. But to have his receptive mind directed to Nietzsche in the opening years of the century gave a particularly significant bent to his thinking and intensified his feeling of intellectual apartness. For at this time Nietzsche was relatively unknown in England, and Orage's books on him, published in 1906 and 1907, must have been among the first in English.[8] And for one who called himself a socialist, the imposition of Nietzschean ideas was bound to lead to interesting results. Later Orage was to move on to Theosophy (though even in this novel and loose body of thought he managed to shock by his unorthodoxy) and then into the Gurdjieff-Ouspensky Institute for the Harmonious Development of Man at Fontainbleau. Even when he returned from America in 1932 to found a new paper, he kept alive his interests in these matters and was on the point of swinging over to advocating them openly when he died.[9] Such a mind as Orage's, then, was quite capable of assimilating Pentyism, for as his closest friend, S. G. Hobson, was to write of him, "In belief he would willingly and knowingly go to the limit."[10] Or as G. K. Chesterton happily put it, he was "emancipated from emancipation."[11] Indeed Orage's open-mindedness was probably the cause of his ultimate failure, for despite the esteem in which he was held during his life, despite the many tributes which leading figures paid to his memory on his sudden and early death, he has left little trace of his power of writing, of his awareness of the changing currents of opinion, and of his ability to charm and influence people. The promise of action never materialized in Orage. No doubt he would have claimed not to have regretted this, for he conceived of his role apart from the hurly-burly of practical politics and decision-making and of himself as *au dessus de la mêlée*.

With such a background and interests, and evidently conscious of his abilities, Orage could have been pardoned for thinking himself out of place in a Leeds primary school. He did what he could locally. Along with Penty and Jackson he began the Leeds Art Club, which flourished and was imitated in Bradford, Hull, and elsewhere. Then

[8] A. R. Orage, *Friedrich Nietzsche: The Dionysian Spirit of the Age* (London, 1906); idem, *Nietzsche in Outline and Aphorism* (London, 1907).

[9] Personal communication from P. Mairet, 1966.

[10] Hobson, p. 141.

[11] NEW 15.11.34.

Penty left for London in 1902, and Orage must have felt the loss. In 1906, however, Orage was surprised to receive sixty pounds in a will. There was little excuse for remaining in Leeds, and with Jackson he followed Penty to conquer wider fields. At first the three worked closely together. Penty's ideas had been published in 1906, and in the same year the Guild Restoration League was set up. Orage became secretary. But, as the fate of Penty's book had indicated, such a venture was premature, and when Penty left soon afterwards, the project was abandoned. Next Orage and Jackson, with the backing of Shaw, attempted to permeate the permeators by founding the Fabian Arts Group; but the Old Guard effectively wrecked this beginning. It was at this point that Orage and Jackson heard of the failing *New Age* and were able to acquire it. Shaw and another backer put up £ 500 apiece to guarantee the first year, and the *New Age* was launched. The change in style which immediately came about under Orage's editor-ship (the more sedate and businesslike Jackson departed after a year) was so marked as to justify the claim that a wholly new paper had been started. The break with the Clayton tradition was complete.

There were two ways in which Orage established the virtually refounded paper in the esteem of the more literate public—by making the paper exciting and by making it significant. In pursuit of the first, Orage was aided by the charm for which he was always remembered. Added to this was the fact that he was a critic of grace and distinction, his taste instinctive and unerring; it was said that he was one of the two people whom T. E. Lawrence thought worthy of consulting on the style of *The Seven Pillars of Wisdom*, the other being Shaw,[12] so that it was not difficult for Orage to appeal to a wide circle of estab-lished and as yet undiscovered writers. The testimony of Ivor Brown, later editor of the *Observer*, is of interest. He has related how, ex-scholar of Balliol, a First, and for two days a member of the Home Office, he was delighted to be given the privilege of writing for the *New Age* for nothing at all, eventually rising to a full ten shillings an article.[13] Ivor Brown was but one of the many outstanding men lured onto the *New Age* or cajoled into writing at absurdly low rates of remuneration. For two years Arnold Bennett wrote a page of literary criticism for a mere guinea a week and, moreover, submerged his identity beneath the pseudonym Jacob Tonson. Even a partial list of the contributors reveals that the *New Age* deserved to be read for its contributors alone: E. Belfort Bax, Max Beer, Cecil Chesterton,

[12] P. Selver, *Orage and The New Age Circle* (London, 1959), p. 52.
[13] I. Brown, *The Way of My World* (London, 1954), p. 136.

G. D. H. Cole, Havelock Ellis, Patrick Geddes, T. E. Hulme, Wyndham Lewis, Katherine Mansfield, J. M. Murry, Ezra Pound, Herbert Read, Walter Sickert, and J. C. Squire were some of the more prominent. But above all there was the occasion when Shaw and Wells took on Belloc and G. K. Chesterton and wrestled over all manner of topics ostensibly on the subject of socialism, one of the encounters resulting in Shaw's happy identification of the Chesterbelloc.

The excitement of the *New Age* was not simply that of the writings of the contributors. There was about it a suggestion of the shocking, indeed almost of the bohemian. Orage himself contributed towards this impression by the air of hidden depths with which he always surrounded himself, an impression which his interest in mysticism fostered and which led Shaw to refer to him as "the mystery man."[14] His background was kept obscure, and it was suspected that his very name had been taken for its "suggestion of tempestuous energy and violence."[15] With some of the circle, the *outre* air was taken further. There was T. E. Hulme, the philosopher, twice sent down from Cambridge and given to riotous conduct and the carrying of knuckle-dusters. Typical of one who was of the *New Age* circle, he had these carved by the sculptor Gaudier Brzeska, himself a fringe member of the group. There was S. Verdad, who beneath this assertive pseudonym was J. M. Kennedy, an extraordinary linguist and member of the Foreign Office, who for over seven years was responsible for the foreign affairs column. Not surprisingly, the air of arcane knowledge which he could impart added to the sense of mystery, of being in touch with the centre of things. The *New Age*'s early advocacy of modern art confirmed this impression, and the reproduction of works by such moderns as Epstein and Picasso, as well as favourable reviews of the other leaders of artistic fashion, settled any doubts about the paper's implied claim to be at the forefront of taste. When Orage held court, open to any with an interest in serious matters and the ability to discourse intelligibly about them, it was quite as exciting as the café society of Paris, though it must be admitted that the ABC tearooms in High Holborn were an inappropriate rendezvous. This sense of commitment, almost of conspiracy, in the service of standards which is captured in the memoirs of those connected with the *New Age* was soon communicated to the readership at large.

14 NEW 15.11.34.
15 Brown, p. 136.

Yet the excitement which the publication engendered was not something accidental, the property of individuals alone. For if Orage was open-minded, prepared to give the run of his paper to all shades of opinion, that did not mean that he or the *New Age* was without a philosophy. There was a very definite course which the paper followed, one whose difference from the normal helped to consolidate the readership in its belief that they were the elect in a world of philistines.

At first this line was expressed negatively. The *New Age* soon quarrelled with the newly established Parliamentary Labour party and the exaggerated hopes placed in that body. The Labour movement was rejected in favour of socialism, a distinction which was crucial to Orage. Criticism of the party began as early as September 1907 and mounted steadily, the main target being the supine opportunism of which organized labour was accused. The Lib-Lab understanding and the 1906 electoral pact were suspected and berated.[16]

Yet no sooner had Orage rejected the Labour movement than he felt obliged to take issue with the existing forms of socialism, too. What appalled him was socialism's crudity. As he put it about this time, but not in the *New Age*, "Writing as a socialist I can sympathize entirely with the sentiments of the early socialists; but I cannot forgive them their political ineptitude nor their betrayal . . . of the interests of artists, craftsmen and imaginative minds generally."[17] Closer contact with the left only confirmed this impression. In 1908 the paper took up the cause of Grayson and even made him joint editor. But the crudities of Grayson's style, acceptable in his Colne Valley constituency but totally out of place in a journal edited by a disciple of Congreve, were too much for Orage, and he was driven to conclude that the extreme left was not to be borne. Grayson soon departed, promoted, as Orage slyly said, to the *Clarion*.[18]

What was happening was that Orage's Nietzschean presuppositions were beginning to shine through. While recognizing that "as a political philosopher Nietzsche is ludicrous [and] as a critic of socialism he is prejudiced and misinformed," Orage also insisted that "as a poet, as a psychologist and above all as a preacher [Nietzsche] belongs to the line of the major prophets." The language of the editorials betrayed the influence. "The Will of Society to perfect itself" was the

[16] NA 6.6.07, 11.7.07, 5.9.07, 11.5.11, 12.10.11.
[17] *Contemporary Review*, 1907, p. 784.
[18] NA 10.10.08, 25.2.09.

essence of socialism; it was a goal "neither exclusively democratic nor aristocratic."[19] The paper was ever open to Oscar Levy, the editor of the definitive English edition of Nietzsche, and to Levy's collaborator, Anthony Ludovici, who stressed the idea of aristocracy. In the end the vicarious impress of Nietzsche on the *New Age* reached such proportions that Belloc was revealed as a Nietzschean[20] (though perhaps understandably he did not know this), and one astute salesman billed his wares as "Sokoro, the cigarette for Supermen."[21]

It was evident that with such an orientation the periodical's socialism would not be of the heart but of the head. To Orage socialism was essentially an intellectual matter; there was no place for sentiment. The only time that Orage seemed to have been carried away in his championing of causes was over the Ferrer affair. The *New Age* became so worked up that banner headlines, never otherwise used, accused Grey, the foreign minister, of murder because he did not intervene to save Ferrer.[22] In general, however, Orage's approach lacked sentimentality, a lack which could emerge with brutal clarity, as when he wrote: "The poor have made themselves an intolerable and disgusting spectacle, unfit for human eyes; they are a running sore. . . . The socialist hates the poor . . . they disgust him, he turns from them with loathing."[23] The class war was never a feature of the paper, the language in this respect nearly always being restrained. It was notable that only one member of the extreme Social Democratic Federation was welcome on the *New Age*; this was E. Belfort Bax, whose philosophical bent and opposition to women's suffrage made him congenial to Orage.[24]

Perhaps after this Orage's unorthodox views on democracy were only to be expected. "There are more genuinely free men to the square mile in Russia at this moment," he stated, "than in any other country in Europe." And he was certain that "unless democracy is regarded merely as a means its modified tyranny is no less a tyranny than any other despotism"; for after all, he noted, "Democracy, which is only

[19] NA 2.5.07, 27.1.10.

[20] NA 2.1.13.

[21] NA 14.8.13.

[22] NA 23.9.09, 21.10.09. Ferrer was the Spanish educationalist of anarchist sympathies executed by the government; shortly before this he had been in London. See H. Belloc, *The Ferrer Case* (London [1910?]).

[23] NA 3.10.07.

[24] See Orage's review of Bax's *The Fraud of Feminism* in NA 4.12.13. See Bax in NA 30.5.08 and 27.6.08, writing against votes for women.

the political device of elective institutions, has no more necessary relationship with socialism, than walking has with any given place."[25] Nor was this merely a theoretical stance. When Cole set up the National Guilds League in pursuit of a goal which was dear to Orage's heart, Orage complained tetchily: "Why democratize it? If you insist upon a movement it will probably not consist of the people whose ideas are of any value or whose action is of any effect."[26] Cole's retort was already on the record. The *New Age*, he had noted, "was always . . . more than a little scornful of democracy."[27]

Orage's outlook was clearly tough-minded, an attitude which his Theosophical interests supported. He himself did not intrude these ideas into his *New Age* writings, but an indication of such thinking can be gathered from a slight book which Dr. L. Haden-Guest wrote, *Theosophy and Social Reconstruction*. Haden-Guest, later a Labour member of Parliament and peer, was a Theosophist, and at the time of writing his book was Orage's first drama critic. The system outlined by Haden-Guest was socialist in that it claimed to be "based on the recognition of Brotherhood [which] would give to each the opportunity of growth" and in its demand that justice should take the place of charity. But since Theosophy was centered upon evolution and reincarnation, and since it encouraged a belief in an astral world beyond the material, it was also possible to hold that "the principle of brotherhood implies that all men are unequal, being at different stages of their evolution."[28] In the background hovered the belief that society was not to be viewed as the mere aggregation of individuals, a belief which came out clearly when the Lloyd George budget of 1909 was being discussed. Orage rejected the proposal that such all-important change should be decided by referendum on the ground that "if democracy means anything at all it means the general will as distinct from the sum total of individual wills."[29]

In fact, Orage could have called himself, perhaps, a Tory democrat. It was the outlook of several writers for the *New Age*. J. M. Kennedy aggressively entitled his book, which first appeared serially in the *New Age*, *Tory Democracy*. Here Kennedy held that only those states were true states which were founded upon an organic basis, contrasting in

[25] NA 2.5.07.

[26] Mairet, p. 69.

[27] G. D. H. Cole, *The World of Labour* (London, 1913), pp. 51–52.

[28] L. Haden-Guest, *Theosophy and Social Reconstruction* (London, 1912), pp. 21 and 48.

[29] NA 9.9.09 and 23.12.09, 8.12.10, 9.3.11.

this respect the ideas of Aristotle, Bolingbroke, and Burke with those of Plato and Rousseau. Kennedy's hope was that the workers would eventually see through the Liberal legislation, which benefited only the manufacturers, and that they would then form an alliance with the aristocracy against the middle classes. A. E. Randall, who wrote a great deal of the *New Age* both under his own name and under the pseudonym J. F. Hope, was another who openly called for a revival of Tory and aristocratic virtues.[30]   The proposal of Sir Francis Fletcher-Vane was slightly different. For him the way out of an admittedly intolerable situation lay through a return to the past, and in answer to his own question, "What is the connection between the feudal and the socialistic idea?" he gave the reply, "There is no connection because they are the same."[31] The significance of all this was noted by Cecil Chesterton, a frequent contributor to the paper and himself a socialist. He acknowledged that "in abstract theory the Tory doctrine is undoubtedly nearer to Socialism than the Liberal doctrine, for Toryism and Socialism are alike in regarding the nation as an organic whole, while Liberalism regards it as a fortuitous concourse of warring atoms."[32]

The best clue, however, to the kind of philosophy which Orage would have liked to formulate (had his gift been for construction rather than for criticism) is provided by the writings of T. E. Hulme. This thinker, belatedly recognized today as a crucial figure in the development of twentieth century English thought, was an Oragean discovery who found the *New Age* the most congenial journal for his writing; indeed, he continued to write for the paper as the war correspondent "North Staffs" until his untimely death in 1917. It was Orage who took care of his correspondence and who arranged for the *New Age* contributor, Herbert Read, to edit these jottings for their appearance as *Speculations*.

Hulme was impressed by the Vitalist philosophers Bergson (whom he knew) and Sorel (whom he translated). Under their impact he discovered the necessity of change, of revolution. At the same time, however, he discovered the centrality of original sin and thereafter had nothing but scorn for those who "chatter about matters which are, in comparison with this, quite secondary notions." From this starting point Hulme developed the idea that people and systems

---

[30] NA 16.2.11, 4.3.15.
[31] NA 6.6.08, 12.9.08.
[32] C. Chesterton, *Party and People* (London, 1910), p. 43.

divided themselves into two kinds, depending upon acceptance or rejection of original sin. The former he termed classical, the latter he termed romantic. It was a syndrome which could be applied to any sphere of thought. "Romanticism in literature, relativism in ethics, idealism in philosophy and modernism in religion" was to Hulme a consistent and objectionable pattern.

What Hulme had managed was a fusion of the revolutionary and the disciplined. The conclusions were inevitably startling. Like so many *New Age* socialists he could dismiss democracy as a "pseudo-category [with] no necessary connection whatever with the working class or revolutionary movement" and scoff that "the amount of freedom in man is much exaggerated." He summed up his own attitude in the following passage: "A . . . combination of the classical ideal with socialism is to be found . . . in Proudhon, but Sorel comes at a happier moment. . . . There are many who begin to be disillusioned with liberal and pacifist democracy while shrinking from the opposed ideology on account of its reactionary associations. To these people Sorel, a revolutionary in economics, but classical in ethics, may prove an emancipator."[33]

The outlook of the *New Age*, then, was singular, but up to this point unexceptional. Unfortunately, one further point must be made. There was an anti-Semitic note to the publication. This first appeared via the pens of Cecil Chesterton and Belloc.[34] But in this attitude they were not alone on the paper. Romney, the military writer, denigrated the fighting qualities of Jews and suggested that they were not quite men. Correspondents on monetary reform could not resist the chance of accusing Jewish money lenders of being worse than Gentiles. The claim was made that the white slave traffic was a Jewish monopoly. Ezra Pound claimed, "The Jew alone can retain his detestable qualities."[35] Orage himself was not wholly immune, and writing as "Chester of Stanhope," commented: "It would be deplorable if anti-semitism were revived in England. But so alarming is the combination of the Jewish international financiers against Democracy that some such movement may be identified." From time to time correspondents wrote to protest against this anti-Semitism, and Orage replied, "The Jews receive no worse criticism in *The New Age* than the Scotch, the Welsh, the American and how many other races and nations."[36]

[33] T. E. Hulme, *Speculations* (London, 1924), pp. 10, 51, 63, 252–60.
[34] NA 7.12.07.
[35] NA 28.4.10, 6.6.12, 27.6.12, 12.9.12 and 24.7.13; this last was by Kitson.
[36] NA 1.7.09, 11.7.12.

There was no suggestion that this anti-Semitism was directed against the Jews as persons; many Jews wrote for the paper, notably the prominent Zionist, Israel Zangwill, and one of the most striking attacks in the *New Age* on Jewish financiers came from M. D. Eder, himself a Jew.[37] Orage has been defended against the charge.[38]

If the tone of the *New Age*, its excitement and unorthodoxy, were apparent from the outset, the positive policy of the paper was not so quick to appear. By 1910, however, disillusioned with the extreme left, Orage felt that it was time to strike a definite line. In the search for a new policy, the way was smoothed by the sudden eruption in England of syndicalism.

Syndicalism was not wholly new to England, but it was not until 1910 that the doctrine became a burning issue. In that year Tom Mann, the socialist who had converted Orage to socialism, reappeared in England, back from Australia, whither both he and syndicalism had travelled. However, it was to France that Mann looked, for there conditions and a writer had given rise to a consistent and formidable philosophy. There dissatisfaction with parliamentary socialism had gone much further than it had in England, and in addition there was the fact that Marxism was temporarily in disarray following the eruption of revisionism. In France an alternative updating of Marx was provided by Georges Sorel.

Sorel was determined to save the essential Marx. In his view this essence was the vitalizing victory of the workers through the agency of the class war. Marx had assumed that the workers would take over from a capitalist system in full bloom. The nineteenth century, however, had shown the decadence of capitalism, alarmingly indicated in the supine desire of the English middle class and the Liberal party to arbitrate rather than to fight. If the workers took over at such a stage in capitalist decline the result would be a repetition of the barbarism which followed Christianity's entering upon a decadent heritage. To prevent this the workers were to provoke middle class anger, solidarity, and determination to fight. If this happened the final resolving smash would come about between two forces at the height of their powers, and the new synthesis would be formed at a favourable juncture. To encourage the capitalists to make a stand it would be necessary to enlist the workers in a programme of violence, which need not be bloody; the culmination of this programme would be, in fact, the

---

[37] NA 4.1.08, 25.4.08.
[38] By P. Mairet, in a personal communication, 1966.

general strike. To Sorel such an approach was not so much a practical step as a myth, a hope to be kept dangling before the worker as a stimulus to further action and a means of whipping the capitalists into the desired state of determination.[39] Sorel, then, had worked in the opposite way to Bernstein's revisionism, for where the latter "endeavoured . . . by changing the theory to fit a democratic and reformist practice . . . syndicalism . . . insisted upon making practice as revolutionary as theory had always been."[40] In this work Sorel put great store by the unions, and in this way his teachings linked up with the heritage of Proudhon, who had always had as great a following in France as had Marx. Consequently the spread of syndicalism was facilitated.

It will be immediately appreciated that Orage was favourably disposed towards syndicalism. Its anticollectivism was in tune with his own. The violence inseparable from syndicalism was attractive to him, and in 1912 the *New Age* noted, "We welcome the present labour revolt and see in it a prospect of fairer days."[41] Above all, syndicalism's emphasis upon the autonomy of the unions fitted very well with his own Penty-inspired ideas about the guilds, and its doctrine of myth was naturally appealing to Orage's cast of mind. But Orage had the sense to see that syndicalism unchecked would be as great a potential tyranny as was state socialism: in place of the tyranny of the consumer would be that of the producer. He was sufficiently orthodox to recognize the need for the state, and he wrote: "It is for the State to play the part of Nature and to maintain by positive means the balance of the contending forms of social organization. That balance is what we call socialism."[42] He knew, then, that he would have to find some means of reconciling the conflicting claims of state socialism and syndicalism. If he could, then the *New Age* might take the lead in progressive thought.

This synthesis was not to be done by Orage, but by his friend and colleague, S. G. Hobson. The one-time secretary to Keir Hardie and once a candidate for Parliament, he was much more of a practical politician than was Orage and a necessary corrective to that editor's speculative nature. From an intimate connection with day-to-day politics he had concluded that the futility of parliamentary action had

---

[39] G. Sorel, *Reflections on Violence* (London, 1916), pp. 92, 102–03, 107, 110, 140.
[40] J. A. Estey, *Revolutionary Syndicalism* (London, 1913), p. 78.
[41] NA 4.4.12, and also see 8.2.12.
[42] NA 29.2.12.

been exposed. "I do not think," he wrote, "that any close observer will disagree with me that as the months go by the Labour Party grows more moderate and reactionary. . . . I confidently anticipate that the next session the Labour Party's meetings will open with prayer."[43] He began to cast about for ways of saving some remnant of true socialism. At the 1909 Fabian Society conference he moved to disaffiliate the society from the tainted Labour party, but his motion was rejected. Even before this he had agitated for the formation of socialist representation committees on the lines of the similar Labour party forerunners, and in fact some were formed. But this was the eve of the syndicalist onrush, and Hobson was led to consider the new philosophy. The approach by way of the socialist representation committees was abandoned, and he set about convincing Orage, who needed little convincing, that it ought to be possible "to build a bridge between the syndicalists and ourselves."[44]

The search for a bridge was no doubt eased by the reappearance in the *New Age* about this time of Penty's ideas. Penty had recently returned from America and was speaking on the subject of restoring the guilds. An incidental remark in an article in the paper opened a correspondence in which Penty joined, claiming that the trade unions could easily be transformed into the guilds which he advocated.[45] This observation highlighted the link between Orage's instinctive belief and the facts of modern industrial life, with which Hobson was more in touch. The synthesis was not long in appearing. Some four months later an article by Hobson was prominently featured; in it the ideas which were later to be identified as guild socialism first appeared. The new line had been heralded by Orage, who announced that the solution to the collectivist-syndicalist antithesis had been discovered. "Syndicalists," he noted, "ask for the Trade Unions exclusive management and control; collectivists ask on behalf of the state for the same autocracy," whereas the way out was "to combine these extremes in a joint management by means of which the state shall be in partnership with everybody and everybody in partnership with the state." The article itself was entitled "Emancipation and the Wage System," and it boldly called for "a new epoch, new not only in social and economic structure but new spiritually."[46] A spate of articles

---

[43] NA 4.7.08, 11.7.08.
[44] Hobson, p. 149.
[45] NA 16.11.11.
[46] NA 25.4.12.

followed, later to be collected and published under the title *National Guilds*, and Hobson began to be joined by other publicists.

The guild movement continued to expand and develop until by 1920 it had become a force to be reckoned with. Some idea of its influence can be gained from a bare list of those who declared their support for it. The most important capture was undoubtedly G. D. H. Cole, the Oxford don and prolific socialist writer. Some of the others were Clifford Allen, the pacifist and leading Independent Labour party politician in the early 1920s; Arthur Greenwood, economist, academic, and later labour minister; Frank Hodges, miners' leader, later of the Central Electricity Board; Rowland Kenny, first labour editor of the *Daily Herald* and brother of Annie Kenny, the suffragette; George Lansbury, leader of the Labour party in the aftermath of the 1931 débâcle; M. I. Postgate, later Mrs. Cole and a socialist leader in her own right; Bertrand Russell, the philosopher and quasi-anarchist; and R. H. Tawney, the economist historian. On the fringe was William Temple, later archbishop of Canterbury. In addition to this was the fact that the miners, the railwaymen, and the post office workers (to mention only members of the most important unions) had declared for some form of guild socialism.[47] Above all, Hobson had actually set up a building guild based on Manchester which built thousands of houses at attractive prices with above-average workmanship until the slump of 1920–21, a lack of efficient control, and the hostility of the established building trade brought it crashing in 1922.[48] For most of the time and for most of the people interested in guild socialism, the *New Age* remained the journal of the movement.

This is not the place to relate the growth of the movement, the formation of the National Guilds League, the Byzantine disputes about the nature of a Guild Socialist state, and the hierarchy of parallel guilds meshing at every level and for every function and culminating in the great Joint Council of the Guild Congress and Parliament. What is important here is an idea of what the Guild Socialist philosophy was. For as the next chapter will relate, the breakup of guild socialism left Social Credit in command of one wing of the movement and naturally susceptible to its basic beliefs.

[47] This list is taken from M. I. Postgate, *Growing up into Revolution* (London, 1949), pp. 66–72; see too *Guildsman*, 3.22.

[48] *Guildsman*, 12.22; Hobson, pp. 226–28; G. D. H. Cole, *Chaos and Order in Industry* (London, 1920), chapter 9.

The basis of the Guild Socialist position, as Hobson had made quite plain, was an attack on wages. The attack was mounted in two waves. The first was an onslaught launched from the Marxian position on economic grounds. Wages represented but a part of the income which the workers ought to receive; the remainder was "surplus value" stolen from the workers to furnish the capitalist's profit. (A salary, on the contrary, did not represent surplus value and was more akin to a wage than a profit.) The second attack was on moral grounds. Wages were paid only for the labour put in and bore no essential relation to the end product; they were paid for a commodity from which all human qualities had been excluded. Inevitably they were contrasted unfavourably with salaries and were a sign of inferior status. A frequent illustration used to indicate the meaning of "wagery" was the Ruskinian one of the armed forces, where all men, of whatever social class and of whatever rank, received "pay," not "wages," and received this pay irrespective of whether they were "employed," that is, fighting, or "unemployed," that is, idling the time away in barracks.[49] While the *New Age* recognized that it had not originated the idea of wage abolition it did claim that it had "translated a theoretical abstraction into an actual living issue."[50]

The development of the Guild Socialist critique on the twin basis of economics and ethics gave Orage the incentive to put out a little book of observations on economics in which he paid tribute to the "sensible" Ruskin. Orage had always been interested in economic thought of an unorthodox kind and had featured Meulen, J. A. Hobson, Donisthorpe, and Kitson in his paper; only the opposition of his backer had prevented his giving them a greater scope.[51] By 1917, however, under cover of a successful guild movement, Orage was emboldened to bring out a more considered view of economics.

The book was a reprint of articles which had appeared in the *New Age*, and although the entries were jottings under alphabetically listed headings, the outline of Orage's thought was clear enough. His motivation, as a good disciple of Ruskin, was presented as follows: "It has long . . . been realized that in thus permitting production to be carried on from an irrelevant motive [the profit motive] we were admitting

[49] NA 25.7.12; J. Ruskin, *Unto This Last* (London, 1907), p. 117.
[50] NA 29.8.12.
[51] For Meulen see NA 3.11.10, 2.2.11, 20.10.11, 30.10.11, 14.12.11, 4.1.12. For J. A. Hobson see NA 16.9.08. For Donisthorpe see NA 14.4.10, 15.12.10, 8.2.12, 7.3.12, 25.4.12, 9.5.12, 11.7.12. For Kitson see NA 29.2.12, 23.5.12, 20.6.12, 25.7.12. The *Eleventh Hour Bulletin*, 28.11.34.

an ethical contradiction into the practices of the state. At the same time, since economists, by means of their analysis of the factors of production, found themselves unable to detect an intellectual defect in the system, the ethical defect was assumed to be either a passing phenomenon, to be remedied by education, or inherent in human nature. Nothing, they concluded, was wrong in the theory of economics." In seeking to resolve the problem, Orage was led to a restatement of much of the Ruskinian position. But he went on to add points which the prophet had not mentioned. Thus where Ruskin attacked the senseless accumulation of profit, Orage went beyond this to attack the very notion of work. "In economics," he said, "progress means the advance towards the idea of production without labour," and he berated the Labour party for its attachment to the Right to Work Bill, which was its favourite standby. "This phrase . . . is terrible in its implications. . . . It implies . . . that the object of modern industry is *not* production." Orage also added a glimpse of the possibility of underconsumption when he wrote, "Over-production is always possible and imminent in societies where spending power is inferior to producing power"; that he really meant "underconsumption" and not "over-production" is indicated by his addition, "Economic saving consists in consuming as much as is necessary for the production of as much as possible."[52]

Where he made the most significant departure, however, was in his clues (they were nothing more) towards the solution of this state of affairs. The law of supply and demand was a questionable economic law, "as easily . . . broken as obeyed." He knew that "the object of all sellers . . . is . . . to extract from the customers as much purchasing power as possible in return for as little as possible." When this particular way of putting the point is placed beside the observation that "in a number of transactions . . . a reserve price is placed on the commodities," it is clear that Orage had come close to a belief which was later to become an important one in the Social Credit case. Another clue towards the solution, and another pointer towards the coming Social Credit, lay in Orage's view of capital. He saw that this economic driving force "exists in two forms, a real and a nominal," the latter reflected in monetary terms, the former the only real quantity. Real capital "consists of Tools of Production," that is, anything and everything which may be used to increase production and consumption.

[52] A. R. Orage, *An Alphabet of Economics* (London: T. Fisher Unwin, 1917), pp. vi, 115, 134, 98, 140 respectively.

But this capital did not exist merely in the present. "Capital . . . consists not only of the actual tools, but of the credit men can establish for themselves that the tools will be usable and will be used."[53] As will be seen, this too was an interesting foreshadowing of the later *New Age* thinking.

The more political implications of guild socialism were developed on these bases by Cole, using a somewhat different approach. For Cole the main attraction of guild socialism was that it made possible active, not passive—positive, not negative—democracy. To him parliamentary democracy was the second. The people did not initiate or control, they merely possessed the power every so many years of rejecting one of the parties. In industrial as opposed to political matters there was not even this freedom, for the owning and managerial classes were absolute. The guild system would change all this. The workers would control production in all its phases through their industrial and craft guilds, the citizen would safeguard his consumption rights through a modified parliamentary system, and finally all would control all through the overriding Joint Council. The bureaucracy of state socialism would be a dead letter. No longer would impersonal authorities care for the old, the sick, the unemployed, but each guild would have the responsibility of looking after its own.[54]

It was not long before the whole of guild socialism, including these two aspects, was examined philosophically and the attempt made to establish it on a firm footing. This was the work of the Spaniard, Ramiro de Maeztu.[55] As his being of the "generation of '98" indicates, de Maeztu, like Orage, had long been a critic of the existing order. And like Orage he had managed to turn a Nietzschean outlook into a form of socialism. His maturer conclusions appeared first in the *New Age* and then in the book *Authority, Liberty and Function in the Light of the War*. At the outset the author acknowledged that he owed "to *The New Age* and its editor . . . the idea of the Guilds; to M. Leon Duguit that of objective rights; to Mr. G. E. Moore that of objective good; to Herr Edmond Husserl that of objective logic; and to Mr. T. E. Hulme the acknowledgement of the political and social

---

[53] Ibid. S. G. Hobson had long been aware of the nature of real credit; see NA 19.11.14, 9.3.16.

[54] G. D. H. Cole, *Guild Socialism Restated* (London, 1920), pp. 31–41; NA 7.11.12.

[55] Details of de Maeztu's life may be found in W. Herda, "Die Geistige Entwicklung von Ramiro de Maeztu," *Spanische Forschungen der Goerresgesellschaft*, ser. 1, vol. 18 (1961).

transcendency of the doctrine of original sin." Yet if the book was derivative it was also valuable. It brought together many contemporary lines of thought and revealed how guild socialism could be reconciled with them.

De Maeztu's starting point was the impact of a war of unprecedented scale which had made him recognize the evil of sovereignty. To him the pope and the kaiser were equally misguided, for they both claimed a general power over their subjects. Even "the perfect liberal" came under this condemnation, for he too made in effect the same claim. Because "the true essence of association does not lie in the unique will but in the common thing," no one man could presume to speak in general for others; but this was just what the liberal member of Parliament claimed to do on behalf of his constituents. The correct basis of society would be the principle that people "ought never to grant powers to anyone except when they are attached to a definite function." When this is done, "the conception of freedom and tyranny lose their antagonism . . . and the outcome is that they define the same thing. Freedom is our own tyranny; tyranny is the freedom of others." De Maeztu went on to add some interesting observations, such as questioning the sacredness of liberty and preferring "organization" in which nobody would have any right other than that of doing his duty, and admitting, "I am not a socialist because I believe the working class will be happy under socialism. I am a socialist because I believe that socialism is just."[56] But these foreshadowings of things to come were not the important thing at that time. What was taken up was the idea of functionalism, the idea that democracy could be meaningful only when set in such a framework that each function had its own representation.

Unfortunately, de Maeztu had not managed to achieve what he set out to do. There was to be no consensus upon functionalism, for it could, of course, go two ways. Quite clearly de Maeztu was tending towards that form of socialism which afterwards became some kind of national socialism, a movement of the right. His later life indicated this more clearly than his writings, perhaps. After serving as Primo de Rivera's ambassador to the Argentine, he was swept up into the civil war and executed by the forces of the left.[57] But it was equally possible to go to the left with a functionalist philosophy, and when

[56] R. de Maeztu, *Authority, Liberty, and Function in the Light of the War* (London, 1916), preface, pp. 51–52, 79, 139, 146.
[57] Herda, p. 214.

Tawney brought out his *Sickness of an Acquisitive Society* it was seen that the doctrine could be presented within a more orthodox socialist tradition.

The fact that guild socialism presented twin appeals, via economics and via morals, was not a source of strength, but of weakness. At first it did not appear so. The economic argument appealed to those inclined to Marxist thought, and the Glasgow and Sheffield shop stewards, Gallacher and Murphy, both of whom later joined the Communist party, were close to the Guild movement, while John Paton, originally of the Clydeside shop stewards, came right over to guild socialism and founded the *Guildsman*. On the other hand, the ethical side of the movement, with the promise of developing a social conscience and doing away with the cold inhuman machine of state socialism, attracted those of other views; a significant group was made up of High Churchmen whom Reckitt, then editing the *Church Socialist*, was able to influence—men such as the Reverend P. E. T. Widdrington, the Reverend Egerton Swann, Father Paul Stacy, Father P. Bull, and R. H. Tawney. Such an alliance was an uneasy one, and the first puff of wind was to expose the brittle nature of the union.

The puff turned out, in fact, to be the hurricane of the Russian Revolution, and its blast was too violent to allow the flowering of so delicate a plant as guild socialism, with its fine balance between "the spirit of solidarity and the spirit of devolution."[58] Even the Bolshevik party itself could not escape the pressure of the times, and Lenin's conveniently ambiguous slogan, Democratic Centralism, revealed how the very Revolution was torn between the two alternatives. What chance was there, then, that guild socialism could withstand such a disruptive choice? The grounds on which the guild movement split were the proposal to change the movement's name, and the question of the correct attitude to be adopted towards the Russian Revolution. In fact, of course, they were one and the same dispute.

The term *guild socialism* had been chosen by Hobson when he first came to write his articles in the *New Age*. At the time, such a term was secured only "with Orage strongly objecting," but it was only natural for Hardie's ex-secretary to insist upon the link with his formative past.[59] When the series was published as a book while Hobson was in Central America, Orage took the opportunity to name it *National Guilds*. Once the title had been chosen, Cole seemed to

[58] Cole, *The World of Labour*, p. 24.
[59] Hobson, p. 177.

have felt it advisable to keep to it in forming and naming the league. But that he was not happy with such a title was made clear by his proposal in 1919 to rechristen the movement Guild Socialist League and to stress the socialist aspect. The proposal to change the name was finally put at the fourth annual conference in June 1919 and was lost, seventy-eight to thirty-nine. The position of Cole, anomalous in the eyes of the majority, was summed up neatly in the following triolet which Reckitt composed:

> Mr. G. D. H. Cole
> Is a bit of a puzzle;
> A curious role
> That of G. D. H. Cole.
> With a bolshevik soul
> In a Fabian muzzle
> Mr. G. D. H. Cole
> *Is* a bit of a puzzle.[60]

The allusion to the Bolsheviks was inevitable. Indeed the change-of-name controversy was but an episode in this developing battle over the significance of the Russian Revolution. The opening salvo had been fired at the third annual conference in May 1918, when M. I. Postgate moved that a message of congratulation be sent to the Bolsheviks in their isolated anticapitalist stand. Several spoke in her support, including Cole, but the proposal was eventually rejected.[61] The discussion then hung fire, but it came to the fore again in the early summer of 1920. It was a time when direct action to prevent arms shipments to Poland for use against the Bolsheviks was being urged. Under such stimulus the Communist-inclined wing grew in strength, and a confrontation at the May conference became inevitable. The *Guildsman* admitted that the movement was "face to face with the biggest crisis of its career." Penty came out against the "sovietists," and Reckitt complained that the determination to secure a clear-cut decision for or against Russia was to introduce a Bolshevik tactic. And at the conference the Bolshevik sympathizers were victorious by sixty-seven to fifty-five in carrying a motion instructing the executive to draw up a report embodying guild policy, especially with regard to the Russian Revolution. Even this, however, was not sufficient for the more extreme members, who seized the opportunity provided

---

[60] *Guildsman*, 1.19, 6.19, 7.19.
[61] *Guildsman*, 6.18.

by the formation of the Communist Party of Great Britain, and Cole
had to admit that "a considerable number of the members . . . joined
it." Meanwhile the executive had delegated the task of preparing the
policy document to Cole, who presented it, the "Programme of Action," at the extraordinary meeting of December 1920. Hardly surprisingly, Cole, who about this time was still playing with the idea of
violent revolution, was unable to satisfy the moderates, and when the
Programme of Action was carried by sixty-eight to forty-eight, six
moderate members of the executive resigned. Their places were taken
by the more extreme socialists, and their influence, despite the seces-
sion to the Communists, became decisive. In July 1921, their predomi-
nance was signalled when the name of the *Guildsman* was changed
to the *Guild Socialist.*[62]

But the movement was at an end. The extreme socialists had been
lost. The moderates had been alienated. The rump occupied an ever-
shrinking no-man's-land. Many erstwhile guildsmen, above all the
middle-class element, were eager to grasp at any straw. And even
while the disintegration was proceeding, and even from the very same
source which had earlier given the lead to the guilds, that straw was
being pushed forward—the straw of Social Credit.

Yet before one takes leave of the *New Age*, certain observations
should be made. As a journal it has been neglected.[63] This was not
so much because of its small circulation, for at first the *New Statesman*'s was little higher, and it was possible in those days to keep going
on far smaller circulations. Rather, it was because the *New Age* was
so hard to categorize. The *New Statesman* carried an unmistakable
Fabian stamp, and moreover the eventual triumph of a Fabian-soaked
Labour party has kept this journal to the fore. The *Labour Leader*
was likewise easy to pigeonhole; it perfectly captured the straightforward Independent Labour Party (ILP) no-truck-with-the-right attitude. But the *New Age*? At times one is tempted to refuse to call it
socialist, but the guild socialism cannot be written off as a cuckoo in
the nest as simply as that. One can only say that the paper was *sui
generis*, a judgement which would have appealed to its editor. In
Orage himself these seemingly conflicting viewpoints were under control and reconciled. But it is evident that in lesser people, or in those
forming their opinions at a later date, when the choice between

[62] *Guildsman*, 4.20, 5.20, 6.20, 9.20, 1.21; the names of the seceders are given in
Postgate, p. 96; N. Carpenter, *Guild Socialism* (New York, 1922), p. 135.

[63] Despite the study of W. Martin, *Orage and The New Age* (London, 1967), this is
still true.

right and left presented itself in a different and more difficult light, such a satisfactory synthesis would not be so easy. The *New Age* marked a watershed; what came after could never hope to recapture the detached yet commanding heights, but would have to be committed to one or the other side in the battle on the plain below.

Clearly there were specific points where the *New Age*'s analysis anticipated Social Credit ideas; this was especially true of Oragean economics. But the significance of the paper was greater than this. There was about it a prestige which demanded that it be read and considered, and this was to be important when Douglas began to put out his ideas through its pages. At the same time, its rejection of the individualistic competitive ethic was still mainly negative. The Guild Socialist solution was not totally satisfying, as Orage was vaguely aware,[64] especially after Cole had come to the fore and had insisted upon emphasizing socialism. The *New Age*'s discovery of Social Credit, therefore, was as important as was Douglas's discovery of Orage.

[64] Mairet, p. 73.

chapter five

MAJOR DOUGLAS THE MAN AND HIS MESSAGE

So far it has been assumed that the main features of Social Credit have been understood by the reader, so that, for instance, at least the contrast with distributism could be appreciated. While a general understanding of Social Credit is adequate for such a purpose, to understand the movement itself demands a much more precise grasp of the technical case for the theory. That will be the purpose of this chapter. But Social Credit theory cannot be understood without knowing something of the man who first formulated it, and so it is with Major Douglas that the chapter begins.

Relatively late in life, when he was approaching forty, Douglas grasped the idea of Social Credit. It was an idea which promised the solution, if not to all the world's problems then at least to the major ones, and it is fair to liken Douglas's discovery to a religious conversion. Certainly it changed his life. From being an unknown engineer, very much a private citizen, he became a world figure and the centre of controversy, and not only to those whose reaction to Social Credit was one of disagreement. Quite untrained and quite unsuited for the role of propagandist, he felt that his discovery obliged him to convert the world. Inevitably the interaction of the man and his message was crucial, and in the case of Douglas and Social Credit more so than is common in such cases. Other movements generally manage to establish a body of belief and of believers who can stand apart from the parent, drawing strength from an already widely known tradition. With Social Credit this never happened. Douglas always retained too crucial a position, and independent Social Credit developments never acquired a healthy life of their own. Doubly unfortunate was the interplay of Douglas the man and Douglas the social saviour, for while the movement suffered, so did Douglas. He died a lonely and embittered man, cut off even from the main body of his own supporters.[1]

Regrettably little is known of Douglas's life. He always had a passion for secrecy. He seems to have written little privately, and one of his closer colleagues remembers that his written communications were restricted to invitations.[2] If any letters have survived, they have not been made known to this writer. Indeed, at one stage a biography of Douglas was announced;[3] it was to form the introduction to Mairet's edited account of Douglas's writings. When *The Douglas Manual* eventually appeared, however, there was no reference to his life whatsoever. This withdrawn attitude was kept up to the last, for in his will Douglas ordered that nothing be written about him other than the customary press notification.[4] His only child, Miss C. M. Douglas, has honoured his wishes and refuses to discuss her father or make available any documents which may still exist.[5] This unsatisfactory state of affairs has been perpetuated in unexpected ways; even when official records ought to be of help, they are strangely silent. There is no question that Douglas was at the Royal Aircraft Establishment, Farnborough, between 1916 and 1918, but today no record of his being there remains.[6]

Naturally the small amount of biographical detail which was allowed to slip through to the Social Credit journals and to the inner circle of acquaintances tended to reveal Douglas in a favourable light.

[1] Personal communication (1967) from Mrs. M. W. Gordon-Cumming, at one time Douglas's secretary.

[2] Personal communication from Rev. V. A. Demant, 1967.

[3] NEW 5.4.34.

[4] His will may be consulted, of course, at Somerset House.

[5] Personal communication from Miss H. Douglas, 1967.

[6] The *Monthly Army List* notes his becoming a captain (temp.) on 1.1.16 and his being promoted to major (temp.) on 1.6.16. The *Air Force List*, 1919, shows that he was demobilized on 1.4.18. Communication from E. E. Stott, Public Relations Officer, Farnborough.

The early Social Credit paper, *Credit Power*, printed a brief outline of his career which had been obtained from *The Engineers' Who's Who*. It ran as follows: "Member of the Institute of Mining Engineers; member of the Institute of Electrical Engineers; educated at Cambridge University; was with the Canadian General Electric Company, Peterborough, Canada; Assistant Engineer, Lachine Rapids Hydraulic Construction; Chief Construction Engineer, British Westinghouse Co.; Chief Engineer and Manager, India Westinghouse Company; Deputy Chief Engineer of Electrification Schemes, Buenos Aires Pacific Railway Company."[7]

All this indicated that Douglas was a man of some substance in the engineering world, though oddly enough he did not feature in *The Engineers' Who's Who* in the first two years of its publication, 1920–21 and 1921–22, and it seems that only his Social Credit standing brought him to the attention of the editor. Also rather strangely, both accounts omitted any mention of his work on the Post Office Tube Railway in London, of which he was to make so much later. Added to the favourable impression given by these entries was that produced by the widely held belief that Douglas was connected with the Scottish aristocracy. His attitude towards his descent was never straightforward, although he is remembered as having shown a pride in family.[8] To some he gave the impression—it was never anything stronger—that he was related to the Sholto-Douglases; others believed that he was related to the Dukes of Hamilton; on one occasion it was stated that he was a cousin of Lord Weir, and Douglas, who was quick to correct misstatements about himself, let this stand. (The present Lord Weir admits that the family had heard something along these lines, but knew of no certain relationship.)[9] Douglas never spoke openly on the subject, just as he never mentioned his schooling or professional training.

This picture, however, collapses immediately any investigation is made. When Douglas went up to Pembroke in the Lent term, 1910, he had himself entered as Clifford Hugh Douglas, son of Hugh Douglas, engineer, of Edgeley, Cheshire.[10] The birth certificate, however,

[7] *Credit Power*, 6.23. The reference to the Institute of Mining Engineers was an error; it should have been the Institute of Mechanical Engineers.

[8] Personal communication from T. M. Heron, 1967.

[9] Personal communications from Mr. and Mrs. M. W. Gordon-Cumming and from Lord Weir, son of the alleged cousin of Douglas, 1967; NA 22.6.33.

[10] Records of Pembroke College, Cambridge.

suggests a different story. Douglas, born 20 January 1879, was indeed the son of Hugh Douglas, but he was named Clifford only. Nor was his father, then at any rate, an engineer, but a draper, and he lived, not at Edgeley, but at 5, Greek Street, Stockport, Manchester. It is always possible that Douglas senior was a prosperous draper and later retired to Edgeley, even that he may have become an engineer. But if so, his fortune must have been late in coming, for the local paper does not reveal the father as a draper of sufficient importance to advertise (unless he traded under some other name), and Douglas's late entry to Cambridge (he was thirty-one) suggests, too, that the father was not able to send his youngest son there.[11]

The entry about Cambridge is also misleading, though it would be understandable and pardonable if, in the climate of those days, Douglas put his father down as an engineer and not as a draper. The Cambridge education was not a preparation for his engineering life, as the *Credit Power* note suggests; as has been observed, Douglas was thirty-one when he went up. Nor was it in truth a Cambridge education in the normally accepted meaning of that term. Douglas remained at Cambridge for four terms only, and that included the Long Vacation term, and so went down without taking a degree. The circumstances of this Cambridge episode are as mysterious as most of Douglas's career. College records of those days were not the detailed dossiers they are today, and they reveal merely his going up, going down, and occupancy of rooms since demolished. He played no part in the College Debating Society, and the library records do not show that he ever borrowed a book. Presumably he was reading for a Tripos in one of the sciences, since later he did remember "the early part of a misspent youth" when for several days his pleasures were interrupted by capped and gowned gentlemen who asked him "awkward questions about, let us say, the relation of the differential calculus to the motions of the moon." Why he chose to go down after so short a stay, and, since he had stayed for the Long Vacation term, so suddenly, is not recorded. It might have been that the travelled engineer of thirty-one found the undergraduate style, dreadfully revealed in the Debating Society minutes, too uncongenial. Yet in later life Douglas was keen to give the impression of being a Cambridge man

[11] The *Cheshire County News and Stockport Chronicle* for 1879, the year of Douglas's birth, and for 1889 were searched, but no reference to a Douglas could be found. Edgeley was a select residential area depending upon Manchester.

in the full sense; "educated Cambridge" was part of his *Who's Who* entry, and when back at Cambridge to give an address, he drew out his stay at Pembroke to "years." One of his few autobiographical references was to his having taken Greek in Little-go, in which, he claimed, he obtained 86 percent, although translating by heart and not knowing where to stop.[12]

The professional career of Douglas is equally suspect. The references to his membership of the two professional bodies are correct. But British Westinghouse has no record of his having worked for the firm.[13] However, since Douglas's first wife was, he claimed, the daughter of an Indian Civil Service official, and since in his evidence to the MacMillan Committee, he provided specific details of his stay in India, it is possible that he was there in some capacity or other, later choosing, perhaps, to identify the firm as British Westinghouse as an indirect way of enhancing his own standing. This tendency to magnify seems to lie behind his claims in respect of the Post Office Tube work. It was always believed, and here Douglas gave support to the notion, that he had been in charge of the project or at least of some significant section of it. The Post Office records show, however, that his connection with the project was minimal. Only two references to Douglas exist. The first acknowledges "Employment of Mr. C. H. Douglas at £ 350 a year for preparation of plans and specifications to form the basis of invitations to tender and preliminary experimental work, with, at a later date, supervision of installation of plant." (The plans and plant referred to were the electrical equipment, not the actual tunnelling.) The salary of £ 350 was a small one when compared with the thousands the leading engineers were receiving, and that Douglas's standing was a lowly one was confirmed in the second reference. It was at this time that the war was interfering with the project and the laying off of staff was being considered. A handwritten comment observed of Douglas, "We may have to give this man a gratuity if his services are not continued"; the reference to "this man" and the possibility of his going without compensation cruelly put Douglas

[12] NA 2.8.23; *Social Credit*, 26.10.34; *Social Crediter*, 29.10.38.

[13] He joined the Institute of Electrical Engineers in 1904 and left in 1920; he was a member of the Institute of Mechanical Engineers between 1918 and 1936. I owe confirmation of these facts to the staff of the two institutes, to whom I am grateful. Communication (1967) from H. R. Baines, Secretary, Westinghouse Brake and Signal Co. Ltd.

beyond the pale of the true professionals.[14]

Douglas must, in fact, have been laid off, because the electrical contracting was not resumed until after the war. It might be that at this time Douglas went to France to help with the organization of railways there. Mr. T. M. Heron remembers Douglas's telling him that while working in that capacity he met and talked with one of the Sassoon banking family, who revealed that the war could, financially speaking, go on forever—an observation which helped Douglas in his later thinking.[15] But if he did work with the railway system, it was in a civilian capacity. For the army lists are silent upon the subject of Douglas until 1916, when he was taken on strength at the Royal Aircraft Establishment, Farnborough, and quickly promoted to major. It was here that the public life of the major began.

Henceforth, the recollection of those who worked with him can be used to fill out the sketchy impression built up from his own activities and statements. Even so, the picture remains blurred, and it is possible to arrive at two quite different interpretations of the man; even during his own lifetime there were two distinct responses to Douglas.

To some, Douglas appeared a hero, almost more than life-size. Indeed, at times he was embarrassed by the adulation which women, especially, showered upon him.[16] More soberly, Orage found him "personally and intellectually attractive" and said that after close association over the years his first impression had "only been intensified." And when Augustus John painted Douglas's portrait he "was impressed by his personal dignity and charm."[17] Lesser people who came into contact with him felt the same, and one particularly liked his absence of "side." They admired, too, his presence, whether at a social gathering, where it was immediately known when he had entered a room, or on a public platform, where although not given to rhetoric, he could hold an audience.[18] He was not intimidated by august figures; indeed, it was quite the reverse, and Wyndham Lewis once remarked, "A long time ago I talked with—or was talked to by —Major Douglas."[19] His devotion to Social Credit was praised, and

[14] *Post Office Records*, E25087/1914, File 4. The entry is undated but would be about 2.9.14. The second entry is ibid., File 3. "The Post Office Tube Railway, London," *Engineering*, 1928.

[15] Personal communication from T. M. Heron, 1967.

[16] Personal communication from Mrs. M. W. Gordon-Cumming, 1967; C. M. Hattersley, *Aberhart and Alberta* (London [1937]), p. 23.

[17] NA 1.4.26; A. John, *Chiaroscuro* (London, 1952), p. 177.

[18] Personal communication with Mrs. W. T. Symons, 1966.

[19] W. K. Rose, ed., *The Letters of Wyndham Lewis* (London, 1963), p. 416.

his onetime secretary remembers how he would give up, a week before any speech, his usual and much appreciated alcohol and tobacco in order to be in the best possible condition to convince his audience. That he would always give the same scrupulous attention to an audience of a handful as to one of thousands was also commented upon favourably. Others were taken by his modesty and his willingness to allow that the germ of Social Credit had been known a century before his formulation.[20]

Yet others found him quite different. They pointed out how difficult it was to work with Douglas. His charm could be turned into an annoying urbanity, and Mr. and Mrs. W. T. Symons, at one time very close workers with Douglas, recall how they visited him with the set intention of challenging him about a vital matter of policy. After a smoothly enjoyable talk in which Douglas refused to approach the topic they had come to discuss, they were forced to depart no wiser, and sadly aware that they would never work with him again. Furthermore, it was Douglas's fault that he could not rest content until he had pointed out all the difficulties and snags in any proposed course of action, and his own writing suffered from this determination to be pedantically precise and to qualify almost every observation. The attempt of the Reverend T. P. Kirk, an Anglican well known for his work with the lower classes, to draw together the different varieties of monetary reform was wrecked by Douglas's inflexible approach. It was claimed that Douglas was arrogant, an attitude into which he retreated whenever the argument was getting too deep for him. Where his admirers would describe him as "squirelike," his detractors preferred to describe him as "autocratic."[21] The later conduct of the Social Credit movement which centred upon Douglas was taken as confirmation of this inherently tyrannical nature.

Of course, both interpretations contained elements of the truth; they were not incompatible. Indeed, they usefully pointed to the correct interpretation. Douglas was essentially a solitary man, and it seems to have been a solitariness which was rooted in a sense of inferiority. That this was his nature was borne out by his lack of real personal contacts, for of all those with whom he worked, only one was

---

[20] Personal communication from Mrs. M. W. Gordon-Cumming, 1967; NA 17.7.30, 9.4.31; also see Ezra Pound in NEW 2.4.36.

[21] Personal communications from M. W. Gordon-Cumming, P. Mairet, M. B. Reckitt, and Mr. and Mrs. W. T. Symons, 1966–67.

acknowledged a friend.[22]   His interests, sailing and fishing, were those of the solitary sportsman, and the only clubs he belonged to were yachting clubs. The inability to find friendship may have been intensified by a deep-seated dissatisfaction with himself. His lack of communication went beyond the merely modest and became unnatural. Such an absence of straightforwardness, together with the allusions to family and his reluctance to mention anything of his life, suggests that perhaps he felt himself to be something of a failure. The Cambridge interlude, so late in life and in the midst of an otherwise orthodox career, may have been an attempt to break away from a profession which he felt in some obscure way to be unworthy of him. Doctor James Young, the favourite pupil of Jung, once observed, "Douglas's walk is that of a paranoic," and he may well have hit upon the truth.[23]   Thus, with those who made him feel his inferiority, as he saw it, he did not get along, whereas with those who did not remind him of missed opportunities, he could be himself and very charming. Significantly he got on well with women, who could not be looked upon as a challenge to his position, and with Orage and with John, both of whom were not members of the establishments. It was significant, too, that he quarrelled with the Chandos Group, an avowedly intellectual Social Credit organization, and equally significant that in the condemnation he exempted Father Demant, who although a university man, was not an Oxbridge product and had a degree in engineering.

Should this interpretation be a correct one, it does not necessarily mean that Douglas was driven to Social Credit by any selfish motive, as a means of making a mark and satisfying a wish to be something more than an engineer. Had this been the case, an orthodox career, say in Parliament, would no doubt have been possible, for he evidently had many of the qualities for success. At the same time it is vital to grasp that in his own estimation his scheme was not one designed to benefit him at all; in all probability he would, relatively speaking, have lost. Under the existing system he was financially well off, able to retire in 1918, not needing at any time to be kept by the movement, and able to live in some style in the Temple, run expensive cars, and undertake world tours; when he died in 1952 he was worth some

---

[22] This friend was William Allen Young, the author of *Dividends for All* (London, 1921) and *Ordeal by Banking* (London, 1931); personal communication from W. T. Symons, 1966.

[23] Personal communication from P. Mairet, 1966.

£ 13,000. Under the existing system he enjoyed a fair share of power, although he would, on his own reckoning, have had less power had Social Credit been adopted, and he could certainly have added to his power by embracing one of the established political philosophies. Nor would a Social Credit state have needed his services as technical adviser for very long. It seems difficult, therefore, to explain Social Credit merely by saying that it answered a need of its inventor. Rather, the point to be made is that Douglas's personality was such that his leadership and the movement suffered as a result of his own shortcomings and inadequacy.

An understanding of Douglas's personality suggests that some of the more general views which he held about the mechanics of society were unduly coloured by his troubled uncertainty. And if he was led in this way to extreme conclusions, he may well have been encouraged along the path by the treatment which he received, or thought he received, from his opponents. For years his attempts to convince the world of Social Credit had been met by a barrage of criticism quite impossibly unfair. In this respect left-wing writers were particularly blameworthy. To take one example only: Barbara Wootton, with claims to the status of intellectual, reviewed Social Credit and managed three times to insinuate that the scheme was inherently inflationary, because, it was alleged, Douglas advocated "an indiscriminate issue of money." This totally ignored the Just Price mechanism designed to prevent inflation. Whether the mechanism would or would not have worked was open to argument, but certainly "the promiscuous issue of money" was not being put forward.[24] On top of this misrepresentation was the belief that Social Credit was being boycotted by the press, naturally on orders from the financiers. Douglas himself wrote, "In this country the Institute of Bankers allocated five million pounds to combat the subversive ideas of ourselves. . . . The large Press Associations were expressly instructed that my own name should not be mentioned in the public Press. . . . During the last five years the seed of Social Credit has been driven underground."[25]

And finally it must be remembered that about the middle 1930s, when the character of Douglas's pronouncements changed for the worse, he was struck down by a crippling and mysterious illness in his leg. He was often in pain, and eventually he died while undergoing

[24] *New Leader*, 22.5.25.
[25] NA 28.3.29.

an operation to amputate.[26] Perhaps the surprise should not be that some of his beliefs were unusual or extreme, but that in holding them he had the sense to resist the temptation to be yet more extreme. As will be seen later, his strong common sense rarely deserted him.

Before moving on to examine this philosophy a word of warning must be given. To begin with, Douglas wrote very poorly, and even the defence which Orage felt called upon to give acknowledged that "Major Douglas's style may be 'involved' for spoiled readers who demand other people's ideas in words of one or two syllables."[27] But the real problem was not style in the narrow sense. It is doubtful whether Douglas ever managed to get down on paper exactly what he wanted to say. For all his scientific attitudes, his was essentially an intuitive mind, which sensed but could never quite capture the truth. The result at times was writing which appears at the best bizarre and at the worst absurd. Thus he was given to such statements as "The Foreign Office is the home of the Roman Catholic interest and the Treasury that of the Jewish," though in this case he did have the sense to warn his readers that this was not quite what he wanted to say, but rather, a hint. Considerably more esoteric was the reference to the "Baconian little ships" at Dunkirk. What is meant is clear to one who has some knowledge of his way of thinking, and it becomes clear when read alongside the quotation below, but as it stands it represents an amazing ellipsis. Or what is to be made of the observation, "The Jew and his philosophy . . . is epitomized in the one way street"? On another occasion he noted, "What bearing, if any, . . . the fairly well established fact that Hitler is the grandson of an illegitimate daughter of Baron Rothschild of Vienna has I do not know."[28] Such a statement, with its qualification and throw-away air, can be taken only in the sense of a "thought out loud"; it may show perhaps that Douglas was losing his grip, but it also shows that the underlying cast of mind was the allusive. It is necessary to approach Douglas's writings with rather more sympathy than is normal, for it is evident that a hostile examination of such works could all too easily reduce Douglas, and the many independent minds who accepted him, to the level of charlatans, rogues, or simpletons.

[26] Personal communication from Mrs. M. W. Gordon-Cumming, 1967.

[27] NA 2.3.22.

[28] NA 28.10.26; C. H. Douglas, *Brief for the Prosecution* (Liverpool, 1945), p. 1; idem, *The Big Idea* (Liverpool [1942]), pp. 50, 64.

On one occasion Douglas revealed to an audience how he came to hit upon Social Credit. Although the quotation, from a book by H.M.M., is a long one, it deserves to be given, for it is revealing in several ways and on several levels.

He said the beginning of this rather long-winded story was about fifteen years ago. He said, he was in India in charge of the Westinghouse interests in the East, and it happened that one of these interests concerned a survey of a large district with a good deal of waterpower. The survey was made at the instance of the Government of India, and there was found to be a good deal of waterpower all right. Major Douglas said he went back to Calcutta and Simla and asked what was going to be done about these. They said, "Well, we have not got any money." At the time manufacturers in Great Britain were hard put to for orders, and prices for machinery were very low indeed. Major Douglas said he accepted the statement made, and, he supposed, pigeon-holed the fact in his mind. At that time, he said, he dined frequently with a gentleman who was the controller-general of India, and he used to bore him very considerably by continually talking about something that he called credit. He used to tell of his experiences in India and Britain with Treasury officials who persisted in melting down and recoining rupees, having regard to what they called "the quantity theory of money." "Silver and gold have nothing to do with the situation; it nearly entirely depends upon credit," his friend used to say. Major Douglas remarked that had his friend given him a short, sharp lecture on Mesopotamia it would have been at that time about as intelligible to him. Nevertheless, that fact also must have got pigeon-holed in his mind.

Major Douglas proceeded to say that just before the war he was employed by the British Government in connection with a railway for the Post Office from Paddington to Whitechapel. There were no physical difficulties with the enterprise at all. He used to get orders to get along with the job. He used to get orders to slow up with the job and pay off the men. . . . Then the war came, said Major Douglas, "and I began to notice you could get money for any purpose." And that struck him again as being curious.

After that there was an interval, so far as he was concerned personally, until he was sent down to Farnborough to the Royal Aircraft Works in connection with a certain amount of muddle into which that institution had got. After some weeks he found that the only way in which he could do anything was to go very carefully into the costing. His friend . . . had suggested to him to get some tabulating machines, which he did, and after a time he began to live with those things, he said, and even to dream of rivers of cards emanating from those machines. One day it struck him, with regard to the figures on those cards, that the wages and the salaries did not represent at the week-end the value or the price of those goods produced. "You say anybody would know that, and I suppose they would," said the Major. But it followed to him if that was true, then it was also true in every factory in every week at the same time. Therefore, it was true that the amount of purchasing power or wages and salaries during that week was not sufficient to buy the product according to the price at that week.[29]

The first interest in this account is the implied claim that Social Credit was the discovery of Douglas's own unaided efforts. This, surprisingly enough, seems to have been the case. It has been shown that no tradition of monetary reform existed in Britain and that it was unlikely that the general public would know of such matters. Moreover, it was certain that Douglas was ignorant of the few monetary reformers of the day; he had to be put on to the *New Age* by Jackson, and only came into contact with Kitson's ideas after this development. Douglas does not seem to have been the man to take another's idea without acknowledgement, and when he did rely upon the Work Study people he said so. Later, when he knew more about monetary reform, he admitted that about one hundred years ago the germ of Social Credit had been known.[30] Above all there was the testimony, both of his colleagues and of his own writings, that he was quite ignorant of any theoretical economics and that his reading was extremely slight.

[29] Quoted in H. M. M., *An Outline of Social Credit* (London, 1929), p. 5.

[30] C. H. Douglas, *Credit-Power and Democracy* (London: Cecil Palmer, 1920), p. 14; idem, *The Big Idea*, pp. 10–11; NA 17.7.30.

Secondly, the quotation is of interest in suggesting that Social Credit was a merely materialistic doctrine and that what was known as the A + B theorem, an amazingly crude account of the industrial process, was an essential foundation for this hedonistic philosophy. Social Credit was nothing of the sort, in fact, but one could be pardoned for thinking so from Douglas's own account of it. What had happened was that by 1923, when the above quotation was made, developments had caused Douglas himself to become a victim of his own propaganda and theory. His earlier views had been effectively overlain by a changed emphasis.

This was partly Douglas's fault. As his theories were examined, the lack of novelty in them became more and more obvious, and there was an understandable tendency to concentrate upon the more characteristically Social Credit ideas. It should also be noted that in these five or so years since he had begun to advocate his theories Douglas had undergone a shock of disillusionment. At the time, he did not have the experience of the fortunes of monetary reform movements which Kitson, say, had had. He was not prepared, like Kitson, for the government's deflationary policy, and when it came his somewhat naive reaction was one of horror, akin to that with which he received the rebuff of his scheme at the hands of the Labour party and other bodies which, he was convinced, ought to have been interested. This revelation, coupled with the disastrous effects of the depression and the beginning of the application about this time of new industrial processes such as electricity, mass production, and time and motion studies—the juxtaposition of poverty and plenty, in fact—seems to have made a big impact upon him. In his earlier writings he had been inclined to see Britain as oversupplied with goods, or even to believe that "the world was over-manufacturing before the war in nearly every direction." He believed too that "the material requirements of the individual are quite definitely limited," and he was more interested in the possibilities of more rational systems leading to shorter hours of work. He was even prepared to agree that the fourteenth century in England had enjoyed an adequate standard of living without excessive labour. But by 1930 he wrote, "The problem . . . is to provide the greatest number of people with the greatest amount of money that they can effectively use."[31] The change of emphasis was as if his

[31] C. H. Douglas, "The Delusion of Super-Production," *English Review*, 1918, pp. 428, 432; idem, *Economic Democracy* (London, 1920), p. 67; idem, *These Present Discontents* (London, 1922), p. 8; NA 30.10.30.

anger with the authorities had pushed him into the belief that their parsimony should be countered by the utmost prodigality. The interest in the power of the machine became sharper, and plenty and its desirability began to be insisted upon.

In the conditions of the depression, then, it was natural and it seemed tactically wiser to play down the aesthetic considerations. And so Douglas hit out at the Penty-Mairet emphasis upon craftsmanship. "Handicraft belongs to . . . amusement," he wrote in a reasonable mood, and "There is absolutely no virtue in taking ten hours to produce by hand a necessary which a machine will produce in ten seconds," in an unreasonable one.[32] For this kind of utterance his follower Reckitt denounced him as "a sub-human thinker."[33] Such a description was not warranted, however. Douglas was responsive towards beauty (his yachting and fishing suggest this), and he could be scathing about the tendency of the world to value the wrong things, deploring "this glorification of Bigness." And he went on, "Bigness for the sake of Bigness, you can't have too much Bigness. . . . The Albert Memorial is bigger than any Cotswold cottage—grade accordingly."[34] It would be wrong, then, to think of Douglas as a crudely materialistic writer; in fact, his main concern was for quite other ends. The age of plenty and the A + B theorem were not the starting point for his system at all. In fact, to understand Social Credit it is necessary not only to set it within the limits of its author's method and style but also to set its mechanisms within the context of the total system. Here one is reminded of Pound's warning.

At the outset Douglas's system appears to be contradictory. At times he was determined to insist upon individualism as the beginning and end of social organization. He was positive that "systems were made for men, and not men for systems, and the interest of man, which is self development, is above all systems." It followed from this that "we must build up from the individual, not down from the state." Beyond this notion of self-development Douglas would not be more precise. He refused to make extravagant claims about the end of man, contenting himself with the observation that "the end of man, while unknown, is something towards which most rapid progress is made by the free expression of individuality." At the same time he insisted that man was not so depraved that freedom would be dangerous for

[32] NA 12.7.28; *Economic Democracy*, p. 45.
[33] Personal communication from M. B. Reckitt, 1967.
[34] *The Big Idea*, p. 25; see also *Economic Democracy*, p. 78.

him. He denied the view that given a state of plenty "Jack Jones would drink himself to death in a week," and he added, "Personally I am all for letting Jack Jones try." He backed up this belief with repeated denunciations of puritanism, which he described as repellent.[35]

On the other hand Douglas stressed the value of the organic, and his approach to Chesterton and the Distributists on this point has been noted. As the years passed, this emphasis grew more pronounced, until he came to lament the breakup of the landed estates and the disruption of the ruling families. The organic, however, was always of negative importance for Douglas, and any attempt to endow the group with a positive purpose always brought forth his scorn; he had early dismissed such claims with the sneer, "We can, I think, safely leave the group consciousness to look after itself," and during the Second World War he attacked the Germans for their exaggerated notions on the point.[36]

The way in which Douglas was torn between these two poles was well illustrated by the problem which America posed for him. At first he was most favourably inclined towards that country, paying tribute to the Declaration of Independence as "an assertion of the supremacy of the individual considered collectively." Soon afterwards he welcomed Wilson's speech at Versailles as "marking the authorative and formal entry of the plain people into that heritage from which they have so long been debarred." But when the idea of the League of Nations emerged he recoiled, protesting that "the very core of the League of Nations idea is power, final and absolute."[37]

What lay behind this judgement was an attitude which Douglas would probably have disowned had it been put to him. Douglas never succeeded in stating his basic objection to such organizations as the League of Nations. His engineering past would have stood in the way of such an admission, but it was really the efficiency of the closed society which he feared. The nearest he got to revealing this belief was in the following very Pentyesque statement: "To strain after 'justice' is not only to miss it, but is the sure and certain way of handing over the world afresh to the tender mercies of the high priest and the scribes." It was this fear which accounted for his horror of the Fabian Society and of its creation, the London School of Economics, an

[35] *Economic Democracy*, pp. 6–7; *Social Credit*, 28.9.34; *This Prosperity*, 11.32; NA 1.11.28, 30.10.30; NEW 9.6.32.

[36] *The Big Idea*, pp. 26–28; *Brief for the Prosecution*, p. 79; NA 30.12.20.

[37] NA 6.2.19 20.11.19; *Economic Democracy*, p. 5.

institution which, Douglas felt, was devoted to running peoples' lives by reducing them to statistics.[38]

What made Douglas fear organization and what made him insist upon the organic was his bold analysis of human nature and especially of human motivation. While holding that most people were good, socially minded creatures, he allowed the existence of a minority whose driving force was the pursuit of power. It was here in the identification of the power complex that Douglas showed his originality. In a pretotalitarian age it was difficult to conceive of anyone's being motivated by power for its own sake. Yet it was this point which Douglas had stressed from his earliest writings onwards; the second of his articles in the *English Review* was entitled "The Pyramid of Power." In that article he described the "will to power" and noted that it was particularly virulent in Germany. The war had encouraged the development of this will, and not only in Germany, so that a new danger faced the world. It was not merely an intensification of previous conflict, for there was a qualitative difference, too. "Strong and embittered differences of opinion resulting in some sort of conflict are nothing new in the history of civilization," Douglas noted, "they recur with dreary monotony. The relative merits of a York or a Lancaster . . . have riven countries from top to bottom without resulting in the emergence of anything very new. . . . But there is a definitely novel component in the present upheaval . . . the cleavage is in the main horizontal and the issue is impersonal." In Douglas's view, then, groups were of two kinds. There were traditional natural groupings which predated the emergence of the "novel component in the present upheaval" and which were to be preserved as essential protection against the coming storm. They would tend to be small, and in fact Douglas once declared that no organization should exceed three thousand. On the other hand there were artificial organizations which had no real purpose but to provide the means by which the power seekers could arrange the people into a perfect hierarchy of obedience. It was for this reason that Douglas was so distrustful of democracy. Not that he was prepared to give up the concept itself. He declared his belief in the "Democracy of the Common Will"; what he rejected was the "Democracy either of the Intellect or of the Emotions, which lead directly to dictatorships." Thus he refused to distinguish between the extreme right and the extreme left. He sensed rather than understood that mass mobilization through the ballot box would lead to "a

[38] *Credit-Power and Democracy*, p. 13; C.H. Douglas, *The Labour Party and Social Credit* (London, 1922), p. 23.

Mussolini and a Lenin or Trotsky who are identical in their contempt for Liberty and passion for the rule of centralizing force." The same intuition led him to oppose the Work Study philosophy and its later manifestation, Technocracy, two movements which maintained that a planned approach to the routine of work at all levels could lead to tremendous increases in output. Such methods demanded a high level of organization and therefore were to be feared. A typical Douglas judgement upon these movements was that they were "Syndicalist in essence and [did] not differ very widely . . . from . . . Fascism."[39]

It was inevitable that sooner or later Douglas should seek to identify more precisely the power-seeking conspiracy. In the beginning he was restrained in his attitude towards it. But from an early belief that it might, "like Topsy, just have growed," he moved to attack "a very deeply laid and well considered plot of enslaving the industrial world to the German-American-Jewish financiers." It was not long before the German-American element faded into the background, leaving the Jews as the real villains of the piece. When asked where real power ultimately lay, Douglas would answer that it was with Sir Basil Zaharoff, the mysterious armament king.[40] But the nature of this anti-Jewish outlook must be probed, for it is doubtful whether it can be called anti-Semitism in the normal sense.

In the early days Douglas always denied any animus against individual Jews. Even in the 1930s he wrote: "It must be emphasized that attacks upon the Jews as a body are wholly indefensible, except in cases where Jews act as a body while utilizing advantages which proceed from their incorporation as individuals in other nations. So far as this review is concerned, only their financial relationships are in question." On a later occasion he asserted, "The very last thing which I should desire . . . would be the association of the Social Credit movement with Jew-baiting," and he acknowledged that the persecution of Jews would mean "an irreparable loss to the rest of the world." He could praise individual Jews and thought highly of Sidney Hillman, the Jewish leader of the American Clothing Workers, whom he met in America and whom he described as "one of the ablest labour

[39] *English Review*, 1919, p. 100; personal communication from Mrs. M. W. Gordon-Cumming, 1967; *Fig Tree*, 6.36; NA 5.7.28, 12.1.33; NEW 12.1.33.

[40] NA 1.1.25; personal communication from T. M. Heron, 1967. Zaharoff was a dealer in armaments, and his sinister appearance and secretive manner were gifts to people like Douglas. For Douglas's considered views on these matters see his *The Big Idea*, p. 49.

leaders I have ever met." But later a harder line began to emerge. Conveniently, Douglas summarized his attitude towards the Jewish question as follows: "If I have, for my own part, come to believe that there is a fundamental relationship between the troubles which afflict Europe and what is known as the Jewish problem I have formed that opinion with reluctance . . . perhaps the first necessity is to explain beyond any risk of misunderstanding, the nature of the charge, and why it is a racial and not a personal indictment. In this connection, Disraeli's description of his people as 'a splendidly organized race' is significant. Organization has much of the tragedy of life to its debt; and organization is a Jewish speciality." The most important point about the Jews was the extent of their exclusiveness. This meant a great amount of inbreeding and there was, too, a reliance upon a narrow tradition, especially upon an education which stressed a detailed knowledge of a restricted number of sacred books. The result of this way of life, thought Douglas, was the breeding of a race which was far more homogenous than any other, a race which tended to think in the same overall way. Because of this it was the ideal vehicle for those seeking power; it provided a ready disciplined army which could be manipulated into doing the will of the real rulers. In fact, to Douglas, the Jews were the unwilling and unknowing dupes of a conspiracy, not the conspiracy itself; some, but not all, of the leaders of this conspiracy would be Jewish. This aspect of the argument was brought out clearly in the case of the Freemasons, who were likewise a tool of a conspiracy. "It must be remembered that the essence of Freemasonry is that 99% of Freemasons don't know what it is about, or what they are doing."[41]

Evidently to Douglas, Jewishness was not a racial term at all, but a philosophical description. This point was made very clearly when he once divided systems into two, the characteristics of the first being "Deductive, Totalitarian, Machiavellian, Idealistic, Jewish, Love of Power, Planned Economy," and of the second and balancing group, "Inductive, Democratic, Baconian, Realistic, Christian, Love of Freedom, Organic Growth."[42] Anti-Semitism of the Douglas kind, if it can be called anti-Semitism at all, may be fantastic, may be dangerous even, in that it may be twisted into a dreadful form, but it is not in itself vicious nor evil. It is merely an extreme form of religio-

[41] *Fig Tree*, 12.36, 3.55; NA 3.6.26, 2.9.26; *Social Credit*, 26.8.38; *The Big Idea*, p. 50.
[42] *Fig Tree*, 6.38.

philosophic propaganda, to be classed with Coulton's anti-Catholic tirades. And finally it must not be forgotten that Douglas did not seek to discriminate against Jews as people; it was never suggested that the National Dividend be withheld from them.

So far, in its concern for the free individual, as free as possible from the state, and in its tendency towards seeing a conspiracy of a personal kind, the analysis has been quite evidently Distributist. But whereas the Distributist answer was to put the clock back, if not to the Middle Ages then to primitive capitalism, Douglas was very different. For a solution he looked to the *New Age*. From that paper he took the idea of devolution. At first he was prepared to see the guild system as providing a satisfactory solution to the problem, and this was considered, though not by name, in his first *English Review* article, "The Delusion of Super Production," in 1918. But as time went on this commitment was weakened. In the first book, he acknowledged, "Among the more important of these forms of positive decentralization is the shop steward or rank-and-file movement in industry and the workmen's councils in politics, both purely decentralizing in tendency." He qualified this by adding that he would not want workers to control everything, for example, distribution, since this notion was "based on the fallacy that labour . . . produces all the wealth, whereas . . . production is 95% a matter of tools and processes." In his second book, which came out soon after the first, the reference to guild socialism had become slighting, and the final impossibility of that system was made plain when it was pointed out that it was producer-centred, whereas for Douglas the consumer was the more important.[43]

Yet if devolution on the Guild Socialist plan was not viable, it was still possible to approach it on a slightly different tack, and that was by taking up de Maeztu's functionalism. Douglas noted: "The vital and probably immortal germ of the Guild Idea is its recognition of function in society as well as in the Individual. . . . A satisfactory modern cooperative State may be broadly expressed as consisting of a functionally aristocratic hierarchy of producers accredited by and serving a democracy of consumers." By "function" was meant what de Maeztu had meant, organization for a specific task, and this was to be contrasted with "the military system," which was de Maeztu's old bugbear, sovereignty. Indeed on one occasion Douglas went very near to a paraphrase of de Maeztu when he wrote, "Any policy which

---

[43] *Economic Democracy*, p. 91; *Credit-Power and Democracy*, p. 76.

aims at the establishment of a complete sovereignty, whether it be a Kaiser, a State, a Trust or a Trade Union, is a policy of Domination, irrespective of the fine words with which it may be accompanied."[44] Years later it was acknowledged that functionalism was the only element of guild socialism which Douglas found congenial, and it was stated that de Maeztu himself accepted Social Credit, "having learned from Douglas that the functional principle shall first of all be applied to the credit monopoly."[45]

Having thus made use of the Distributist and *New Age* philosophies to form the basis of his own system, Douglas introduced something more specifically his own. This was a more precise account of the part which economics should play in society. The existing system was totally unacceptable, for it tolerated poverty. In two ways poverty militated against the flowering of individuality which Douglas insisted upon. To begin with, he held that "the basis of independence . . . is most definitely economic; it is simply hypocrisy . . . to discuss freedom of any description which does not secure to the individual . . . an average economic equivalent of the effort made." The test of an economic system was therefore the Ruskinian one, that "economic organization is most efficient when it most easily and rapidly supplies economic wants," that is, not a value system but a wealth system.[46]

Secondly, and more importantly, poverty was accompanied by its "twin evil . . . servility." Physical want was bad enough, yet after all it was only a "transient phenomenon." Servility, however, was "a definite component of a system having centralized control of policy as its apex."[47] By this Douglas meant that continual want was the lever by which the conspiracy was enabled to do its work. A full understanding of the economic system would pinpoint the way in which the conspirators were enslaving the world, and yet at the same time it would show the people the way in which this and other conspiracies could be crushed beyond any possibility of resurgence. It is at this point, and only at this point, that the technical side of Social Credit is to be considered.

The Douglas of the later years always rested his case upon the A + B theorem and claimed it was the test of Social Credit genuineness. With this wish his critics have been in agreement, claiming that

[44] *Credit-Power and Democracy,* p. 94; *These Present Discontents,* p. 5.
[45] *Fig Tree,* 9.37.
[46] *Economic Democracy,* p. 6; *Social Credit,* 28.9.34.
[47] *Economic Democracy,* pp. 16–17.

a repudiation of A+B meant a repudiation of Social Credit itself. It is important then to see just what the A + B theorem stated. For this purpose it is necessary to go, not to Douglas's earlier writings, but to his second book, *Credit-Power and Democracy*, for it was there that the A + B theorem made its first appearance. This in itself should be sufficient to call a halt before rushing to assume certain things about A + B, for it suggests that it was not the foundation of the doctrine so much as an indication of it. What was it that Douglas actually said?

The key passage reads as follows:

> Payments may be divided into two groups: Group A—All payments made to individuals (wages, salaries and dividends). Group B—All payments made to other organizations (raw materials, bank charges, and other external costs.) Now the rate of flow of purchasing power to individuals is represented by A, but since all payments go into prices the rate of flow of prices cannot be less than A + B. The product of any factory may be considered as something which the public ought to be able to buy, although in many cases it is an intermediate product of no use to individuals, but only to a subsequent manufacture; but since A will not purchase A + B, a proportion of the product at least equivalent to B must be distributed by some form of purchasing power which is not comprised in the descriptions grouped under A. It will be necessary at a later stage to show that this additional purchasing power is provided by loan credits (bank overdrafts) or export credit.[48]

It is unfortunately necessary to begin by showing what A + B did *not* say. In the first place it was not saying that there was a growing inability on the part of the community to buy the *consumable* goods being produced; the inclusion of the phrase, "ought to be able to buy although . . . of no use to individuals" is unambiguous. Secondly, it was not saying that the system was breaking down. It allowed that the system would be kept going by the injection of purchasing power equal to B, and it was pointed out that there were organizations willing and eager to provide the required amounts; they would come

[48] *Credit-Power and Democracy*, p. 22.

from "loan credits." In other words the A + B theorem was not an argument devoted to establishing the increasing poverty of the community or to showing the contradictions of the productive system which would inevitably produce a smash. It was an argument devoted primarily to showing the inevitability of servility, for since the people could never buy the whole product, the plant owners retained power.

> The unregulated system of credit issue and price making distributes purchasing power both in respect of capital production . . . and ultimate products . . . it takes back in the prices of ultimate products only practically the whole of this purchasing power, leaving the community . . . in the position of having bought both the plants and the product, but having only got delivery, i.e. control, of the product.[49]

This was bad enough, but what was worse was the other truth which A + B taught; it established that the continuance of the system depended upon the whim of those who controlled the supply of B payments, in other words, the financiers. Capitalism had given way to creditism, the objectionable to the diabolical.

The A + B theorem does not support the general interpretation that the capitalist system was inherently unstable and that the community was becoming poorer and poorer. Yet Social Credit has always been assumed to mean this. Is it then a complete misunderstanding? Not at all, for Douglas, the prophet of doom, did believe in the "coming crash," and he did believe that the community was being deprived of goods "by the most gigantic and organized sabotage on the part of the capitalistic system and Labour itself."[50] Where then was the basis for such a belief, if not in A + B?

In Douglas's view the nature of advanced industrial technique meant that an ever-growing number of projects were intricate undertakings which could only begin to produce wealth after a long period of time; indeed, it might be several years before the products came onto the market. In the meantime, however, the wages and salaries of those working on the project, and the cost of the materials which were being used, were being paid throughout this long unproductive period. Two results flowed from this arrangement. In the first place

[49] *Credit-Power and Democracy,* p. 35.
[50] "The Coming Crash" was the title of a series of Social Credit lectures; see NA 25.9.24. *Credit-Power and Democracy,* p. 12.

a large amount of money was being fed into the existing supply, an amount which, because it related to products not yet in existence, caused inflation. This point was a minor one, however, and was subordinate to the second and main result. This argument held that none of this extra money was on hand to pay for the extra goods when eventually they came onto the market. It was this point which was the basis of the Douglas analysis, and as such it demands careful consideration.

To Douglas the main point of attack was upon the "so-called" law of supply and demand. It was a law which, he was convinced, was used by the power seekers to hoodwink the people. In theory, supply and demand was a process which, given time for equilibrium to be found, ensured justice between the two parties to a contract and so enabled the economic cycle to continue. Douglas spotted, however, that in any but utopian conditions the process was a hypocritical one, working in one direction only. "It is," he wrote, "a widespread delusion that price is simply a question of supply and demand, whereas, of course, only the upper limit of price is thus governed, the lower limit, which under free competition would be the ruling limit, being fixed by cost plus the minimum profit which will provide a financial inducement to produce."[51]

Douglas was claiming, then, that within the capitalist system, driven by the need to maximize profits, the money in any market was completely removed by the working of supply and demand. It did not matter if extra money was appearing, money in respect of extra but future goods; that extra money would be removed, too, by the same operation of the same law of supply and demand, working within the premise of the need to maximize profits. But what happened when a sudden increase in the amount of goods in the market took place, when, in fact, the future goods became present goods? The extra money had already been recovered. In theory, supply and demand dictated that price equal total money divided by total goods. But the costs of production had been incurred in a past cycle (which incidentally had been subject to inflationary pressure, thus aggravating the situation) and so bore no essential relation to the present position. Nevertheless, the manufacturer had to cover these past costs (or go out of business), and to do this meant selling above the theoretical supply and demand price. It followed that not all the extra goods could be removed from the market. In certain areas gluts would take

[51] *Economic Democracy,* p. 55.

place, and a chain reaction leading to depression would be under way. Only the bankruptcy of a sufficient number of traders would release the required free purchasing power into the system to enable expansion to get under way again.

The difficult point of this argument is the assertion that the increased supply of goods encounters a more or less static and insufficient supply of money. It was urged against Douglas that he had ignored the fact that industry is a continuous process and that money taken off the market in price is simultaneously and just as quickly reentering the market as wages, salaries, payments for raw materials, and so on. This was the point where Douglas introduced the "rate of flow" argument.

From the beginning Douglas had realized that this objection would be brought up, and he warned: "Let not the patient reader allow himself to become confused by the fact that B has at some previous time been represented by payments of wages, salaries and dividends. While this is of course true it is irrelevant—it is the rate of flow which is vital."[52] He knew that the rate of invention and of industrial expansion was a tremendous one and that new processes were being added in great numbers at every possible point in the productive system. As he put it in one of his high-flown moments: "The industrial machine is a lever, continuously being lengthened by progress, which enables the burden of Atlas to be lifted with ever increasing ease. As the number of men required to work the lever decreases, so the number set free to lengthen it increases."[53] It is clear, then, what he meant by the rate of flow; he meant that the rate at which B payments were being incurred (that is, new processes added to the productive system) was greater than that at which they were being transformed into A payments. Significantly, he allowed that the Social Credit analysis would not have been applicable to a pre-machine-age society.[54] It is this which made nonsense of the criticism offered by E. F. M. Durbin, the promising young Labour politician, whose argument relied upon the Hayek model for a refutation of A + B. That model was a static one, in that it assumed that the number of manufacturing processes did not increase, or if they did increase they did so only in step with the population; that is, the model ignores a qualitative difference in the profile of industry. And it also makes nonsense

[52] *Credit-Power and Democracy,* pp. 24–25.
[53] *Credit-Power and Democracy,* p. 20.
[54] *Economic Democracy,* p. 40.

of C. B. Macpherson's claim, "Douglas assumed that the economy is neither expanding nor contracting," for which statement of course no documentation was or can be given.[55] It was unfortunately typical that the clearest statement of the basis of Social Credit had to come from a pen other than Douglas's.

That it was official may be judged from the fact that it appeared in the *Fig Tree*, Douglas's own journal, of which he was editor. The author in question, R. L. Northridge, wrote inter alia, "Since the number of machines in use has been, and is, constantly increasing having started from zero, and since during their life all are collecting money which is to be disbursed only after they are scrapped, a very considerable deficiency must arise from the mere increase of capital assets."[56] Douglas had said as much years before, but unfortunately not nearly clearly enough.

It will be appreciated that the rate-of-flow concept was a vital factor in both the Douglas arguments. It explained how supply and demand brought about increasing poverty amidst plenty by impeding, not fostering, the rapid distribution of an ever-increasing supply of goods. But it was also essential to the concept of increasing servility, the A + B theorem itself. The rate-of-flow argument drew attention to the fact that the profile of industry was ever changing as a continually increasing number of processes was inserted into industry. In this broadening of the industrial pyramid the providers of loan capital played a controlling part. Consequently, as the rate of flow became bigger and faster, these providers of credit came to exercise an ever-increasing dictatorship over the organization of industry. In step with the quickening of the rate of flow went the hardening of financial monopoly.

The rate-of-flow concept was therefore the bridge by which the two basic, but quite distinct, ideas of Douglas's Social Credit were joined. Indeed, so inextricably did the two ideas become entwined that they became fused, not only in the mind of the public but in the mind of the inventor himself. Now, having disentangled the two strands, it is possible to attempt an evaluation of Social Credit.

The socialist element in Social Credit was patent. To begin with, the A + B theorem was an argument directed to proving what Marxists would have had no hesitation in calling surplus value.

[55] E. F. M. Durbin, *The Problem of Credit Policy* (London, 1935), p. 41; C. B. Macpherson, *Democracy in Alberta* (Toronto, 1962), pp. 110–11.
[56] *Fig Tree*, 6.36.

Douglas came near to saying so when he spoke of "the constant filching of purchasing power from the individual in favour of the financier." Similarly socialistic was his idea of the Cultural Heritage. He believed along with the socialists that "natural resources are common property, and the means of exploitation should also be common property"; he also believed that "the industrial machine is a common heritage, the result of the labours of untold generations of people whose names are for the most part forgotten . . . therefore . . . society as a whole . . . has a right to the product." This notion of the Cultural Heritage was made more specific, and the general attack broadened, by the attention devoted to the concept of real and financial credit. This followed from the previous idea that only the Cultural Heritage and the present use made of it by society can represent wealth and that financial credit is merely a convenient way of representing this *real* wealth. But such a mirror should, like the original, be a communal possession, whereas it had fallen into the hands of the bankers, whose granting of an "overdraft is just as absolutely new money as if the banker had coined it or printed bank-notes for the amount." Not that Douglas had any objection to the expansion of currency in this bookkeeping way, but he wanted the community to have the control of this useful power.[57]

Securely based on such socialist grounds, Douglas could afford to be far more radical than the Labour party of that day. While that body hivered and hovered over the advisability of a capital levy, Douglas was quite clear in his own mind. The alternative form of nationalizing he rejected on the Bellocian ground that it would be found to benefit those already in possession of the wealth, and he contemplated the outright confiscation of all factories, plants, railways, et cetera. It would be no outrage because the community had "already bought and paid for many times over the whole of the plant used for manufacturing processes."[58]

Despite this, Douglas has always been seen as an antisocialist. Certainly he revealed on occasion a strong dislike, amounting to loathing, for socialism. But when he named the three forms of socialism in vogue when he began writing—Fabianism, or state socialism as practised in Prussia, guild socialism, and bolshevism—it was

[57] *Credit-Power and Democracy*, pp. 18, 31, 32; *Economic Democracy*, pp. 69, 110.
[58] *Economic Democracy*, p. 112; *Credit-Power and Democracy*, pp. 69, 72.

evident that he was objecting not to their assumptions about the final goal, but to their assumptions about the methods to be adopted. Douglas felt that all three believed, in varying degrees, in the need to discipline the great mass of the people and run their lives for them through a bureaucracy. His own pet name for socialism was "monopoly." The objection to socialism was summed up in the following examination of what might happen under "a Labour administration of a nationalized state":

> Now the State being the only producer, intermediate products would have no external market in the country, with this interesting result—that either all capital production costs would be allocated against ultimate products, in which case the ultimate products would absorb at least the total earnings of the whole population, or alternatively only maintenance, depreciation and obsolescence . . . would be charged against ultimate products, in which case prices would be less than costs by the ratio that capital would bear to consumption, but the community would have no possible means of utilizing its cash savings. In either case the community would have no financial control whatsoever over the capital it had helped to produce.[59]

In other words, the socialist solution was no solution at all, since the individual would have even less chance than he enjoyed under capitalism of asserting his freedom. Once again it is seen that to Douglas increasing servility was the more important consideration.

The problem then was to bring about a socialist commonwealth without, however, replacing it with an even worse state of affairs. Socialism or any form of planning was totalitarian and fraught with danger, though its efficiency could not be denied and though the national control of, say, the railways and electricity supplies could be envisaged. At the same time the drawbacks of capitalism, that its concept of ownership was socially impossible and that its basis in supply and demand played into the hands of the financial conspirators, meant that a change was absolutely essential. However, not everything should be given up, for capitalism had the supreme merit of fostering independence and inventive skill; it was important not to

[59] *Credit-Power and Democracy*, p. 56.

tip the baby out with the bathwater. The middle way was to leave the administration of enterprises to private individuals but to remove the possibility of exploitation which depended upon ownership. Douglas looked to the day when an owner's factory would have lost "all its property value, leaving only the administrative value"—when, in fact, the owner would cease to draw a profit and would begin to draw a commission, based on a turnover dictated by public estimation of his products.[60] Douglas thought that he had a simple method of doing this.

It will be remembered that to Douglas the real crux of the problem was supply and demand, a faulty law which enabled the real rulers to retain their hold on the source of consumable goods and which, at the same time, prevented the smooth transfer of goods from producers to consumers. The solution, then, lay in cutting the Gordian knot and making the law a valid one, applying not only to consumable goods but also to capital goods (this would end servility) and also applying to the present, not to a past accounting system (this would end the increasing poverty). The mechanism was the Just Price.

The method was simplicity itself, and as will be seen, it did not depend upon the A + B theorem. At the root lay a grasp of what cost was when expressed in nonmonetary, but real, terms. Cost was "the price of consumption," according to one of Douglas's favorite aphorisms.[61] The meaning of this statement may be judged from the examination of a static economy, merely content to replace the productive agencies and to maintain the volume of production. In that condition price must be such as to replace, and just replace, the consumed goods, both consumer goods and capital goods. If, however, the economy expands for any reason, and a surplus over the last accounting period is produced, then the cost of replacing the consumption will be less than it was in the previous case. Conversely, any extraordinary consumption, say a war, will mean a deficiency to be made up and so a need for cost to rise above the normal. In fact, Douglas was concerned with the first case, since he believed that the normal economic state was one of expansion. Thus, to take an extreme example, assume a 100 percent increase in goods coming onto the market; if the price prevailing at the time of their production, plus profit (that is, the old selling price of goods immediately prior to the arrival of the new batch), is charged, then only the old quantity can

---

[60] *Credit-Power and Democracy*, p. 51; *Economic Democracy*, pp. 18, 21.

[61] Personal communication from Mrs. W. T. Symons, 1966.

be disposed of, and the increase must remain unsold. However, the reduction of the price to 50 percent of the old price will enable all the goods to be taken off the market. Douglas summerized this as follows: "The Just Price of an article bears the same ratio to the cost of production that the total consumption and depreciation of the community bears to the total production."[62] It was held to be simple for a nongovernmental body of statistical experts to compute the required figures. The mechanism, it should be noted, was self-regulatory. If the community at any moment decided to rest on its laurels and relax its effort, the consumption would approach, maybe even surpass, production, and the price would rise to and possibly above the cost price. It was also proof against inflation, for by definition price would be such that all money would be removed from the market; there could be no money free to chase prices.

The scheme, however, could not be allowed to rest there. The Just Price, while it would benefit everyone, was essentially a development of the existing system of rewarding effort. Douglas was prepared to go some way with this principle, for he believed that a person should be free to make the most of his talents. But to *base* any system upon such a principle would be to accept puritanism and its own basis, a world of scarcity. In the age of plenty there was no need for abstemiousness. Moreover, the concept of scarcity was the main weapon with which those with the will to power worked; remove this weapon and the conspiracy would become powerless. Therefore, an equally important element in Social Credit thinking was the National Dividend, to be given as of right and inalienably to every citizen. Furthermore, such a payment was demanded by the logic of the Cultural Heritage. In the twentieth century, Douglas claimed, "the dividend is the logical successor to the wage."[63]

It was recognized that the National Dividend might open the door to inflation, since here was free money being injected into the system. The problem was never squarely faced, it must be admitted, though bows were made in the direction of some form of control over prices. It was felt that the wartime experience had shown the possibility of such controls, and the only remaining problem was that of the danger of too much state power. But in the condition of the times—depression, poverty in the midst of plenty—there was some justification for Social Credit's impatience with the argument. Indeed Kitson, always

[62] *Economic Democracy*, p. 134.
[63] *Credit-Power and Democracy*, p. 43.

unorthodox, went so far as to deny the practical possibility of inflation, pointing out that the "inflations" which had followed the fortuitous discoveries of gold in the middle of the nineteenth century and
again at the end of the century had been followed in turn by a
tremendous industrial expansion.[64] Social Crediters were never prepared to go this far, but their attitude did veer in this direction.

It is customary to dismiss the technical side of Social Credit as
fantastic and illogical. Douglas himself did not help matters by using
an awkward style and by throwing in a great deal of extraneous matter
which was bound to antagonize many of the sections of opinion which
he should have been attracting. But it is hoped that this account has
revealed the sane basis which Social Credit possessed and that it has
also made clear why so many people, among them several prominent
thinkers, gave their allegiance to the doctrine in the period between
the wars.

Was Douglas a Positivist? The case for identifying a Positivist
background to Douglasism is a powerful one. In general terms there
was the fact that his solution, by stressing consumer credit and an
absolute definition of price, was within the anarchist-Positivist tradition rather than the Individualist. But the links with Comte can be
pressed more closely. Both were engineers who became sociological
catholics in outlook, objecting to atheism and to Protestantism-
puritanism in particular; both used the notion of the Cultural Heritage and accepted the value of organic growth, leading to a common
rejection of socialist, that is, planned, solutions; both believed that the
scientific method was to be used, yet never allowed to become more
than a method, and on this point there was an identical appeal to
Bacon. As a consequence of this functional stance they agreed in
allowing the people a decision on matters of fundamental choice, yet
refusing them a general sovereignty. Finally, there is the fact that
Douglas knew French, well enough to translate a book from that
language into English.[65] Did a young, bored engineer—in India,
say—while away the time in teaching himself the language by plod-
ding through a forgotten volume of Comte? Did the ideas of positivism soak into him in this half-conscious, half-understood way, to
lie dormant until later experience quickened them to life? How intriguing would be even a glance at the Douglas library!

[64] *New Albion*, 4.34.
[65] J. L. Chastenet, *The Bankers' Republic*, trans. C. H. Douglas (London, 1926).

chapter six

THE SOCIAL CREDIT MOVEMENT 1918-1936

One of the lessons which Social Credit learnt from the parent guild socialism was the advisability of avoiding formal organization. But even before the idea of guild socialism had been compromised by the collapse of the National Guilds League, Orage had distrusted movements and had preferred to remain on the level of academic discussion. As far back as 1912, when a correspondent had suggested "a League of Guild Socialists or at least a preliminary committee," Orage had done nothing. The establishment of a National Guilds League had had to wait until 1915, when Cole could give his attention to the venture. Even then Orage, "an individualist who hated societies and dreaded the influence of the mass mind," was sceptical; he joined only later, and then for tactical, internal reasons. Later the league was to take him to task for failing to give league activities sufficient support in the *New Age*.[1] Something of this way of thinking no doubt rubbed off onto Douglas, either planting the seeds of later development or else reinforcing notions already held. Certainly Orage and Douglas were

[1] NA 11.7.12, 13.5.15, 26.10.16; M. B. Reckitt, *As It Happened* (London, 1940), p. 132; P. Mairet, *A. R. Orage: A Memoir* (London, 1936), p. 69; N. Carpenter, *Guild Socialism* (New York, 1922), p. 95.

close in their outlooks, especially at this period, and when Orage was ill at the beginning of 1919, it was Douglas whom he chose to write "The Notes of the Week."

More importantly, the emergence of Social Credit from the disintegrating guild movement meant that the early form of Douglasism was fixed and identified with a particular kind of support. As was explained, the guild movement was wrecked on the rocks of communism. It was almost inevitable that a large number of those who were not prepared to follow the extremists should have been attracted to the ready-made alternative being championed so energetically by Orage. By the time the split came, Douglas had become well known within the Guild Socialist ranks. His first article in the *New Age* had appeared in the first issue of 1919. In a more formal way Social Credit had been brought to the attention of the National Guilds League when Douglas addressed the members in September 1919 and was praised for the "brilliant and entertaining character of the address." Some weeks later the column "Towards National Guilds" accepted the Douglas analysis as an integral part of guild method. It was an acceptance confirmed by the rewriting of the guild textbook to allow a place for the doctrine.[2]

But Social Credit did not have it all its own way. Cole was ready to fight acceptance. When, in March 1920, H.M.M. asked in the *Guildsman* why there was no discussion of an idea which he felt would "lead automatically to National Guilds," he was answered by Cole, who pointed out that while he was in agreement with much of the Social Credit analysis, especially approving the connection noted between price and purchasing power, he felt that Douglas's tactics were wrong and that it was best to go for production first and then later for the control of finance.[3] But Cole's criticisms were not sufficient to kill all discussion. In 1919–20 M. B. Reckitt, a convert to Social Credit, was secretary of the National Guilds League.[4] At the May conference of 1920, battle between the believers and the nonbelievers was joined when the Liverpool and Glasgow groups brought forward motions supporting Douglas. The outcome was the appointment of a committee, which included Penty and Reckitt, to consider the doctrine. An interim report was soon produced which noted that

[2] *Guildsman*, 11.19; NA 2.10.19; M. B. Reckitt and C. E. Bechhofer, *The Meaning of National Guilds* (London, 1920). The first edition had appeared two years earlier.
[3] *Guildsman*, 3.20.
[4] *Guildsman*, 9.19.

the National Guilds movement had now come to the point of considering not merely the workers but also the general public—in other words, the producer orientation was tilting towards the consumer. The imminence of a capitalist smash was pointed out, but this report did not judge the Douglas proposals themselves. This task was left to the extraordinary conference of December 1920, the one which discussed the league's standing vis-à-vis Bolshevik Russia. The scheme was attacked by several members: by Penty, on the ground that there was too great an emphasis upon currency as the way out; by S. G. Hobson, because he believed financiers depended just as much upon the workers as the other way round and because "this was the first time he had heard of an ethical proposition coming out of a mathematical formula, and he thought that Bertrand Russell should be told of it"; and by Cole, who repeated his earlier argument about tactics, adding that there was a danger of inflation and that it would be difficult to approach the Labour party if profit were kept. By thirteen to forty-one the Douglas scheme was rejected, a decision rubbed in by the savage review which Cole gave to *Credit-Power and Democracy* in the following issue of the *Guildsman*, in which he stated, "I believe this scheme to be unworkable practically, unsound economically and undesirable morally." What was worse, Cole had seen through Douglas. "Indeed, the truth is out, Major Douglas is in no sense a Guildsman. He is simply a Distributist and one who believes that control should rest with the consumer exercising power through the expert and not with the producers as a self-governing industrial democracy." The review ended by comparing Douglas with another writer, who, according to Cole, possessed the gift of clear writing, which Douglas lacked. "Perhaps," he said of the other writer, "this is because he knows what he means."[5]

But not all sections of the league were prepared to agree with Cole. The Coventry, Glasgow, and Paisley groups all broke away in protest against this treatment of Social Credit. The appeal of the Douglas scheme, which had "done more to revive the drooping spirits of Guildsmen than anything else of recent years," was noted.[6] A new stage in the spread of Social Credit ideas now began. The natural attempt to convince the guild movement had failed. The section which accepted the Douglas analysis now started to organize on a more

[5] *Guildsman*, 4.20, 9.20, 1.21, 2.21.
[6] *Guildsman*, 2.21, 4.21.

formal basis. During 1921 groups were formed across Britain for the study and propagation of Social Credit. The signal for this was given in March of that year when the Glasgow Guild Socialist, H. M. Murray, the disappearance of whose branch has been noted above, wrote to the *New Age* of 3 March 1921, pointing out that a study circle was being founded in that city. Other groups followed, and by the end of April eighteen groups had been set up; by the end of the next year this figure had risen to thirty-four.[7] There was, too, a permanent organization in existence (at least in 1921 a coordinating secretary was referred to), but this machinery cannot have had much life, because it was necessary to refound the movement in 1923.

Yet already morale was failing. In part this was inevitable with a scheme which claimed to be a mathematically demonstrable solution to the world's problems and yet failed to be accepted. As Douglas admitted some years later, "I had the idea that I had got hold of some specific technical information and I had only to get it accepted; I had the idea that I had only to run to father and he would be very pleased about it." In fact, Douglas was to run to two fathers. First, he and Orage submitted the scheme to the Ministry of Reconstruction. Later, he demanded an interview with Lloyd George to protest against the repayment of the United States loan in gold rather than in goods. Both times he was refused, in the first instance without being granted an interview.[8] But on top of this strange reluctance to take up the scheme which was shown by the leading men of the day, there were internal difficulties experienced by the movement. In 1922 two heavy blows fell.

The Labour party committee set up to examine Social Credit—and at this date both Douglas and Orage expected that it was through organized labour that their scheme stood the best chance of success—at last made its report and rejected the proposals. The reaction of Social Crediters was one of pained surprise. "It might have been expected," Douglas complained, "that the Labour Movement would be the first and most influential supporter of the claim to the social dividend."[9]

The second blow, and it may well have been triggered off by this

[7] The totals are approximate; at this stage no central authority published definitive lists, and these totals have been pieced together from notices in NA.

[8] *Social Crediter*, 14.1.39; NA 21.9.22; *Millgate Monthly*, 8.32.

[9] The Labour Party, *Labour and Social Credit* (London [1922]); this report is discussed below in chapter 9. NA 31.8.22.

rebuff, was the decision of Orage to give up journalism and retreat into the mysticism of the Gurdjieff-Ouspensky school at Fontainebleau. Such a loss was a grievous one for the movement, but far worse was the irresponsible way in which Orage disposed of his paper. A tentative offer to J. M. Murry was rejected, and the new owner and editor was to be Major William A. Moore, at one period a foreign correspondent for the *Times*. Moore had no interest in Social Credit and even began to point out what he considered to be the fallacies of the analysis. Before long he was revealed as a believer in a strong state which would dictate prices and would receive interest upon its, and not the community's, credit. Kitson was brought to the point of protesting, "In common with many others . . . I have been somewhat startled to see the change in the tone of *The New Age* since its change of ownership." The Central Advisory Council began to doubt that anything could "be got out of the paper," and it suggested, "The quicker we drop all reference to it in connection with Social Credit the better."[10] Fortunately, Moore found the *New Age* too uncongenial to remain for long in charge of it, and perhaps the implied boycott by the Social Credit movement exposed the paper's inability to keep going as an independent journal. In June 1923, Moore's retirement was announced. The editorship was taken over by Arthur Brenton, who had been running *Credit Power* since 1920.[11] Brenton was not the intellectual that Orage was, and under him the *New Age* never built up the following which the paper had enjoyed from 1907. But he was a competent editor from the narrow point of view of monetary reform. His commentary upon world affairs from the Social Credit angle, usually given in the form of extended analogies, which were his forte, ensured that the cause never lacked an adequate if not brilliant presentation. To him the message was all that mattered, and he was accustomed to dismiss the remainder as "wrapping."[12] Perhaps as important as the loss of Orage's pen was the disappearance of an undisputed authority which could give a central direction to the whole. At a time when the inevitable disillusionment gave rise to

[10] Reckitt, in a personal communication (1967) to the present writer, has stressed the irresponsibility of Orage at this point; NA 28.9.22, 7.12.22, 15.11.34; undated letter from H. Cousens to N. Egerton Swann in Reckitt's papers.

[11] NA 28.6.23. *Credit Power* began as *Public Welfare*, a private venture restricted to the Social Credit world. I have not been able to find copies of *Public Welfare*.

[12] Personal communications from M. B. Reckitt and W. T. Symons, 1966–67.

questioning over the most effective way of spreading Social Credit, the only force which might have been able to hold the movement together was absent, devoting his days to manual labour in a flight from the external, mechanized world.

The first sign that the initiative was being taken out of the hands of the entourage which till now had controlled Social Credit was the appeal made via the *New Age* for joint action between all monetary reform groups. The writer of the letter, G. F. Powell, mentioned the ideas of Kitson, Meulen, and Stoll in addition to the *New Age* advocates.[13] The proposal was not acted upon, and before long another criticism was heard. This time it was that the appeal of Social Credit had been too much directed at the middle classes and the intelligentsia and that what was needed was "the language of the pothouse." However, this too was rejected, because Douglasism, it was claimed, was too intellectual for popularizing; the attempt to do so would pervert the meaning. At the same time, the belief in the imminent breakdown of the existing system was insisted on, and the necessity of taking up Social Credit as the only possible solution was confidently awaited. The coming conference in January 1924 was expected to answer many problems on the correct strategy to be followed. The outcome of the conference was not helpful, however. Nothing was said which gave a clear indication of the way to a more effective approach. At least one Social Crediter felt more could be done by taking the message to the people, and he became a solitary speaker for Douglasism in Hyde Park.[14] Letters continued to be sent to the *New Age* demanding that attraction succeed demonstration, and that *something* be done. Towards the end of 1924 a pamphlet was circulated drawing attention to the lack of action and suggesting that Douglas himself was of this opinion, a suggestion which brought forth an indignant denial from Douglas.[15] A conference which was held at Swanwick in 1925 saw the difference brought into the open and marked the first of the many splits which distinguished the Social Credit movement in England.

The lead in pressing for a more organized and purposeful movement had been taken by a group centred on Sheffield. As befitted a city with a rich past of agitation for workers' control, Sheffield sported no fewer than three Social Credit study circles, one an ILP creation,

[13] NA 8.2.23.

[14] NA 4.10.23, 8.11.23, 29.5.24.

[15] The Open Letter and a draft reply by W. T. Symons are in Reckitt's papers; they date from April-May 1925. See also NA 23.4.25, 12.5.25.

and one, run by W. H. Bolton, which was theosophical.[16] It was from Bolton that a series of centralizing proposals came in May 1924. The contrary idea had been championed by the London establishment, a group which had had some experience, via the guild failure, of organized movements; when later in 1925 a coordinating secretary was appointed, the London members refused to participate or to contribute towards the cost.[17]

The Sheffield members went to the conference confident that they could impose their views upon the movement, for they had made their preparations well. The conference committee, charged with organizing the conference itself, had been packed by the Sheffield contingent; of the four members of this committee two were Sheffield men, A. L. Gibson and W. H. Bolton, while a third was Miss M. Alexander.[18] Although Miss Alexander originally came from Belfast, she was a protégée of the two just named, who had indeed been responsible for bringing her over from Northern Ireland. The last member was J. E. Tuke, who was not a strong character and was no doubt swayed by the others.[19] This inner group had produced an agenda which had been supported by eighty-seven Social Crediters, with six more qualified approvals, against only three decided negatives. Having prepared the ground so well, these activists felt optimistic about the outcome.

However, in some way which is not clear, the conference at Swanwick repudiated the prepared agenda. The person responsible for this defeat was W. T. Symons, a leading London member. His argument was, "The movement as such is a spiritual association." He also pointed out how a certain comrade in Manchester, a prominent industrialist there, could not "even use the title Social Credit in his approaches."[20] The plan for a centralized organization pursuing a policy of action was defeated. But those who supported the original Sheffield proposals, to the total of twenty-seven, decided to withdraw from the conference and organize their own movement. They in-

[16] NA 17.3.21. Bolton also had links with the Positivists—at least, one W. H. Bolton edited the *Positivist Year Book* (Liverpool, 1929); see J. E. McGee, *A Crusade for Humanity* (London, 1931), bibliography.

[17] E. E. McCarthy, "A History of the Social Credit Movement" (M.A. thesis, Leeds, 1947), p. 27.

[18] Reckitt's papers, Open Letter.

[19] Personal communication from Miss H. Corke, 1967. Tuke will be met with again in chapter 10.

[20] For Symon's part, a draft letter in Reckitt's papers. Symons is discussed in more detail in chapter 8.

cluded Kitson and Frederick Soddy, the Oxford chemist and
Nobel Prize winner, a certain Dr. Rice, who headed the new organization, and H. E. B. Ludlam, a Coventry printer who had been most
vociferous in the *New Age* in calling for the new line. [21] This group
later called itself the Economic Freedom League and, within a short
while, had its own journal, the *Age of Plenty*, edited by Ludlam.

The issue of centralized versus decentralized organization had been
one ground for the split. There had been a second ground, too—this
time the nature of the technical case for monetary reform. The difficulty which many near to Douglasism most commonly felt was the
interpretation of the A + B theorem—the hallmark, in fact, of pure
Douglas Social Credit—and there had always been those to play down
this aspect. When Soddy began to outline a brand of new economics
which dispensed with this concept, the way was open for a new
grouping to form of those who preferred to seek a lower common
denominator. Symons was as deeply opposed to this as he was to the
centralizing schemes. He pointed out that only Douglasism, making
use of the A + B theorem, had that new philosophic basis which
could commend the idea on other than economic grounds and make
it far superior to any of the other suggestions, which were but tinker-
ings with an outworn liberalism. The resolution which Symons carried brought out the commitment to the founder. "That the Social
Credit movement consists of those persons who wish to associate
themselves with the principles of Social Credit as enunciated by Major
Douglas"—that was the form of words which the rebels could not
accept and which was responsible for the split. [22]

Ostensibly the split had occurred over the question of strategy. But
at the same time there were those who distrusted Douglas's personal
qualities and his ability other than that for economic analysis. For
while the preliminaries for the conference were under way, the Sheffield group had been in touch with Douglas himself. The conference
committee had asked Douglas to become president of the Social

[21] Dr. Rice was of no account. Frederick Soddy, professor of chemistry at Oxford,
was an opponent of conspiracy; see F. Soddy, *Frederick Soddy Calling All Taxpayers*
(n.p. [1950]). His major, and very difficult, work was *Wealth, Virtual Wealth, and Debt*
(London, 1926), which was dedicated to Kitson. He also paid tribute to Douglas; see
his *The Inversion of Science* (London, 1924), p. iv. Ludlam is treated below in this
chapter.

[22] *Report of the Second Social Credit Conference* (n.p., n.d.), in Reckitt's papers.

Credit movement, but Douglas had declined this honour. Puzzled by this stance, the committee had interviewed Douglas but had not found the interview satisfactory. To them it appeared that Douglas was prepared to see the movement broken up and refounded in a completely new way. If the committee members were convinced that in representing Douglas in this light they were giving a true picture, then they were justified in feeling aggrieved some two months later. In April Douglas announced, "Good progress has been made in a short time on the present lines," and nothing more was said of the plans to reform the movement.[23] Miss Alexander, for one, felt that Douglas was an obstacle, and she gave his obstruction as the reason why she resigned from her position as coordinating secretary before the end of the year.[24]

From 1925, then, there existed two kinds of Social Credit. The majority, under the presumed leadership of Douglas (since he never repudiated this position after the uncertainties of the pre-1925 conference wrangling), numbered the greater part of the guild heritage, and they had settled down to the task of converting by gentle persuasion, using the still helpful appeal of the *New Age*. The other brand promised a more active propaganda and, in the first number of the *Age of Plenty*, claimed to be spearheading "a healthy discontent . . . that knows what it wants and is determined to get it." But it should be made clear that at this period the gap between the two kinds of Social Credit was not unbridgeable; Douglas himself contributed an article to an early issue of Ludlam's paper.[25]

It was not long, however, before the Economic Freedom League began to follow a policy which Douglas and many others could not accept. Early in 1928 Ludlam's need for action had led him to stand in the Coventry municipal election, and he had been gratified by a vote of 1,092 for a candidature unaccompanied by any campaign. But he had failed, by 323 votes, to be elected.[26] Soon afterwards John Hargrave, who will be considered more fully in the following chapter, attended the Second Conference of the Economic Freedom League, where he made a great impression on some of those present. The activists now had in Hargrave the dynamic leader they needed and in his following the nucleus for a real party of action. A new grouping, the Economic party, was founded.

[23] Ibid.; NA 23.4.25.
[24] McCarthy, p. 28.
[25] *Age of Plenty*, 7.26, 10.26.
[26] *Age of Plenty*, 4.28.

But soon it was announced that the organization would no longer run as a party.[27] The breakdown of the Coventry experiment was brought nearer when personal antagonisms began to disrupt the city's Social Credit community. Much of the blame for this disintegration must be laid at the door of Ludlam himself. Few could work with him, and by 1930 Kitson had departed to found the Monetary Reform Association, though no doubt he was helped on his way by the prominence of Hargrave, whom he disliked intensely.[28] There was an unpleasant side to Ludlam. He is remembered by a former colleague as "a little man who wanted to be a god" and as one, moreover, who could "believe whatever [he wanted] to believe."[29] There was a strain of mental unbalance in the man which revealed itself increasingly as he was left behind by the movement. The sub-title "The Mighty Atom of Journalism" was added to the diminutive, amateur sheet which he edited, and soon afterwards the paper announced the policy of "unifism," in which the drift towards concentration in industry and government was now accepted as inevitable and desirable. At the same time the futilities of the monetary reformers were paraded. The root of the trouble, as Ludlam saw it, was the attempt to use the "so-called democratic parties," which, he said, had been good listeners, but were "hopeless as 'actors'." From this he jumped to the conclusion that the choice was simply between communist collectivism and fascist corporateness, and remembering and drawing attention to his Guild Socialist past, he came down on the side of fascism. The inclusion of a passage from Mosley's *The Greater Britain* and the outright soliciting of subscriptions for the British Union of Fascists in the next issue of the *Age of Plenty* signalled the lapse of Ludlam from Social Credit. Poor Ludlam! He was not to find peace of mind in the fascist camp. Almost at once, he began to publish a series of slight works, calling for a return to the land and for national guilds, in which there was no mention of fascism. His book, *The Essence of the Wisdom of Unifism*, was directed at those who had "entered into the domain of spiritual, ethical, evolutionary elevation," and it was given over to such pious injunctions as "In your business transactions be satisfied with just prices and honor and pay your creditors."[30] In such a way, then, did this one branch of Social Credit peter out.

[27] *Age of Plenty*, 11.28, 8.30. These developments are treated more fully in the following chapter.

[28] Monetary Reform Association, *Monetary Reform by Reflation* (Manchester [1932]); NA 3.5.28.

[29] Personal communication from M. B. Reckitt, 1967.

[30] *Age of Plenty*, no. 13 (first quarter, 1933); ibid., no. 14 and no. 16, vol. 2, no. 1. The work referred to (Coventry, 1942) was seven pages long.

This failure of the Economic Freedom League seemed to confirm the wisdom of the more orthodox Social Credit movement. The danger of broadening the appeal of Social Credit was seen to lie in the fact that it both opened the door to all manner of opportunists and missed the mark, leaving the real evil untouched. The way in which Ludlam had been captured by the fascists was an outstanding indication of this. The *New Age* felt the need to reassert its belief in the objective of the movement as follows: "Costing Reform must supersede credit reform as the conscious objective of the Social Credit movement. ... The quantity of credit is not the vital point; it is the proportionate allocation of credit as between capital development and consumable output which makes all the practical difference to the personal prosperity of every member of the population."[31] Exposed at the same time had been the impossibility of a centrally organized activist movement. And so the orthodox Social Credit development during the 1920s reflected the wish to remain a loosely articulated body of students and propagandists. Dining clubs, both for the more intellectual and for the rank and file, were the preferred method of spreading the doctrine; there was, too, the annual dinner.

Such a quiet approach was, of course, inevitable. To begin with, the improving economic conditions after 1925 ruled out any other way. Social Credit is a theory which stands the best chance of success in periods of deflation and/or unemployment, for it is at such times that the contradiction between promise and performance is most starkly expressed. During the late twenties more and more people were finding work and keeping it and for those in work, times were relatively good. And secondly, to Douglas and his close followers, the need for any organization, whether centralized or not, had yet to be proved. It was a cardinal point of their argument that since the economy was poised on the brink of an alarming catastrophe which traditional finance could not prevent and would be powerless to cure, the acceptance of Social Credit was inevitable and but a matter of time. The nearness of the crash was constantly reiterated, and Douglas himself predicted, in 1928, a smash towards the end of 1929.[32] Indeed, so widely held was this apocalyptic interpretation that there was anxiety over the restricted scope of Social Credit activity. The movement, it was contended, should be extended to the masses, since with the truth confined to dining clubs there was the danger of its total

[31] NA 3.1.29.
[32] NA 1.11.28.

annihilation in the event of a gas attack.[33] But this was an extreme view, even among the prophets of doom, and for most members the coming crash was rather a ground for being satisfied with progress.

Thus, the small size of the movement did not trouble the convinced. It might have been true, as Miss Alexander had discovered, that of the many Social Credit groups the majority existed only "on the back page of *The New Age*," that only fourteen groups had any real life, and that some of these had as few as 4 members. It might have been that she could enroll but 278 in the movement and that even the number with whom she was in touch was no more than 1,000. *New Age* dinners might count themselves lucky with 120 in attendance, and the movement might split at a conference totalling 45 members.[34] Such considerations meant little. So long as the key was understood and known to exist, circumstances would bring about the eventual triumph of right and the acceptance of Social Credit. Thus did the movement jog along towards the end of the roaring twenties.

By the early 1930s, however, it had become evident that some accommodation would have to be made to change circumstances. The crash had taken place as predicted, but for some reason the orthodox financiers and governments were managing to struggle along without any need to call in Douglas. To rub in this rejection was the handling of Douglas by the Macmillan committee. In 1929 the government had appointed the Macmillan committee to decide whether the banking and financial systems were helping or handicapping industry and trade. Douglas had been invited to give evidence, but he had been roughly criticized and his ideas had been dismissed. Yet, at the same time the depression and the dramatic rise in unemployment brought Social Credit to the fore and gave it a news coverage which it had never before enjoyed. As the movement began to gain new members and old groups were revived, pressure again began to mount for a more formal organization, especially so when the growth of Social Credit in the Commonwealth began to demand some central clearing house. Then, too, the return of Orage and the founding by him of the *New English Weekly* in 1932 meant a partial revival at least of the intellectual appeal of the old days.

But, as always, Douglas himself was against any highly organized movement, for he feared that to form a party or even anything similar would be to run the danger of putting up an even stronger tyranny

[33] NA 18.10.28.
[34] McCarthy, p. 27; NA 5.2.25.

in place of the one to be attacked.[35] As before, the lead had to come from other quarters, and in fact at this time there was a spate of independent initiative. One of the most ambitious ventures came from Coventry. This time the lead was taken by Robert J. Scrutton, a devout but not intellectual Christian and a friend of Rev. Paul Stacy, vicar of St. Peter's in the city and long-time guildsman and Social Crediter. In April 1932 the first issue of the monthly *This Prosperity* appeared. It was edited by Scrutton and was the organ of the Social Credit Association of Producers, Distributors, and Consumers. Scrutton accepted the Douglas analysis in its entirety, and he showed a deep respect for Douglas personally. The distinguishing feature of his campaign and the one which justified his initiative was the policy he advocated in an article entitled "Forcing the Issue." In it he outlined the need for a mandate party, that is, a party outside politics, made up of pledged supporters who could dictate an election over the heads of the normal political parties and dedicated to forcing the hidden financial power in the open.[36] Taking the example of the members of the Free Churches, who in 1902 refused to pay that part of the tax assessment intended for the support of Anglican schools, Scrutton urged a similar withholding of taxes. Under the slogan No Taxation without Explanation the taxpayer should refuse that proportion of his taxes which went to pay the interest on the national debt. The inability of the government to provide an adequate reason why such a sum should be paid would lead to the setting up of a royal commission to look into the whole matter, and assuredly the commission would be driven to the acceptance of Social Credit.

As the first step in such a campaign, Social Crediters were asked to write to newspapers, raise the question in clubs, churches, and other groups, and in this way interest people in the scheme. From this beginning the Prosperity Campaign began to develop, evolving in three distinct stages. The first would take the form of intensive propaganda at the local level directed towards the demand that Social Credit be given an impartial examination, and to this end Scrutton travelled the country, lecturing and forming groups. The second stage would consist of the compilation of a campaign manifesto. This meant that the local groups and other interested individuals were requested to submit clauses on policy, not means—that is, those broad aims

[35] In 1934 Douglas was to repeat this refusal, as he had already in 1924–25; see NEW 13.12.34.

[36] *This Prosperity*, 8.32.

which were desired in the ideal commonwealth. In the final stage a national conference would be held to discuss the suggested clauses, weld them into one coherent document, and submit them to the people, asking orthodoxy to show how it proposed to put them into practice and at the same time showing how Social Credit alone was able to do this. In the meantime the direct democracy implicit in this approach was put to work through a petition, whose tremendous number of signatures would reinforce the demands expressed by representative bodies for a royal commission. Before long the petition came to be seen as the be-all and end-all of the campaign.[37]

Scrutton's direct methods stood at one end of the spectrum of Social Credit effort at this time. At the other extreme was the Leisure Society. The avowed aim of this group was that of "putting the cart before the horse" and insisting not that Social Credit led to a leisure state but that a leisure state, the true aim of society, was only to be achieved by Social Credit.[38] The society was little more than a dining club; the only obligation upon members, who were organized in "messes," was the eating together once a month of a simple meal. Orage, as might have been expected, was taken by the idea of the society, and it was to them that he gave his talk upon the psychological resistance to leisure and man's slavish subservience to the work fetish.[39] The society also produced a series of pamphlets; these were mainly the work of Eimar O'Duffy, a Catholic Irishman educated at Stoneyhurst and University College, Dublin, and known in Social Credit circles for his satirical writings against the myths of the work state. But his untimely death was too great a blow for the society, and it soon disappeared.[40]

Between the appeals of Scrutton and of O'Duffy came those of the National Credit Association and of the West Riding Douglas Social Credit Association. The former was set up sometime in 1932 with Lord Tavistock, the eccentric heir to the Duke of Bedford, as the leading figure. The exact time and circumstances of its formation are obscure, but the first conference of this new group was held in May 1933, and the aim of "establishing within Great Britain a just and equitable system of finance, scientifically adjusted to the needs of the nation" was outlined there.[41]

[37] *This Prosperity,* 4.33, 3.34, 2.35.
[38] NA 10.9.31.
[39] A. R. Orage, *The Fear of Leisure* (London, 1935). The talk was noted in NA 11.2.32, however.
[40] *This Prosperity,* 6.35; an obituary appeared in NA 13.6.35.
[41] NEW 8.6.33.

The foundation of the West Riding group was more truthfully the reorganization of what had once been a flourishing centre. This reestablishment took place on 17 August 1932.[42] The leading member in the north was C. M. Hattersley, a Cambridge-educated mathematician and a practising lawyer. He had been an early member of the movement, and yet his writings showed that he was able to strike out on an independent line of his own which owed little to Douglas beyond the original impetus. He had also been prominent in the Economic Freedom League and so shown his belief in a more direct form of propaganda than Douglas's.

It was in fact the northern group which set the ball rolling in a new attempt to reorganize the movement. On 11 February 1933, J. J. Taylor, the secretary of the West Riding Association, wrote to Douglas suggesting that the time was ripe for a national organization. The way to bring this about would be for the West Riding group to affiliate with the National Credit Association and so form a broadly based nucleus for future growth. Douglas, as ever, demurred at the idea of any organization, let alone a centralized one. Without getting directly involved, but using a favoured device of a front man, Douglas replied to Taylor with a series of impossible demands; they included a conference to set up a loosely based organization which would recognize Douglas's absolute authority, a Douglas veto over any proposed members of the conference, and a preliminary agenda committee appointed by Douglas personally. Not surprisingly, the Yorkshire contingent had nothing to do with such a suggestion.

This episode has been used to explain the establishment some little time later of the Social Credit Secretariat. The precise moment of its formation is not clear, but it was being discussed in *This Prosperity* in the April issue of 1933. It has been claimed that its setting up was the hurried response of Douglas to the threat posed by the northerners to his undisputed control of the movement. In addition to the fact that no reason was given for this claim, other than a generalized appeal to the known character of Douglas, itself but vaguely established, this explanation is unsatisfactory. It ignores the fact that on many occasions in the past Douglas had refused offers to take a commanding position within the movement and that only recently he had turned down the offer by the West Riding Association itself that he take the lead in organizing on a national scale. Moreover, about this time, Douglas granted recognition to Hargrave's followers, a group which

42 McCarthy, pp. 34, 41–42.

made no secret of its dissatisfaction with the Douglas leadership. Furthermore, it ignores the belief held by those connected with the setting up of the secretariat that the idea was not that of Douglas himself but was a development forced by the pressure of events and formalized by the efforts of others.[43] Indeed, the reason given for the establishment of the secretariat was the sudden growth of the Social Credit doctrine in the dominions, which demanded the existence of a central coordinating centre, and there is no good reason to doubt this statement; the planning of such a departure would probably have been a lengthy process, and that the secretariat could be announced as early as April suggests that the first steps were taken some time in 1932, that is, before the proposal made by the West Riding Association. And it is perhaps significant that the person primarily responsible for the setting up of the secretariat was Symons. It will be remembered that Symons had been the speaker at Swanwick in 1925 responsible for defeating the earlier attempts of the northerners to set up a centralized organization. He would not have been willing to see the secretariat as a vehicle for Douglas's personal aggrandizement. Finally, it must be remembered that at this period the secretariat made no claim to exclusive control of the movement. It took the self-denying pledge that it would be nothing more than an advisory body, and it showed its willingness to work with existing groups by agreeing to supervise the technical side of the Prosperity Campaign which was just then being worked out.[44]

About the end of 1933, then, there seemed every chance that a unified movement would be maintained in which Douglas would retain his unofficial preeminence and which would not be too deeply committed to political action. The tendency was towards unity. The secretariat was working with the Prosperity Campaign. At the summer school held by the National Credit Association in August 1933, a merger had been agreed upon which incorporated the Prosperity Campaign, though it left *This Prosperity* as the organ of the new movement. Scrutton was justified in his announcement: "The day of the Social Crediter ploughing his lonely furrow of economic sanity . . . has gone by. . . . The movement is taking up a nation wide co-ordinated policy of action wherein each individual supporter and

[43] NA 15.3.34; M. B. Reckitt told the present author that W. T. Symons was the originator of this scheme, and Symons, when pressed, admitted the truth of this.
[44] NA 15.3.34; *This Prosperity*, 4.33.

group will be in the position to receive the support and facilities of the whole." Finally, in the first months of 1934, the National Credit Association and the secretariat themselves merged, and there developed a block of interrelated Social Credit activity which promised well.[45] Somewhat to one side stood Hargrave's group and the West Riding Association, the latter giving its approval to the former. But it was not true at this moment that there was any fundamental split between these groupings. Thus, the secretariat published in the *New Age* a list of accredited groups in which was included *Attack*, Hargrave's paper (though it must be admitted that no mention was made of the *Leadswinger*, the organ of the West Riding Association).[46] Yet, within a year further developments had so rocked the movement that this unity was shattered beyond all hope of recovery.

What caused the new split was the result of Major Douglas's tour of the Commonwealth. Sailing from England at the end of 1933, he visited Australia, New Zealand, and Canada, rounding off his trip by a visit to the United States. The tour was a triumphant personal success. In Australia he was met by the leading citizens and overwhelmed by the intensity of the interest in Social Credit. In Sydney his visit was climaxed by an address in the stadium at Rushcutters' Bay, where twelve thousand listened to him, five thousand were turned away, and an estimated one million across the continent heard him on the radio. New Zealand was again a most welcome change from the comparative indifference of Britain, while in western Canada he found the slumbering seeds of Social Credit within the United Farmers of Alberta springing into new life, and his newspaper coverage and the official notice taken of him by the Albertan government must have been sweet. In the United States, after meetings with prominent politicians and other monetary reformers, including Father Coughlin, Douglas addressed the nation in a coast-to-coast broadcast which, he claimed, reached an audience of ninety million. The impression of the tour upon Douglas was a profound one, and upon his return to England it was announced that he would address Social Crediters on a very important development at a special conference to be held in Buxton.[47]

[45] *This Prosperity,* 8.33, 10.33, 2.34.

[46] NA 5.10.33, 12.10.33; I have not been able to find copies of the *Leadswinger.*

[47] NEW 29.3.34, 31.5.34; the Buxton speech of 9.6.34 was printed in *Social Credit,* 24.8.34; NA 24.5.34.

In his speech to this conference, later published under the title *The Nature of Democracy*, Douglas applied the lessons of the Commonwealth movements to Britain. Now that the stage of indifference had been succeeded by one of hostility, and it was now active opposition which was preventing the acceptance of the doctrine, it was time to go on to the third stage, in which the people would be called upon to impose their wishes upon their leaders. This could be done by mounting an electoral campaign, by which local groups would approach their parliamentary candidates and ask them to give a pledge to work, if elected, for the National Dividend; at the same time the electors were to be asked to promise to vote for the candidate offering to support the National Dividend, and for no other. Thus, the plan envisaged the possibility of asking lifelong Conservatives, say, to vote for a Labour candidate, since this candidate would be willing, where the Conservative would not, to sign the Social Credit pledge. In this way it was hoped to organize a body of voters large enough to threaten the success of the sitting member, who would, in the interest of self-preservation, be forced to agree to the pledge.

Such a departure antagonized many of the faithful. In the first place, the decision to take part, even in this way, in elections seemed to run counter to Douglas's earlier views upon the subject. Previously, he had written of elections that they were "a cold and calculated fraud" and had counselled Social Crediters to "go to the polling booth and spoil your voting paper by writing on it some such remark as 'A plague on all your houses'."[48] Of course, the new policy was not necessarily a reversal of this earlier stand, and in fact could be interpreted as a realization that now, and only now, was the time ripe for such an intervention. However, there was a second consideration, which counted with those not opposed to political intervention as such. The method advocated was, they maintained, doomed to failure; such an external interference might have been suitable in some contexts, but in the politics of an entrenched party system it could only do harm. To Douglas, asking a Conservative to vote Labour was a reasonable request; after all, following Belloc, he saw the antics of party as a sham fight. To the more realistically minded, however, the plan was impossible.[49]

[48] NA 30.5.29.
[49] Even Mrs. M. W. Gordon-Cumming, an admirer of Douglas, admitted to the present author the unpopularity of the electoral campaign and the difficulty of undertaking it.

There was a further way in which Social Credit opinion was shocked by the revelation made at Buxton. The campaign was to proceed without mentioning Social Credit by name. The canvassers were instructed to ask voters to give a pledge for the National Dividend in general terms only, and they were advised to avoid discussing methods. Once again, this was in one sense a justifiable tactic. Douglas had experienced time and again the difficulty of getting across the technical aspect, and he also believed that aims, not methods, were the proper concern of a democracy. It could also be argued that hostile propaganda had so queered the pitch that discussion of Social Credit could only antagonize a prospective pledger. On the other hand, however, those whose estimation of human nature and abilities was rather higher than Douglas's and who had the actual canvassing to do could not be expected to share this outlook.

But what was most disturbing in the new developments was the role of the secretariat. The whole campaign was to be run by this organization, which therefore had quickly abandoned its original intention of being an advisory body only.[50] The view began to grow that Douglas and the secretariat were taking on a dictatorial aspect. When the balance sheet of the secretariat for 1934 was published, it was seen that those who thought so had been provided with ammunition enough. It was revealed that while a paltry sixteen pounds and seven shillings had been spent on stationery, no less than forty-three pounds had been voted for a portrait of the major.[51]

The way in which the Buxton conference had antagonized supporters was well illustrated in the case of Scrutton and the Prosperity Campaign. The similarity between the two plans of action was patent, and Scrutton could be excused for thinking that his own plan would be sidetracked. From being an enthusiastic admirer of Douglas, Scrutton became a vociferous critic. For a long while, Scrutton claimed, he had sought to work the two campaigns together, believing that while Douglas's would work only when the politicians decided to hold an election—that is, at their own convenience—his campaign could force an election against the will of the politicians and so wrest an important initial advantage from them. Plaintively Scrutton noted, "We have yet to discover the real reason why our policy of action does not meet with the approval of the Social Credit Secretariat," and *This Prosperity* dropped the reference in its subtitle to *Douglas* Social Credit.[52]

[50] NA 15.3.34.
[51] McCarthy, p. 47.
[52] McCarthy, p. 48; *This Prosperity*, 4.35, 10.35.

In this change of allegiance Scrutton was helped by a development in the wings of the movement. In April 1934, the first steps were taken towards the setting up of the League to Abolish Poverty. Initially, at least, the leading figure in the new venture was William Ward, who as far back as 1898 had been prominent in launching the Old Age Pension movement. By 1934 Ward realized that his pioneer effort had been but a stage in a campaign now broadened by the developments of technology and that a National Dividend was the logical next step. For his second stage Ward had secured an impressive backing. The two leading figures were the avowed Social Crediters Lord Tavistock, who was the president, and the Reverend Hewlett Johnson, the secretary, and the General Council included Professor Bonamy Dobrée, Father F. H. Drinkwater, and the novelists Storm Jameson, Compton Mackenzie, and J. B. Priestley. At a meeting held at Friends House on 19 September 1934, the league was officially launched, supported by the Theosophical Order of Service, among others.[53] The method for demanding the National Dividend was to be the setting up of organizations in every parliamentary constituency to enroll voters pledged to vote for candidates in favour of the National Dividend. Scrutton, having been disappointed by the secretariat, began to support the league in his paper, and as time went on he allowed this new development to absorb his own plans. The Prosperity Campaign began to restrict itself to petitioning, and the second and third stages were allowed to be forgotten. Eventually, the establishment of a Petition Council formally merged the league and the Prosperity Campaign into one organization, and *This Prosperity*, refusing to "dogmatize as to what those anomalies of the economic system are," was stated to be open to all shades of monetary reform. A break with the official Social Credit campaign had taken place, and when Kitson noted that the Social Credit movement was "being run more like a proprietary article like well known pills than as a great public institution for remedying a political as well as an economic crime," the split had become patent.[54]

While the movement was reeling from the blow wielded by the new-style secretariat, a fresh source of discontent broke out.

---

[53] *This Prosperity*, 10.34, 11.34; W. Ward, ed., *The National Dividend* (London, 1935); *This Prosperity*, 8.34. Dobrée was a professor of English at Leeds University and, like Drinkwater and Jameson, was a Social Crediter; Mackenzie was close to that position.

[54] *This Prosperity*, 12.35.

It concerned the *New Age* and the secretariat's need to possess a journal firmly committed to its own line. Brenton's freedom of action had long been limited. The paper had always needed to be subsidized, and ever since 1923 its finances had been taken care of by the New Age Trust Fund, which each year raised the £ 500 or so needed to ensure publication.[55] This fund had been run by W. T. Symons and was therefore closely connected with the secretariat. Because of this link, the secretariat seemed to have believed that it could pressure Brenton into taking orders. When Brenton showed independence, and worse, a tendency to criticize the secretariat, matters came to a head. Brenton had printed the correspondence between the secretariat and the *News Chronicle* in which the latter's offer of space for Social Credit advocacy had been turned down because, the secretariat claimed, the space promised had been inadequate.[56] The secretariat was furious that its dealings and failures had been given publicity, and it made open attempts to oust Brenton. The editor fought back, however, and managed to hang on to his paper for a while longer; but cut off from support, the *New Age* dwindled and finally died with the issue of 7 April 1938. The secretariat, meanwhile, began to issue its own weekly, *Social Credit*, which first appeared on 17 August 1934.

The founding of *Social Credit* and the rapidly increasing impotence of the *New Age* should have given the secretariat a breathing space in which to become established. But its fortunes were smitten by the coincidence of two developments which put further pressure upon the new organization and which led to a further weakening of the movement. In 1935 the general election exposed the hollowness of the Electoral Campaign. The total failure of a committed band of supporters pledged to back candidates who had agreed to support the National Dividend was revealed; in no case did the Social Credit vote influence the outcome. In particular, the fate of two specifically National Dividend candidates was not encouraging. At Erdington, Birmingham, where Father Drinkwater was a leading figure in the campaign, H. G. Bell, a small-scale manufacturer, polled 2,050 votes in a total vote of 43,523, and in North Bradford, Reginald Kenny secured 4,684 out of 39,881 votes. But what was especially distressing was the revelation made when these two candidates met to discuss the results: Kenny admitted that he had had 8,000 pledges, while Bell had had 3,000, and so it was evident that they could not count even upon

[55] NA 20.8.25, 15.8.29; McCarthy, p. 44.
[56] NA 31.5.34.

holding people to their promises. In addition, both agreed that the secretariat's direction left much to be desired and that if the campaign were to be kept going, a reassessment of the democratic nature of the movement would have to be made.[57]

The second source of trouble was the aftermath of the Albertan election, also in 1935. Before the election, the secretariat had been opposed to Aberhart, preferring to support the more orthodox, more technically correct, New Age League. Moreover, Douglas was already on record as stating that in view of the British North America Act, Alberta lacked the basic powers required to put Social Credit into operation.[58] But the Aberhart victory was supposed to have changed this in some way, and it was generally expected that Douglas would throw unambiguous support behind the new premier. Certainly, Douglas was never open in his distrust of Aberhart, claiming that Aberhart's Social Credit had at least shown the people the truth, for in preventing Social Credit legislation, the money power had been forced to come out into the open. But the relationship with Aberhart and with Alberta was never a warm one, and so when Aberhart cabled Douglas to come to Alberta and Douglas chose to interpret this as a general inquiry for some uncertain future arrangement, the opportunity of any fruitful cooperation was lost. Many were shocked by Douglas's attitude and to this day hold his refusal against him.[59]

During 1924–35, then, the movement had passed through an agonizing series of crises and misunderstandings. Now there was a quite unmistakable split between the two wings, the out-and-out activists confronting a secretariat now beginning to reassess the value of even qualified political action. In between, a number of bewildered individuals clustered, some driven to back the Prosperity Campaign, some clinging to a *New Age* now rapidly becoming isolated and meaningless. The only Social Credit opinion which could command any degree of respect in the movement at large was that represented by the *New English Weekly*. Thus, during 1935–36 it fell to this group to take the initiative in an attempt to put the movement back on its feet. Through the *New English Weekly*, Reckitt called for a conference. This, to be held at York, was intended to be a comprehensive

[57] NA 21.11.35, 30.1.36.

[58] *Social Credit*, 29.3.35; NEW 7.5.34.

[59] For comment at the time, NA 23.4.36 and NEW 15.10.36; M. B. Reckitt and P. Mairet mentioned to the present author that they held this refusal against Douglas.

meeting of all shades of Social Credit opinion, and the following invitation was sent by Reckitt to Douglas: "We quite understand that, as Chairman of the Secretariat, you will most probably feel unable to take any part in the Conference. But it is not in this capacity that we write to you, but as one to whom we shall always look with gratitude and admiration as the inspirer of a worldwide movement."[60]   But Douglas was not to be drawn; he disliked Reckitt and his friends intensely, and in *Social Credit* a little later he summed them up as "malcontents . . . of a well known type and almost of a uniform history of socialism, National Guildism, etc.," adding that he wished "most clearly to except Demant."[61]

The conference was attended by some eighty-five members, but not by Douglas. Nor was Reckitt there, for he was ill, but his speech was read for him. It was an outspoken attack upon the state of the movement. "Of the three existing nuclei of national action," he claimed, "two are in essence dictatorships, however they may formally disavow such a character." Here Reckitt was condemning the secretariat and the party. The other organization was the League to Abolish Poverty, but, Reckitt felt, the day of petition campaigns had passed, and moreover it carried the danger, all too real as later events were to show, of drifting away from Social Credit and becoming, as the Economic Freedom League had done six years before, a mere monetary reform group.[62]   As the first step towards the reconstitution of a healthy, genuine Social Credit movement, the York conference set up a liaison committee to plan the eventual formation of a national federation, a loose organization of autonomous groups. The secretariat would be allowed to join such a scheme if it revised its dictatorial character. This beginning was followed up, not as had been hoped in 1937 but a year later, when the Yorkshire groups, the remnants in the main of the old West Riding Association, took the initiative in calling a conference in March. It was here that the Social Credit Co-ordinating Committee was set up to bring together the scattered groups and to act as a genuine clearing house—what the original secretariat had set out to do but had abandoned.

Unfortunately, this does not exhaust the tale of dissension and recrimination which beset the movement in the period before the

[60] McCarthy, p. 73.

[61] *Social Credit*, 9.10.36. Reckitt's group will be discussed in more detail in chapter 8.

[62] NEW 15.10.36.

Second World War. The secretariat itself was passing through a crisis. It had begun as a democratically controlled body, and Douglas had been elected to the leadership at the end of 1934, securing seventy-nine votes to the seven of his only rival. At the lower levels the procedure was not so straightforward. First, a selection committee was appointed by a proportional voting system of election, and these members, normally five, then proceeded to nominate people to the offices.[63] This procedure was to give rise to disputes, however, for it was not made clear whether these officers enjoyed security of tenure or under what conditions they could be given orders from above. The position was complicated by the fact that the secretariat became a limited company in 1935, and it was not clear what legal obligations lay upon the officers of the company.[64] Matters came to a head in 1938. Despite the fact that the secretariat was pressed for money, Douglas began to urge the spending of greater and greater sums, and when the officers in charge of the relevant departments protested, he sought to remove them. But legally the appointed officers remained liable for any deficit, and so even if they had been willing to acquiesce in Douglas's high-handed interference, they were forced to question his actions. An attempt by the secretary to sort out the muddle produced this riposte from Douglas: "You are not the Secretary. . . . You are not a judge as to whether the Social Credit Secretariat is conducted in accordance with my views, but if you do not think it is, you can always resign. I would point out to you that the Social Credit Secretariat Ltd. and the Social Credit Secretariat are not the same thing. Neither possess the other."[65] Douglas, however, was legally in the wrong, and there was no step open to him but that of removing himself from the organization. The annual conference of the secretariat was due to meet in a few days. Such a consideration did not deter Douglas. The supporters of the secretariat presented themselves for the meeting only to find that the founder and his henchmen were not to be in attendance. Douglas withdrew to Liverpool, whose section was behind him, and from there he began the *Social Crediter.* The Social Credit Secretariat Ltd., admitting that realization would show a deficit of £ 1,100, decided to keep going for as long as possible. But in April 1939, the editor was obliged to suspend publication of *Social Credit.* It was succeeded by *Reality,* a weekly newssheet produced in Coventry, which made little attempt to argue the Social

[63] *Social Credit,* 9.11.34, 13.12.35.
[64] McCarthy, p. 86.
[65] *Social Credit,* 14.10.38.

Credit case; this was merely assumed and the news commented upon from this standpoint. The effects of the secretariat were bought by the Co-ordinating Committee, and the way was open for Douglas's group to reemerge as the sole and orthodox secretariat.[66]

By 1938, then, the movement in England had taken on the form which it retains to the present day. The Social Credit party claims some eighty to one hundred members. The Co-ordinating Committee claims about twice that number. The secretariat, become conspiratorially minded, gives no information; it has affiliated with the John Birch Society. The Petition Council and other monetary reform schemes of a non–Social Credit sort have been channelled via the Economic Reform Club, a still existing organization, which, set up as the Petition Council in 1936, took its present name in 1937.[67] In this form the movement stagnated. No new talent came forward to take the place of those who had been attracted into the circle in the early days, while at the same time more and more of the important names began to cease their declarations of faith in Social Credit. Today Reckitt looks back upon the York conference as an end, not as a beginning.[68]

The story of the Social Credit movement in Britain is a disspiriting one. Too many divergent and weakening methods were allowed to rack the movement before any effective attempt was made to impose order upon the chaos. Three main salvage attempts were made: that of 1925 failed because Douglas would not take the responsibility which the situation demanded he take; in 1933 the position was reversed, and Douglas tried to claim too dominant a role; by 1936 it was too late to do anything. Douglas's lack of political sense must be considered a reason for failure. Yet, the idea that it was his tyranny which was responsible should be treated with caution. It must not be forgotten that when he could most easily have acted dictatorially he chose not to do so, even when the Sheffield group offered him the crown. Later, it is true, he showed an intolerant streak, but that was

[66] *Social Credit*, 2.9.38, 14.10.38; personal communication from Miss H. Corke, 1967; McCarthy, p. 86. The first issue of the *Social Crediter* was 17.9.38 and of *Reality*, 5.5.39.

[67] These developments were gathered from secretariat literature; from Dr. Philips, a leading member of the Social Credit party; and from V. L. Hadkins, secretary of the Co-ordinating Committee. The author met these two gentlemen at the Social Credit Co-ordinating Committee Conference, Nottingham, 1.4.66. McCarthy, p. 80.

[68] Personal communication from M. B. Reckitt, 1967.

under the combined effects of the flush of his world tour and a crippling illness. Even so, he refused to allow personal feelings to stand in the way of the success of the message. Hilderic Cousens disagreed with Douglas on many matters, and did not hesitate to declare in print, "The trouble frankly is that Major Douglas as a political thinker is not in the same class as he is as an economist or social philosopher."[69] But Douglas did not break with him, and at a date later than this Cousens contributed an article to Douglas's own paper, the *Fig Tree*.[70] Douglas made many mistakes, but seldom seems to have acted out of personal pique.

The problem still remains, however, of why no leader arose to fill the vacuum caused by Douglas's withdrawal. This question will be considered in the following chapters, especially in the next one, which is devoted to John Hargrave.

[69] NA 26.3.36.
[70] *Fig Tree*, 12.38.

chapter seven

JOHN HARGRAVE AND THE MILITANT MOVEMENT

John Hargrave, obeyed as a dictator in the various guises of White Fox, Wa-Whaw-Goosh, headman of the Kibbo Kift, and finally, leader of the Social Credit Party of Great Britain and Northern Ireland, was born in 1894, the son of Gordon Hargrave, a nominal Quaker. To his father, to whom he was devoted, the young Hargrave owed much, especially an amateur but wide knowledge of sociology and anthropology, and also a love of the countryside, but he was not given a specifically religious outlook. Of formal schooling he had little, and by the age of fifteen he was working as an illustrator for Nelson's, going on to become cartoonist for the *Evening Times* at the early age of seventeen; later he worked in advertising. In 1908 he began to take an interest in the new Scouting movement, in which he soon became prominent. At one stage, indeed, he seemed to be marked out as Baden-Powell's successor; at least his appointment as Headquarters' Commissioner for Camping and Woodcraft has been interpreted in this way. But even in nonconformity—and at this date Scouting was outlandish—Hargrave found it difficult to be orthodox, and his first book, *Lonecraft* (published in 1913), was directed to those Scouts who for one reason or another did not belong to any troop. It was dedicated to Ernest Thompson Seton, whose Indian-inspired movement in the United States so influenced Hargrave. He had given notice of his independence.[1]

At this point, when relations with the official Scouting movement were already strained, the war intervened. Hargrave served as a stretcher-bearer, probably the role most likely to intensify a loathing of war, until he was invalided out in 1916.[2] He returned to England to find, to his dismay, that the Scouting movement was being used by the ultrapatriotic forces as an instrument of war. The breach continued to widen, and in 1920 Hargrave withdrew to set up his own brand of antiwar, outdoor philosophy under the name of Kibbo Kift.[3]

The mood which gave rise to the Kibbo Kift was widespread in the years immediately after the war. In part it was a response to the same inchoate feelings which had inspired Baden-Powell, but not entirely, for as the parallel but more extensive youth movement in Germany showed, revulsion from the war was a strong element, and unlike the Scouts (originally directed primarily at children), the postwar movements embraced all age groups and amounted in effect to a whole way of life. Not that Hargrave borrowed from Germany; the influence was, if anything, the other way, and Hargrave's books were popular in translation.

Along with opposition to war went a rejection of what was considered part and parcel of a war-prone civilization—the unhealthy tedium of the towns and the stultifying monotony of a mechanical world. In political matters there was an equally clear-cut repudiation of traditional practices. When the Kibbo Kift proclaimed that it "began as a body impulse to get Earth contact in a mechanical age," and when it was "bold enough to say openly, what we all know in our secret hearts to be the truth, that our political machinery is out-of-date, is breaking down, and must be scrapped,"[4] it was showing itself to be part of a broad and influential body of opinion, as can be seen from the list of those who agreed to act as advisory counsellors

[1] For Hargrave's early life see NA 4.4.35; *Broadsheet,* 8.26, 1.27; *Nomad,* 5.24; *Pine Cone,* 4.25; *Social Credit,* 1.11.35; L. A. Paul, *Angry Young Man* (London, 1951), p. 54.

[2] J. Hargrave, *The Great War Brings It Home* (London, 1919), pp. 49–51.

[3] *The Mark,* 9.22. At the time, Hargrave was accused by the Scouts of "socialist and bolshevik tendencies"; see I. O. Evans, *Woodcraft and World Service* (London, 1930), p. 63.

[4] J. Hargrave, *The Confession of the Kibbo Kift* (London, 1927), p. 56.

to the Kin (the term members of the Kibbo Kift used for themselves).
It included Sir Norman Angell, known especially for *The Great Illusion*; Havelock Ellis, writer on sex education; Sir Patrick Geddes; Sir
Julian Huxley, biologist and writer; Vilhjalmur Stefansson, arctic
explorer; Sir Rabindranath Tagore, the Bengali poet; and H. G. Wells.
It must be confessed, however, that only Geddes seemed to take his
office at all seriously.[5] Despite these initial advantages, the Kift
never numbered more than a handful, and it never seemed likely to
reflect at all adequately the general mood which it claimed to represent. Numbers are difficult to establish, but in 1924, the peak year, the
total attendance at the annual camp was 236, by 1927 a series of
Easter hikes organized in various centres brought out no more than
58 members, and in 1931 the number of names inscribed in the Kinlog
was only 185.[6] These figures were tiny beside those of the Scouts or
of the German movements. The reasons are not difficult to establish.

To begin with, the Kibbo Kift had to compete against an existing
alternative, the Scouts, and about this time other groups had been set
up, notably the Order of Woodcraft Chivalry. This was founded in
1916 by Ernest Westlake, a Quaker, in the belief that until instinct was
recognized and fitted into a scheme of education, no lasting improvement in society could be hoped for.[7] Before Hargrave took up the
idea, Westlake's group was working on the basis of the recapitulation
theory, the belief that the child has to live through all the stages of
mankind before he can come to a full appreciation and acceptance of
the present stage in evolution. These and other ready-made alternatives were always prepared to provide a refuge for those of the Kin
whose sole quarrel was with Hargrave's tendency to end all discussion
with the drastic "I have spoken."[8] Moreover, the ethos which he
imposed on his following was calculated to deter rather than to attract, a serious misjudgement in one whose grasp of propaganda was
unusually strong. The very name, from an old Cheshire phrase meaning "proof of great strength,"[9] indicated the founder's mystic attachment to a folk past, and the use of such terms as *Althing* to

---

[5] *The Mark,* 6.22, 10.22; *Broadsheet,* 8.28; Evans, p. 127. Geddes gave Hargrave's
Confession an enthusiastic notice in the *Sociological Review,* 1928.

[6] *Nomad,* 7.24; *Broadsheet,* 5.27, 3.31.

[7] *Pine Cone,* 7.23, 7.24.

[8] *The Mark,* 6.22.

[9] There was, however, a school of thought which interpreted it as meaning "skilled
left-handed"; see *Front Line,* 5.32. For Hargrave's meaning, *Confession,* p. 60.

indicate the annual council and *Kinlog* for the membership roll created an Anglo-Saxon ambiance more ludicrous than similar borrowing from Kiplingesque India could manage to be. Nor could the Kin hide their folk revival from the world, for a uniform, in green and brown, of Saxon cowl and jerkin and Prussian-style army cloak, was decreed.

Most inimical, perhaps, to Hargrave's desire to lead a movement of national regeneration was the attempt to impose a pretentious and muddled philosophy upon his following. It opened with this assertion: "All Life is Life. There is no Life but Life. Everything is Everything and we are part of It all . . . there is One Great Life, Force, Power, Soul, Will, Unit, Cause, Being—*and we are actually part of It.*"[10] The hint of eclecticism in this statement came out strongly in the following description of a Kibbo Kift camp fire ceremony recorded by a participant: "The Keeper of the Council Fire, over whose scarlet costume gold flames snaked, stepped out swinging a censer and intoning a collect beginning

> Energy, energy, ceaseless energy,
> The silent terrific energy of the Universe.
> The fearful and wonderful energy of the electron.
> Microcosm and macrocosm.
> One, One, One is One.
> All is energy. The energy of One.
> Fire, the great symbol of energy.
> Fire which leaps before us,
> The Fire of Althing.
> O Mighty Fire of Life!"

The philosophy went on, predictably enough, to proclaim, "The Kindred have one common aim, world unity."[11] Such an extreme beginning might understandably have led either to anarchist egalitarianism or to individualist survival of the fittest, and indeed Hargrave did pay tribute to Thoreau on the one hand and Herbert Spencer on the other; in fact the preferred conclusion was that society should breed a superior strain, and that to this end citizenship and the right to marry should be withheld until the candidate had successfully completed a

[10] *The Great War Brings It Home*, p. xv.
[11] L. A. Paul, *The Living Hedge* (London, 1946), p. 154.

system of training. But since such eugenics was not immediately practicable, a system of child education based upon recapitulation, which would reveal the true nature of man and suggest ways to perfection, was advocated.[12]

Eugenic conclusions, no matter how modified, presupposed a superior organism or a directing idea against which the progress of the strain could be measured, and they would therefore seem incompatible with the Kin's premise, especially when that premise was expressed in the form "the proper function of the individual is to live splendidly"—a nod in the direction of Nietzsche, who had influenced the Order of Woodcraft Chivalry too. Equally curious, in one who was such an immanentist, was the belief in the idea of an élite. For this was how Hargrave encouraged the Kin to think of itself, and how in fact it did see itself. "We were the Elect," one ex-member recalled. And in a magazine article, Hargrave catechized himself thus: "Do you expect to be a big, popular movement? No. Big, popular movements have to appeal to big, popular sentiments, and big, popular sentiments reflect herd instincts and catchpenny catchwords".[13]

For Hargrave the élite was vital in imposing order upon "the hot-headed, unsteady, easily gulled Mass-mind," or, as he put it in one of his less felicitous moments, the Kin's function was that of "a Positive Upright Fertilizing Principle [whose] creative climax of Lingam in Yoni is reached when it has penetrated inertia and given form to formlessness." And as the Kin was to the people, so was Hargrave to the Kin. When at all feasible, a Hargrave *diktat* settled policy, and where discussion was considered unavoidable, no vote was taken; the sense of the meeting was relied upon (here Hargrave's Quaker ancestry may be discerned).[14] It was a disastrous attitude to adopt, however, for in 1924 serious dissension occurred when the South-East London section withdrew after losing a motion challenging Hargrave's dictatorship and began a new organization (the Woodcraft Folk) with a marked leftward tendency.[15] This was a serious blow to the movement, but it is only fair to point out that the élite-minded Kibbo Kift was not misled, as so many élite groups were, especially at that time, into hatred for any person or group. In particular, the

[12] *The Great War Brings It Home*, pp. 21, 80, 159, and especially the closing chapter; *Confession*, p. 62; Paul, *The Living Hedge*, p. 121; Paul, *Angry Young Man*, p. 57.

[13] Paul, *The Living Hedge*, p. 155; *Healthy Life*, 10.32.

[14] *Broadsheet*, 8.26; *Confession*, pp. 94, 120.

[15] Paul, *Angry Young Man*, p. 56; *Nomad*, 7.24.

Kin went out of its way to praise the Jews for their contribution to progress.[16]

Even if this self-contradiction of an élite-dominated group in an immanentist setting could be accepted, there still remained the problem of what the Kibbo Kift was to do (apart from the children's activities, for which a case could be made out); all-night hikes might be good for training, but training to what end? When Hargrave described the Kin as existing "to act as an instrument of social regeneration," he presumably meant something like the Bolshevik role as the vanguard of the proletariat, or what later the storm troopers were to be for national socialism. But the Kin was not a political vanguard; it was apolitical and hostile to any kind of parliamentarism, which it saw as "one of the channels of mass-suggestion." Yet if the Kin's role was to convert by example rather than by direction, its policy of arrogant withdrawal from society was psychologically wrong. The truth was that Hargrave's vision was an impossible one. When he noted, "The Kindred have one common enemy: Sloth," he was acknowledging that his movement was one of pure action, a reflex devoid of intelligent purpose.[17]

Weighed down by such an incubus, the Kibbo Kift ceased to grow as early as 1924. As war memories faded and as the economic situation began to improve and the challenge to parliamentarism to recede, the Kin was driven to rely more and more on the personal magnetism of the founder. This was considerable enough; one ex-follower, L. A. Paul, remembers him as the one other man, in addition to Ramsay MacDonald, in whom he had met "the consciousness of greatness." Even sober intellectuals would testify to his powers, for a man who could surprise an initially hostile gathering of monetary reformers into standing at his bidding clearly possessed an unusual gift of persuasion. But in the circumstances such talents could only just hold the converted, and sometimes not even that. Hargrave must have sensed that something was missing and that some overriding purpose would have to be found. Those who were used to his messianic behaviour might have detected an impending change, for in the late summer of 1924 the headman and one lieutenant withdrew for fourteen days into the mountains of Wales; but for those unprepared for the Dispensation of the New Law, the later issues of *Nomad* (the Kibbo Kift journal at that time) must have come as a surprise. Without any

[16] *The Mark*, 1.23; *Confession*, pp. 44–45; *Broadsheet*, 9.26, 4.28.
[17] *Broadsheet*, 11.25; *Nomad*, 10.23; *Confession*, pp. 62–63, 199.

preparatory message the faithful were bidden to read books on New Economics, including Douglas's *Economic Democracy* and *Credit-Power and Democracy* and Soddy's *Cartesian Economics* and *The Inversion of Science.* [18]

The agent responsible for sowing the seed in such a receptive mind would seem to have been Rolf Gardiner. In 1923 Gardiner, then reading modern languages at Cambridge, became assistant editor, then editor, of *Youth,* a university magazine started in 1920 with a strong leftward slant and a leaning towards guild socialism. In 1921, when Social Credit ideas began to permeate the guild philosophy, Gardiner founded the Cambridge Social Credit study circle. At the same time his interest in Germany brought him into contact with the German youth movement, which he admired intensely, and under his editorship *Youth* began to reflect these changes. Hargrave became a contributor and found his articles featured along with those of Douglas. The usefulness of Social Credit ideas for the Kibbo Kift movement was plain. Hargrave recognized the importance of his conversion to monetary reform and later acknowledged: "Half our problem is psychological and the other half is economic. The psychological complex of industrial mankind can only be released by solving the economic impasse." [19] Previously, the Kibbo Kift had been an idealist movement prepared to ignore the material spheres. Now the emphasis was changed, but in such a way that while the economic basis was given due importance, it was not allowed to become the final end.

The transformation had to be effected slowly, for action that was too precipitate would have antagonized too many of the Kin. As it was, the Kin passed through an anxious period of realignment. Moreover, the existence of other monetary reform groups meant that Hargrave would have to step warily if he were not to find his movement dismissed as unnecessary. It was a year before Social Credit was mentioned by name; then it was brusquely announced, "We believe in Social Credit, the Just Price and the release of the individual from the position of machine minder." [20] Not before 1927 did monetary reform become an official part of the Kin's creed, and even then the declaration did not commit the Kin to any specific brand of reform. Meanwhile, Hargrave was feeling his way to a criticism of the existing

[18] Paul, *Angry Young Man,* p. 49; *Nomad,* 8.24, 12.24.
[19] NA 1.12.21; *Youth,* 3.23, 7.23; *Confession,* p. 49.
[20] *Broadsheet,* 8.26.

Social Credit movement which would allow a role to the Kin. Shortly after the general declaration of belief in some form of Social Credit, he noted, "The whole of the Social Credit movement is very weak in its psycho-sensory faculties."[21] This was his way of saying that he could improve their propaganda.

Hargrave's bargaining position was strengthened by the fact that two branches of the Social Credit movement were in existence at this time, the orthodox group around Douglas and the *New Age* and the upstart Economic Freedom League centered in Coventry. Hargrave therefore had a choice. The *New Age* was a long-established weekly with a brilliant past; still the official organ of the movement, it was able to count on the contributions of well-placed men. The Economic Freedom League's paper, the *Age of Plenty*, an erratic monthly, was not so professionally produced as the *New Age* and could not command a readership of the same calibre, but its supporters were activists who might well prove the better material for welding into the paramilitary organization to which Hargrave instinctively gravitated. Moreover, under John Strachey's influence, they paid attention to a section of the population which the *New Age* people totally ignored—the masses, especially the unemployed masses. Strachey at that time was all but a Social Crediter. He had attended the 1926 conference of the Economic Freedom League and there advocated making use of the "tremendous latent powers of the working class."[22] A year later the unemployed of the northeast began to demand an inquiry into the country's financial methods. Hargrave soon showed himself in agreement with this approach, and after a visit to the northeast began the swearing in of Surplus Labour Groups whose members agreed to the following statement: "To back the kindred of the Kibbo Kift in making One Great National Demand for the proper supply of Money to buy the Goods produced by the Community and I undertake to back the kindred of the Kibbo Kift towards this Economic Change by means of Unarmed Mass Pressure; and to this end I place myself here and now willingly under the strict discipline and direct leadership of the Kindred. So be it."[23]

The *Age of Plenty* was the first to take note of Hargrave's conversion. In its issue of January 1928 a correspondent said of the Kindred,

[21] *Broadsheet,* 8.27, 4.28.

[22] E. E. McCarthy, "A History of the Social Credit Movement" (M.A. thesis, Leeds, 1947), p. 29.

[23] *Broadsheet,* 10.28, 11.32; NA 18.10.28.

"This is a very healthy movement, and any man worth his salt should be with it." This overture was followed two months later by the announcement that Hargrave would be the main speaker at the 1928 conference of the Economic Freedom League. The *New Age* had earlier taken note of Hargrave the youth leader and amateur philosopher when it reviewed his book *Winkle* and when his major work, *The Confession of the Kibbo Kift*, was enthusiastically praised; it was seen as a sign of strength that the author had been sufficiently eclectic to have drawn "something useful from St. Paul, Mme. Blavatsky, Charlie Chaplin, Cromwell, Lao Tze, Nietzsche, Noah and Tolstoy."[24] But it was not until it reported the meeting of the Economic Freedom League that the *New Age* appreciated Hargrave's role as a Social Credit publicist. The correspondent found Hargrave, who appeared in Kin uniform, a welcome change from the others, whose "speeches and discussions clogged like cold suet pudding." For this correspondent the highlight of the meeting was when Hargrave called successfully for the delegates to stand at his bidding, a practical demonstration of the power of the emotions over the intellect. The account closed with the observation that the Kin had something, "some throb of life—which the Social Credit Movement will need; *Faith* in themselves."[25] Evidently Hargrave was someone to be cultivated, and when the Kin annual camp took place soon afterwards, both the editor of the *New Age* and a representative of the Economic Freedom League were in attendance.[26]

The former must have been the more persuasive. The issue of Hargrave's paper, *Broadsheet* (July 1928), which followed the Althing urged its readers to take the *New Age*, but it made no mention of the *Age of Plenty*. A little later Hargrave's cat's-paw began to make more open moves through the *New Age*. This agent was Philip Kenway, a retired New Zealand sheep farmer, an ex-Quaker, and a generous supporter of Social Credit causes. He developed an intense admiration for Hargrave and was pleased to act as his "front" man. Through the correspondence columns of the *New Age* he put forward the suggestion that some third way could surely be found between the Social Credit movement and the Economic League. His inquiry was taken up by others, who wrote in to advocate mass action and called for a disciplined core of one thousand members commanding the

[24] NA 28.5.25, 8.12.27.
[25] NA 3.5.28.
[26] *Broadsheet*, 6.28.

unquestioning allegiance of at least two hundred fifty thousand followers; this approach was christened the Third Line by Hargrave, who himself entered the field to reveal his plans to enlist the aid of Surplus Labour Groups. At this point, however, the *New Age* had second thoughts. Douglas's distrust of political movements was referred to, and Douglas himself contributed an article predicting the 1929 smash, thus by implication rejecting the need for any plan for action. When the *New Age* dining club members discussed Hargrave, they presumably concluded against him, for in the same month Kin interest was switched to the *Age of Plenty*.[27]

Again the lead was taken by Kenway. And again it was planned not to use the Kin directly, even though by this time it stood unequivocally for monetary reform, or as it was put, for the "economic Runnymede." Rather, an intermediate group was set up, the Economic party, with the sole aim of creating "an effective propaganda instrument." That the Economic party was a front was soon made clear when it was announced that its officers would be appointed by Kin headquarters in London. But the usefulness of a separate organization was shown by the way in which it could attract members who presumably would not have joined the Kibbo Kift. Compton Mackenzie was one of them.[28]

The Economic party was organized on a businesslike basis, as would have been expected from Hargrave and Kenway, its secretary. A clear statement of aims was recorded in the charter, published in the *Age of Plenty* in July 1929:

1. That the credit power of a Community belongs to the Community as a whole and may not be restricted or withheld by any private individual or group whatsoever

2. That the cash credits of the population of this country shall at any moment be collectively equal to the collective cash prices for consumable goods for sale

3. That the sole function of finance is to make available for consumption and use the total goods and services produced

---

[27] P. Kenway, *Quondam Quaker* (Birmingham, 1947), a book dedicated to Hargrave; NA 6.9.28, 27.9.28, 11.10.28, 18.10.28, 25.10.28, 1.11.28, 13.2.29; *Broadsheet*, 11.28.

[28] *Age of Plenty*, 7.28, 1.29, 2.29, 10.29; NA 31.7.29; Mackenzie chaired a meeting for Douglas in Glasgow, NEW 25.5.33; *Gramaphone*, 5.33.

4. That banking organizations shall act as the Public
   Accountants of the British people, and not as private
   monopolies of the Nation's Credit Power

To carry on the day-to-day propaganda, Worker's Educational
Groups (WEG) were established; these were shop organizations not
unlike communist cells but probably a heritage of the Guild Socialist
past. The first were set up in Coventry with George Hickling, an
unemployed mechanic, as secretary. Coventry, however, was a hotbed
of intrigue and personal feuds, and the scheme was soon abandoned.
In the disorganization the *Age of Plenty* suspended publication for two
months.[29]

If this particular project came to nothing, there was another development in Coventry which did have a significant result. From being
a subordinate, Hickling had developed ideas of his own importance
and an impressive-sounding organization to embody them. Towards
the end of 1930—that is, soon after the collapse of the Economic
party—he began to organize the unemployed of Coventry into the
Crusader Legion. In this venture he had the active support of Father
Paul Stacy. Father Stacy consented to act as chaplain to the Legion;
he opened his church to Freedom Sunday Services, blessed Legion
banners, and brought down Father Demant, a prominent Social Crediter from London, to preach to the men. Douglas himself addressed
the Legion. Soon the organization had thrown up an inner élite, first
known as the Iron Guard, but later, because of the quasi uniform
which they adopted, as the Green Shirts.[30] The threat posed by this
new group lay in its directness. In this respect it proved an advance
on the Economic party, for in place of their four demands, the Legion
put forward three slogans: Demand the National Credit Office;
Demand the Price Calculus; Demand the National Industrial
Dividend.[31]

Hargrave's own following seemed menaced, especially when branches of the Legion appeared in Glasgow and London. There was,
however, little need for concern, for in personality Hargrave so out-
shone Hickling that he had no difficulty in sweeping the Legion into
the Kin. Yet the threat was not without its effects. When the Legion
went into uniform at the end of 1931, the Kin responded to the

[29] *Age of Plenty*, 6.29, 7.29, 2.30.
[30] *Age of Plenty*, nos. 4, 5, 6; *This Prosperity*, 11.32; NA 26.2.31, 14.5.31, 23.8.31;
The Crusader Legion, *The Coventry Charter* (Coventry [1932]).
[31] NA 26.2.31; *Age of Plenty*, no. 4.

implied challenge by a ruthless modernization: the old lodges were reorganized; the archaisms were dropped, "gear" becoming "equipment," the Thingcouncil appearing as the District Head-Quarter Staff, and the delightful Big Smoke Middle Thing turned prosaically into the London Headquarters; the Saxon-Prussian uniform was replaced by a more up-to-date military variant using the green shirts of the Legion. At the same time, the Legion seems to have been equally impressed by Hargrave and his organization, and at the 1932 camp, attended by forty Legionnaires, agreed to become associated with the Kin, though retaining its own identity. Eventually, the Legion broke up in 1933, the old name Kibbo Kift had been relegated to a subordinate position, and the new title became Green Shirt Movement for Social Credit. As the Kin candidly announced: "That is going to be the popular name of this movement—the Green Shirts! Kibbo Kift is too difficult and the Legion of the Unemployed is too much of a mouthful. We've been misnamed Green Shirts, the name will stick to us—let's stick to it." The remaining links with the Kin past were gradually dropped or modified in such a way as to maintain continuity without jeopardizing the new look; thus the old ⫣K sign was retained but was now referred to as the Double Key symbol, unlocking the Douglas door into the Promised Land.[32]

The reconstructed movement got off to a good start when it received recognition from Major Douglas himself. In a revealing letter addressed to Hargrave, the major wrote, "As I understand that the objects and organization of the Green Shirt movement are based on the ideal, firstly, that it is the business of leaders to lead, so that it may be easier for others to follow, and secondly, that this ideal may be realized by grafting the progress of the present on sound traditions of the past, I think that I can claim a real kinship with it, and I shall feel honored if the green tartan now worn by my family is adopted for the facings of its uniform." He continued to speak highly of the Green Shirts and commended them to his Australian audience in 1934.[33] And with the working class the Green Shirts did enjoy a fleeting popularity. Partly this was due to the fact that desperate men are willing to consider desperate remedies, but there was more to it than that. In many ways the Green Shirt appeal was well suited to the

[32] NA 20.8.31, 21.1.32, 9.2.33; *This Prosperity,* 4.33; *Broadsheet,* 7.31, 6.32, 7.34; *Annual Report of the Green Shirt Movement for Social Credit, 1932–33*; *Social Credit,* 1.11.35.

[33] *Broadsheet,* 2.33; NA 19.4.34.

needs of the unemployed. Hargrave recognized the importance of giving a purpose to empty lives (this had been one of the original Kibbo Kift impulses), and branch life was kept busy. Thus the Bradford branch demanded attendance six days a week: two nights devoted to drill and street patrol, one evening to business, another to recreation, the Saturday to selling literature, and one evening to the study of Social Credit. Efforts were made to find premises which could be used as a club by the members, and a big point was made of the London Headquarters' ability to offer "anything from a cup of tea to a full meal any evening of the week."[34]

The need for colour in the lives of the unemployed held high priority with Hargrave, who from the start had insisted on emotional values. The drums and the banners which were such a feature of the Green Shirt's public appearances, and the use of striking literature, for the publication of which Hargrave's experience was invaluable, were naturally attractive to many whose days were drab and featureless. Even the Kin tradition had its use, for in such times the possibility of camping was better than no holiday at all, and the flying columns by Green Shirt lorry to fresh districts, with accommodation provided by sympathizers in the area, had some of the exciting camaraderie which had last been experienced in Britain in the prewar days of the Labour party. At its height, the movement had a chain of some sixteen groups across Britain, mainly in industrial centres. The membership was not revealed, but it was claimed that *Attack*, the most successful of the Green Shirt organs, was selling seven thousand copies a week. Whatever the numbers at his disposal, Hargrave managed to make a sizable impact. Under his leadership the marching columns of Green Shirts joined in the hunger marches organized by the unemployed, and on these occasions their soldierly bearing contrasted splendidly with the bedraggled appearance of the others. Even the Blackshirts, it was claimed, were impressed by Green Shirt spirit and discipline and paid tribute to their appearance.[35]

It quickly became evident that growth had been too rapid and that the end of the depression spelled the decline of the Green Shirts. After Douglas's recognition, few others came forward to endorse the movement. Ezra Pound did give a banner, and Lord Strabolgi, ex-Liberal

---

[34] NA 19.10.33; *Broadsheet*, 10.32.

[35] *Annual Report of the Green Shirt Movement for Social Credit, 1933–34*; NA 19.10.33; *Broadsheet*, 1.33, 8.34.

and now Labour M.P., received a deputation of Green Shirts at Westminster. This was all, however, and so short of reputable backing were they that one M. F. Cullis, whose only claim to distinction was the fact that he was then a scholar of Brasenose, had his photograph and curriculum vitae printed in *Attack* when he announced his adherence. The established Social Credit membership, where not hostile, was privately amused by Hargrave's antics and gave him no support. Hargrave himself admitted that branch life was precarious; attention was drawn to one branch which had managed to build up a backing of between two and three thousand but which had totally disintegrated within a few weeks of this count.[36]

Yet Hargrave refused to admit defeat. In 1935 the chance to make two fresh bids for a hearing occurred. The first occasion was the unexpected victory of a party advocating Social Credit in Alberta. The Green Shirts knew that the Albertan leader, William Aberhart, did not fully understand Social Credit, and they suspected that the Albertan party was nothing more than a tool of financiers who were using the Social Credit title to discredit the genuine message of Douglas. To prevent anything similar in Britain, Hargrave decided to transform his organization into the Social Credit Party of Great Britain. The second opportunity soon followed. The 1935 general election gave the newly born party the chance to go before the voters, repeat in miniature the Alberta triumph, and shock the tools of the money power at Westminster into mending their ways. At short notice the Green Shirt tradition of antiparliamentary, direct-mandate thinking was abandoned and a candidate for South Leeds decided upon.

The party was lucky in its choice. Wilfred Townend was a strong candidate. Locally born, he had served in the navy during the war, and upon graduating from Leeds University had become divinity master in a local school. Although he had originally been a Labour party supporter, he was converted to Social Credit in 1932.[37] Behind him stood one of the more active branches of the party, in which Townend himself had recently enrolled twenty-one members, and they were helped by squads of Green Shirts from London and other parts of the country. Their cause was also helped by the circumstances of the election; the country was passing through one of its bouts of disillusionment with orthodoxy and with the main political parties

[36] *Annual Report of the Green Shirt Movement for Social Credit, 1934–35*; NA 23.2.33; *Attack,* 7.34; *Broadsheet,* 6.35.

[37] NA 26.9.35, 16.4.36.

(this was the time of the Peace Pledge Union), and locally the with-drawal of the Liberals from a constituency where previously they had polled a respectable vote helped the novel appeal of Hargrave. His flair for publicity got the party a news coverage which was considera-bly more than most minor parties could manage. For instance, the deposit money was presented in silver, and the Returning Officer was allowed to count as far as two pounds before legal tender was sub-stituted; it was both an eye-catching trick and the occasion for a lecture on money, bankers' monopoly, and the rest of the Social Credit party case.[38]   In the end the result was a respectable 11 per-cent of the poll. By the standards of minor parties this was a fair result, and the party was justified in crowing over Mosley's New party.[39] Unfortunately, it remained true that no dent had been made in the two-party system.

The reaction to the events of 1935 and to subsequent developments did the party no good. Douglas could no longer countenance a party which was not merely an organization with inherently dangerous tendencies towards dictatorship, but also had the effrontery to imply that amateurs should dictate to the experts. Recognition was with-drawn, and the Douglas flash disappeared from the uniforms. Later developments only widened the gap, and they reached a showdown over Alberta. Telegrams having proved useless, Hargrave went out at his own expense to put the Albertan Social Crediters right. He was furious to discover that his chances had been jeopardized by Doug-las's forewarning that he was not to be trusted and that he was not technically competent.[40] After such high hopes, and being so near to leading a successful revolt against Aberhart, Hargrave never forgave Douglas. These setbacks and fading hopes were reflected in his behav-iour. He rounded on Douglas and took his revenge for Alberta. When G. F. Powell, Douglas's unfortunate emissary, was welcomed back to England at a Social Credit reception, Kenway and the Green Shirts broke up the meeting. Chanting slogans, hurling objects, and finally rushing the platform, they effectively prevented Powell from present-ing his report. Hargrave jumped up and shouted his repudiation of

---

[38] *Attack,* no. 32; NA 19.10.33, 10.10.35, 17.10.35; *Yorkshire Evening News,* 7.10.35, 15.10.35, 4.11.35; *Leeds Weekly Citizen,* 22.11.35. The Leeds Social Credit group had gone over to the Green Shirts *en bloc;* see NA 4.5.33.

[39] NA 21.11.35. The New Party figures were those for 1931, when of twenty-four candidates only four polled over 1,000 votes; see C. Cross, *The Fascists in Britain* (London, 1961), p. 52.

[40] Personal communication from Miss H. Corke, 1967.

any leadership of Social Credit, in England or anywhere in the world, other than his own. The police had to be called in before order could be restored.[41]

Hargrave's language began to show a return to his Kibbo Kift mysticism; his demand, "Drums, drums—get drums! More drums, more flags, more marching. Make the Drum-thunder roll and the Green Flag of Freedom rise like a forest from the Pentland Coast to Lizard Head," was a hysterical repudiation of the moderation of 1929–35. In turning on Montagu Norman, the governor of the Bank of England, and attacking him as a "sinister Banker Ringleader [who] dresses and acts like a conspirator," he was tempted into the only example of smear technique that can be found in his public utterances.[42] Such an organization was in no state to withstand the Public Order Act which outlawed the use of uniforms for political purposes, although a brave and typical attempt to circumvent the act was made by parading with shirts held aloft on hangers. When war came and suspended operations, the party was dealt a blow from which it never recovered. It still exists in Britain, but Hargrave, though alive at the time of writing, no longer directs it, and its influence is nil.

What is interesting about the Green Shirts is not, however, their fortunes as a political force in Britain; even in their own opinion this was insignificant. Green Shirt activity has an interest because it has been used to support the case that Social Credit is essentially fascist and because the transformation of an already existing organization serves as a means of evaluating the significance of Social Credit philosophy.

The nature of the party was a difficult question for contemporary observers, for action for its own sake and externals tended to bulk so large. On this ground those who discerned a fascist streak could be pardoned; the uniforms, the marching, the drums, the notion of an élite—in the early 1930s all these were to the left wing as red rags to a bull. Social Credit itself was already suspect on the left because of its petit bourgeois appeal, and the association with quasi-fascist characters had already been made.[43] The party had continually to

---

[41] *Social Credit,* 29.7.38. The text of this repudiation may be found in *This Week's Message from Hargrave,* no. 21.

[42] *Broadsheet,* 1.36; *Attack,* no. 38.

[43] *Communist Review,* 5.22, 1.26.

protest against this superficial identification. It could be pointed out that to non–left wingers the Social Credit party appeared as a socialist movement, promising wealth and security to all, regardless of effort or merit. Especially annoying to the fascists was the refusal to accept the idea of an organic state. And in truth the "unarmed military technique" which Hargrave saw as the secret of success was almost entirely symbolic. The frequent Green Shirt marches were either a part of the demonstrations of the unemployed, to which little exception could be taken, or small pacific demonstrations against institutions, as when a section marched to the Bank of England, marched round the building three times, and presented a petition to the governor. When violence did occur, it was more likely to be of the kind that the public found endearing, as when one Michael Murphy hurled a green-painted brick through the window of 11 Downing Street; for this signal act he was awarded the Green Oak Leaf, the highest Green Shirt award. Moreover, it must be added that the Kibbo Kift tradition of championing the oppressed was never given up, and vigorous attacks were directed against anti-Semitism and racial theories.[44]

In short, the Green Shirts saw themselves as equally firm in their rejection of both communism and fascism. They described their philosophy as "the third resolvent factor."[45] In 1933 they had the perfect chance to show their impartiality. That year, the first of May, Labour Day, fell in midweek, and the question was whether to march on the weekend before or after the first. Left and right chose differently; Hargrave's men marched on both occasions.

But if Hargrave was clear in his own mind that the Green Shirts stood for a third philosophy, it must be admitted that it was still far from being convincing. Yet the adoption of Social Credit had at least removed the grosser blemishes which had marked the Kibbo Kift outlook. The old individualism, the reason why totalitarianism, whether of the left or right, could not be accepted, was still a central belief. However, the previous immanentism was no longer insisted upon, and the call for world unity was in consequence muted. What was now wanted was an economic nationalism which, within a self-sufficient area, would insist upon the greatest possible amount of home rule; Social Credit party flags were, by order, to carry not only the Union Jack but also the emblems of the four constituent

[44] NA 23.3.33, 17.8.33, 25.4.34; *Broadsheet*, 4.34, 7.35; *Attack*, 9.12.33, no. 29; *Age of Plenty*, 5.28, 7.28.

[45] The Kibbo Kift, *Miscellaneous Pamphlets* (n.p., 1939).

countries.[46] World unity was suspect, for it was held to increase the chance that the money powers would take absolute control. At the same time there was a new emphasis on the monarchy. A king, it was felt, was the only individual who would find it possible to withstand the pressure of the conspiracy of the money trust. Therefore it was not surprising when the Green Shirts vociferously took the side of Edward VIII in the abdication crisis; on the strength of his comments deploring unemployment, they presented him as the sworn foe and victim of the bankers. Indeed, hopes for legitimacy lived on and as late as 1937 the Green Shirts presented a loyal address to the Duke of Windsor, then at Schloss Wasserlemburg.[47]

An even greater change in outlook, however, was the abandonment of the nonpolitical tradition of the Kin. Ultimately, the Green Shirt state would have been a repudiation of traditional parliamentary democracy, an end which Hargrave proclaimed in 1932 in an address entitled "A Popular Mandate versus Ballot Box Democracy."[48] But as communists and fascists alike had found before this, it was tactically necessary to come down into the political arena. The Kin, lacking any goal which would have justified such a course of action, had not been able to take this step and had been condemned to aimless and contradictory policies. The breaking of the "bankers' combine" and the establishment of a Social Credit world of plenty not only justified but positively compelled political participation and, in so doing, injected a vital sense of purpose. The idea of an élite whose pageantry and symbolism would serve to awaken the masses to a realization of the new order—"We are the Spearhead of the New Life breaking into the mass apathy of this banker ridden community"—was a belief which transformed the Kin élite-for-its-own-sake into the Green Shirt executive, an élite with a purpose.[49] And so without necessarily impugning Hargrave's or the Kin's sincerity in their acceptance of Social Credit, it may perhaps be observed that its discovery was a most fortunate one for them, accepted with all the drowning man's gratitude for the proverbial straw.

The final word on Hargrave and his Kibbo Kift–Green Shirt party may be left to D. H. Lawrence. In a letter to Rolf Gardiner, his

---

[46] *Broadsheet,* 11.36.

[47] This line had emerged as early as 1932; see *Age of Plenty,* no. 9. *Broadsheet,* 7.37.

[48] *Annual Report of the Green Shirt Movement for Social Credit, 1932–33.*

[49] *Broadsheet,* 11.35.

enthusiastic admirer, Lawrence wrote of Hargrave and his *Confession*:

> Of course, it won't work: not quite flesh and blood. The ideas are sound, but flesh and blood won't take 'em till a great deal of flesh and blood has been destroyed. Of course, the birthright credit too is sound enough—but to nationalize capital is a good deal harder than to nationalize industries. . . . [Hargrave] alternates between idealism pure and simple and a sort of mummery: and then a compromise with practicality. What he wants is all right. I agree with him on the whole, and I respect him as a straightforward fighter. But he knows there's no hope, his way *en masse*. And therefore, underneath, he's full of hate. He's ambitious: and his ambition isn't practical: so he's full of hate, underneath. He's overweening and he's cold. But, for all that, on the whole, he's *right*, and I respect him for it. I respect his courage and aloneness. If it weren't for his ambition and his lack of warmth, I'd go and Kibbo Kift along with him. . . . But by wanting to rope in *all* mankind it shows he wants to have his cake and eat it.[50]

[50] R. Gardiner, *World Without End* (London: Cobden-Sanderson, 1932), p. 37.

chapter eight

SOCIAL CREDIT AND THE INTELLECTUALS

The title to this chapter is not a wholly satisfactory one. Not all the people discussed here were, or would have wished to call themselves, intellectuals. Yet there is very little choice in the matter, and if some of these individuals were not, strictly speaking, intellectuals, then at least their interest in and connection with groups which were essentially intellectual justifies their inclusion in this chapter. Above all, it has been pointed out how Social Credit was first seriously developed and championed through the pages of the *New Age,* a journal of uncompromising intellectual appeal and one which commanded a respectful hearing as the herald of a philosophy. And although it has been noted that after Major Moore's disastrous tenure of the editorship, and despite the rescue attempted by Brenton, the old éclat and standing were never regained, yet it is true that the *New Age* tradition never became completely a thing of the past; in different ways, it lingered on to keep the spirit of Orage and his paper alive.

How this came about, the forms which the tradition assumed, and the new influences it attracted to itself will be the subject of this chapter, for they are of special importance in helping to fix the character of Social Credit. By definition, the intellectual reaction was one of which the philosophic bases had already been stated; they could be traced in the activities and thinking of groups which had been established quite independently of Social Credit. That they naturally turned in the direction of Social Credit when those ideas became current is therefore interesting, and an examination of this response should indicate the way in which Social Credit, as an ideology, was regarded at the time.

But to begin with, the older Oragean tradition must be considered, for the first attempt to give a sustained analysis of the deeper implications of a Social Credit state was the result of developments stemming directly from the *New Age*. In particular, they were due to the initiative of a *New Age* contributor who owed a great deal to Orage's encouragement. This was the Serbian, Dimitrije Mitrinovic, whose articles had appeared over the signature of M. M. Cosmoi. This pseudonym, in fact, concealed a double identity, for Mitrinovic's English was poor, and it was necessary for him to convey his ideas to Orage, who then transposed them into a form intelligible enough for printing. But even after passing through the winnowing stage of Oragean translation, these ideas remained mystical and elusive, and when Orage left to pursue his own mystical studies in 1922, the offerings of Mitrinovic began to border upon the unreal. After one particularly obscure article had appeared, the downright Philip Kenway did not hesitate to describe such writing as rubbish.[1] Mitrinovic could hardly be expected to feel kindly towards the new editor, Brenton, who printed such an outspoken letter and who was so far removed from the ideal of Orage. On 12 May 1926, Mitrinovic called together four acquaintances who met at the Ship Restaurant; these four, who first took the name Thursday Group but later became the Chandos Group, from the name of the restaurant to which they transferred their loyalties, were Maurice Reckitt, Travers Symons, Philip Mairet and Alan Porter.[2]

The first-named was a member of the Quaker dyer family, though this religious allegiance had become a thing of the past. In fact, he had been educated, under the shadow of a strong-willed grandmother, into a High Church Anglican, and several years at Balliol had helped to complete the transformation into a potential member of the establishment. The Tory sympathies of the grandmother, however, never came completely to the surface. At Oxford, Reckitt's social conscience and Christian belief took the form of a championing of Christian Socialist principles, and after graduation and a spell of tutoring at Oxford, he

---

[1] NA 13.8.25.

[2] I am grateful to Messrs. Mairet, Reckitt, and Symons for much of the material for this chapter. I thank them, too, for their most useful insights.

became the editor of the *Church Socialist*, the organ of the Church Socialist League. It was only natural that a man who had a keen social awareness, whose Christianity made him instinctively recoil from theories of class war, and who had studied under Cole, should find the guild movement an attractive one. In 1915, he took part in the establishment of the National Guilds League, and three years later collaborated with C. E. Bechhofer in writing the textbook of the guild movement. It was he who had led the opposition to the swing to the left which marked the movement in the period just after the war, and it was he who had taken the lead in accepting the Social Credit analysis within the guild movement. Reckitt frankly admitted that his discovery of Social Credit and his experience of communist leanings at this time made him abandon any formal socialism which he had once accepted.

W. Travers Symons was a socialist of a different stamp, an old ILP man who was proud to have known Keir Hardie. Unlike Reckitt, whose private means freed him from worry about earning his living, Symons had enjoyed a more practical life and had followed his father into a Lloyd's insurance brokerage firm. It was through the *New Age* that he came to know of Social Credit, especially through a study of *Economic Democracy*, the more general observations of which made a far greater impact upon him than did the purely economic. Symons had retained his links with the ILP and had spoken at ILP conferences in favour of Social Credit. He was in consequence a more experienced public figure than was Reckitt, and he had a more practical understanding of the financial world.

The third member, Philip Mairet, had been a worker in the Arts and Crafts movement at Chipping Campden under C. R. Ashbee (an admirer of Ruskin and Morris, on whom he wrote) and also had been connected for a time with the Ditchling Community; he had worked in stained glass and published a pamphlet upon the meaning of craftsmanship. During the war Mairet had been a conscientious objector and had spent part of the time working for Patrick Geddes, producing the charts which were so important a part of that teacher's methods. After the war, Mairet found an outlet for his writings in the *New Age* and began to contribute just about the time when Douglasism was becoming the all-important topic.

The last of the original members, Alan Porter, was a poet and writer who eventually left England for the United States, where he became a professor of literature at Vassar. Unlike the other three, he had no belief in Social Credit, and within a short while he had left the group.[3]

With such a core of followers, Mitrinovic began a tradition of regular meetings to discuss problems of the day from a Social Credit standpoint, and then he promptly left the group to its own devices while he developed new interests. He did not, however, repudiate Social Credit, and he was later to be caught up in the movement in other ways. Meanwhile, the members of the original group added to their number. Soon to join were Albert Newsome, a Post Office engineer and close friend of Mairet; Geoffrey Davies, town clerk of Watford and ex-Distributist; the Reverend Egerton Swann, an Anglican and old Guild Socialist; the Reverend Vico August Demant, now a professor of moral theology at Oxford but at the time a parish priest of Richmond (as his first names hinted, he came from a Positivist family, and he had taken an engineering degree at Durham and had contemplated a Unitarian ministry before taking Anglican orders); Hilderic Cousens, a Cambridge First in classics and one-time secretary to Bertrand Russell; Colonel J. H. Delahaye, an independent politician who stood in the 1931 election; T. M. Heron, director of Cresta Silks, a small firm in a market dominated by the giant Imperial Chemical Industries (ICI), and an active High Churchman, though he had originally been a Presbyterian; R. S. J. Rands, a schoolmaster and ex-pupil of Reckitt; and Basil Boothroyd, a contributor to the *Socialist Leader*, to *Punch*, and to other papers, frequently under the pen name Yaffle.[4]

This completed the regular membership, but in addition G. D. H. Cole, Lewis Mumford, and T. S. Eliot attended on a semiregular basis. Cole was prepared to go a good deal of the way with Social Credit, for instance advocating some form of national dividends; Mumford was at least sympathetic; and Eliot was a crypto-Social Crediter.[5]

At first, the Chandos Group directed its efforts toward discussion of the problems of the day and publishing the conclusions in the form of books. The earliest such effort was edited by Porter and dealt with

[3] This did not prevent his editing a book with a Social Credit slant; see below, n. 6.

[4] I also wish to thank Rev. V. A. Demant and Messrs. Heron and Rands for providing me with valuable material and insights.

[5] For Cole see M. Butchard, ed., *Tomorrow's Money* (London, 1936), p. 185. Mumford had been editor of the *Sociological Review*, 1920. Eliot always hung back from complete endorsement, feigning lack of an economic mind. But see his "all-but" letter in *Social Credit*, 7.9.34.

a problem which must have dominated the minds of the contributors —the coal problem—for the Chandos Group was founded in the shadow of the General Strike, which ended in the very week that the group was inaugurated.

The title of the book, *Coal*, and the circumstances in which it came to be written gave the impression that a specific problem was to be discussed and specific remedies suggested. In fact, the book was merely a peg on which to hang general observations about the nature of politics. The aim of the contributors was to get away from the taking of sides and the mutual accusations which had characterized the dispute up to then. "It is," claimed the Chandos Group, "our chief aim to treat of universal guilt and communal responsibility." And another aim was to accept the fact that attacks of one nation upon another could only destroy the fabric of society. The only way out would be a radical rethinking of political principles. Certainly, the group believed that present politics were irredeemably tainted. This was so on the practical level, for the conduct of politicians gave grounds for the gravest anxiety. Baldwin might be the individual who came in for specific attack as a leader who could not "do more than offer to take the chair in a crisis," but if he was attacked it was only as the personification of a system in which all the parties were considered to be unprincipled. "The nearer we approach . . . the more we are disgusted by the utter absence of a whole policy for the whole community." Yet, if day-to-day politics were bad, the assumptions on which the political system itself was based were worse. Representative government amounted in fact to "quinquennial abdications of responsibility," and the much-vaunted spirit of compromise was really "mutual sacrifice."[6]

This initial stance was easily recognizable as a memory of the Guild Socialist days, and it was scarcely surprising, because Mairet, Reckitt, and Swann had been avowed guildsmen, while the others were more than sympathetic. Accordingly, the solution which they offered might have been easily forecast; it was functionalism. Functionalism would provide for a decentralization which would call forth a more active participation on the part of the citizens. This truth was obvious, had been said before, and did not need to be repeated. But on this occasion a new idea was added to functionalism, an idea which would have appealed to de Maeztu but which had not been stressed in the days of the National Guilds League. This was the idea that each nation had

[6] A. Porter, ed., *Coal* (London, 1927), pp. 8, 10, 36–37, 41–47.

its own function, a way of living which marked it off from all other nations and by which standard it judged its own actions and purposes. "A nation should have character in its actions. It should have a mode of life, a peculiar realization of truth, to declare and exemplify." That was the new conclusion of Chandos, which looked back nostalgically to the days of mid-Victorian England when the country had a sense of function, of purpose, crude perhaps and needing refinement, but an idea to work for, a faith in itself.[7]

It was upon such a beginning that the advocacy of Social Credit was built. It came as something of an anticlimax, for there was no mention of the doctrine by name, merely the statements that wage reductions curtailed purchasing power; that "debts are contracted, property is mortgaged against repayment, but reduced wages and increased productivity per man-hour have already cancelled out of circulation the only means of gaining enough money to pay the debts"; and that the way out lay through cost accountancy and had been discovered.[8]

This was not, however, the only anticlimax. The analysis showed that the existing state of affairs was far from satisfactory, but it made no attempt to show that the sole solution was Social Credit. It was perfectly possible to agree with the denunciations of the opening pages, even that what was needed was a functional society, without seeing how this demanded or even led to Social Credit. When this was written, however, it was already the late 1920s, and it had become evident that Social Credit roused considerable prejudice. A circumspect approach, therefore, had much to recommend it.

The second publication of the Chandos Group was an elaboration of these points. The same ennui with the state of affairs in which "it seems . . . to matter very little what political party is in power" was expressed; the same disillusionment with democracy was noted, its faulty basis unacceptable to the citizen who "cannot delegate his political responsibility." Also objected to was the stultifying practice that "opposition must always oppose rather than contribute." As a remedy, the same functionalism was insisted upon. Indeed, the only difference between the two offerings was that the first declared for Social Credit views, if not by name, while the second contented itself

[7] Ibid., pp. 43–44.
[8] Ibid., p. 65.

with criticism of "the Banks which constitute a Government above the Government."[9]

If the occasional flysheet be excepted, this was the last publication of the Chandos Group.[10] On this basis the importance of the group would seem to be small. In fact, the publications were a minor part of the group's activities. Much more important was the part played in helping Orage reenter journalism on his return from the United States. In 1932, Orage had once again taken up the Social Credit banner in England. On landing he had been surprised to find that Brenton had no intention of giving up the *New Age*, and he was forced to begin a fresh venture, the *New English Weekly*. The risk of such a departure was made more bearable because he knew that Chandos Group members would stand behind him, ready and eager to provide the required articles of the necessary excellence; the Social Credit commentaries written over the pseudonyms Pontifex I, II, and III were provided by Newsome, Cousens, and Symons respectively.[11] Reckitt and Demant were regular contributors, and Mairet was so prominent that upon Orage's untimely death it was he who was chosen to carry on the paper. The *New English Weekly* deserves to be examined because, understandably enough, it showed some of the traits of the *New Age* developed in the light of the interwar trends.

The *New English Weekly* was never the paper which the *New Age* had been, though the sense of continuity was maintained at all costs. The former *New Age* offices were secured, and contributors from its heyday—Penty, Bechhofer, Belloc, Cole, and of course Chandos Group members—were featured; there were even offerings from "Young Nietzschean," from RHC (which had been Orage's old nom de plume), and from "The Ghost of Stanhope of Chester." But Orage was older now, and his long exile in the United States had broken that influence which in some mysterious way he had wielded over the literary world of prewar days. Moreover, the guild idea had been discredited by the failure of the twenties, and what is more, the rise of totalitarianism in its two forms had made such discussion seem academic. Of course, Orage's temperament made him insist on proclaiming his opposition to both variants of totalitarianism. But it was not possible to take that line, the issues being such that a leaning to

[9] J. V. Delahaye, *Politics: A Discussion of Realities* (London, 1929), pp. 11, 19, 22, 44.

[10] Reckitt's papers, dated 6.33.

[11] Personal communication from P. Mairet, 1966.

one or the other direction had to be made. How, then, did the successor to the *New Age* respond to the new mood of the thirties?

The direction which Orage felt obliged to take was almost immediately evident; it amounted to a development of the idea of functionalism as transmitted by the Chandos Group. The second issue of the new paper carried an article by the Marquis of Tavistock, entitled "Economic Nationalism," which accepted the idea of autarchy. The complete repudiation of the liberal-socialist past was clearly intended. It was not to be half measures for the *New English Weekly*. The implications of the decision to endorse economic nationalism were recognized, and the paper did not shrink from defending the positive aspects of this belief. H. G. Wells was selected for attack when he made one of his periodic defences of internationalism; the *New English Weekly* found such an attitude intolerable. "Nationality," it stated, "is as natural a fact as individuality and is one of the essential characteristics of the species Man." Indeed, the paper was prepared to extend this attack on internationalism in such a way as to link up communism and international finance, and on one occasion it hailed the day when "marxian internationalism—the labour equivalent of financial internationalism" would be defeated.[12]

The natural consequence of such a stance was perhaps a turning towards Italy's corporate state, and since Ezra Pound, a Social Crediter since at least 1920,[13] was at this time living in Italy and defending the regime there, and since the Italian apologist, Odon Por, an old Guild Socialist, still kept up his association with the *New English Weekly*,[14] this rapprochement was even more understandable.

Others who wrote for the paper, however, wanted to include the German variant of fascism in their design for the future. The most outspoken of these were Horsfall Carter, an Oxford-educated linguist and publicist, and Rolf Gardiner. The former seems to have had little to do with Social Credit itself, but he found Orage's paper a congenial outlet and made the most of his opportunity. For Carter the appeal of German fascism was the use of youth to defeat orthodoxy. Hitler was praised as the man who had "set all the youth of Germany on fire [and who] determined to demolish 'the system'." Oswald Mosley was likewise praised, on the ground that he was "the one political

---

[12] NEW 28.4.32, 25.8.32, 27.7.33.

[13] *Little Review*, 4.20. Pound had contempt for national socialism.

[14] O. Por, *Guilds and Co-operatives in Italy* (London, 1923); see his articles in NA 15.1.14, 2.7.14, 17.9.14; also NEW 22.11.34, 24.10.35.

paladin who . . . attempted to give expression to this revolt of youth" in England. He recognized that fascism had been accompanied by violence, but he pleaded, "Excesses that have given it a bad name are as peculiar to Italy as are particular manifestations of communism to Russia."[15]

Rolf Gardiner, as has been seen, was also impressed by the German emphasis on youth. In his case he praised the Nazi interest in the land. Hitler's Germany struck Gardiner as "a resurgence of the soil against the asphalt, of the land against the big city." Thus far no exception could be taken to his stance. Unfortunately, he was too ready to accept the current German explanation for the ruin of the countryside. It was the Jews who were responsible, those "Easterners . . . who come with the smell of Asia still in their beards." They had no grasp of the value of the land, for who had "ever known a Jewish poet who came of farming stock outside Palestine?"[16] If the argument lacked cogency, it was only anchoring itself the more firmly in the anti-Semitic tradition.

Naturally, this anti-Semitism brought forth letters of protest. To these the *New English Weekly* replied that the position was very simple: the Catholics and the Anglicans had found spokesmen to come out for Social Credit, but never yet had a Jewish rabbi declared for Douglasism. If the Jews were sincere in not wanting to be known as the enemies of mankind, then let them endorse the only plan which could save the world and enrich the lives of every one. Once again the logic of the argument is defective, but to a convinced Social Crediter it must have had a certain attraction and confirmed perhaps some waverers in their beliefs. At the same time a more reasonable defence was attempted. "Nothing," claimed the *New English Weekly*, "can ever be used in extenuation . . . of the fiendish anti-semitism of medieval Germany." Yet, it was no use blinking the fact that the Jews had themselves to blame for much of their plight. To insist upon anti-European ways was a gratuitous insult to the host culture, and the Jews should adopt western ways—as "Gens" put it, "re-adapt themselves to Western Life."[17]

Support on other grounds for the profascist attitude was forthcoming from those two Nietzschean extremists who had long been colleagues of Orage, Oscar Levy and Anthony Ludovici. Since the former believed that political liberty had "led to Democracy and

[15] NEW 12.5.32, 6.10.32, 24.11.32.
[16] NEW 8.6.33, 22.6.33.
[17] NEW 3.8.33, 21.9.33, 14.6.34, 5.7.34.

Democracy on to Bolshevism,"[18] he was delighted to find developing in Italy a system which promised to lead back to the older purity, which would be rooted in the Catholic Europe of pre-Reformation days; the Christian heresy began to work its poison, he held, only when in its Protestant form. Ludovici did not write so frequently for the new paper as he had done for the old. He had found a new outlet via the Red Rose League and its successor, the English Mistery, a royalist, chivalric, magical, antidemocratic, back-to-the-land organization of quite outstanding impotence. But he did on occasion write in the *New English Weekly*, adding his contribution to the diatribe against "emasculated intellectualism," an undefined bogey which was understood to mean any liberal modernism.[19]

It will be seen, then, that what commended itself in fascism and nationalism was not so much those aspects which came to the fore at a later period as the promise which had lain behind both movements for a totally new start. In fairness to the *New English Weekly*, then, it should also be noted that disillusionment with Nazi Germany and the other totalitarianisms soon became evident. On 6 April 1933, the "Notes of the Week" commented, "Not for some years to come will it be known exactly upon what terms Chancellor Hitler sold his programme for power, but between all the lines it is now clearly written that nothing distinguishes the new German dictatorship from the dictatorship of Central Banks in general." The article went on to show how anti-Semitism might be used as a blind to cover the drift to the servile state. Even Carter came to admit that the Nazis had perverted the revolution, a judgement which seemed to have been triggered off by the recent throwing over of Gottfried Feder, the economic theorist. Douglas himself was always very clear in his own mind that fascism was an evil, and he would not respect the *New English Weekly*'s leanings in that direction. Writing in that paper an article identifying the "enemy," he made a special point of naming fascism and particularizing the Irish Blueshirts and Mosley as examples of the evil.[20]

That this change of outlook on the part of the *New English Weekly*

---

[18] NEW 3.11.32.

[19] The *Red Rose Pamphlets* ran from 1913–23; the English Mistery was set up in 1930 and may be followed in its *Orders*; see, too, A. M. Ludovici, *Creation or Recreation* (London, 1934); NEW 22.2.34, 17.11.34.

[20] NEW 14.9.33, 20.12.34, 3.1.35.

was a painful one was clear. An example of this reluctance to reassess was seen as late as 26 July 1934, when the paper commented as follows upon the state of English fascism: "The press magnate Lord Rothermere's desertion of Sir Oswald Mosley is the final proof that fascism in this country is about to sink. But, at the same time, it is not all together a matter of rejoicing. Though Sir Oswald's programme has been anything but consistent and his own tactics anything but consonant with the English character, both he and his movement represent the nearest approach to practical idealism in current politics; and it will be a tragedy if the wine he brewed for youth is allowed to go sour because he could not bottle it." What made the necessary realignment even harder to bear was the way which Hitler was regarded by some of the leading lights in the movement. Within the movement several grounds existed for the belief that Hitler was on the point of coming out for some form of Social Credit. The Marquis of Tavistock, whose position gave him an entrée into circles normally closed and who later acted as an unofficial peace envoy via Dublin,[21] claimed, "I have personally interested Herr Hitler in our programme," though he did go on to confess, "I am unable to say how far he or the Nazis are committed to it in Germany." Somewhat later a letter appeared in the *New English Weekly* over the signature of Emil Van Loo, Amsterdam, noting, "One of Herr Hitler's envoys told me personally . . . that the financial system in the new Germany would be based on National Credit and I understand that it was Lord Tavistock who brought the new thesis to Hitler's notice." Within the movement it was also believed that Douglas himself was in touch with Hitler. Not that this was done directly; the channel of communication was a devious one, via Gurdjieff, the Russian mystic who knew Orage and whose methods might be considered acceptable to Hitler. Even after the war had begun, a Social Credit source was claiming that in 1939 Göring was having enquiries made in England about the working of the doctrine.[22] These reports were shadowy, and although, of course, Germany did use novel ideas of economics with rather more verve than the democracies, such reports were no doubt the product of much wishful thinking. The very fact, however, that such beliefs were current at the time meant that it was doubly regrettable to many of

---

[21] John, Duke of Bedford, *Silver Plated Spoon* (London, 1962), p. 137.

[22] NEW 6.10.32, 27.7.33; *Reality,* 15.3.40; for Hitler's links with the Theosophists see G. L. Mosse, *The Crisis of German Ideology* (London, 1966), pp. 75–76; personal communication from W. T. Symons, 1966.

the *New English Weekly* circle that Nazi Germany had to be thrown over. The fact that it was speaks in favor of the *New English Weekly*. Finally, the reaction of the periodical to the Spanish civil war may be noted, for there was a case where it was possible to look upon the conflict in its origins as one innocent of fascist-communist complications. At the time of the outbreak of hostilities the paper came out clearly for the cause of "the Spanish left [which] may fade for a time . . . but will not die."[23] If this meant, metaphorically speaking, that de Maeztu had been dropped, it also meant that George Orwell, who wrote for the *New English Weekly* in the late 1930s, had been taken on board. In conclusion, it can be said that if at times the paper sailed close to the extreme right it did so for reasons which, in the main, were defensible and that when the negative aspects of fascism came to the surface they were repudiated.

The Chandos Group, then, was significant in its ability to act as a reservoir of talent from which a wide Social Credit advocacy could be drawn. There was another importance to the group, however, for it acted as a link organization between other and quite different groupings which, if not wholly Social Credit, did give a sympathetic hearing to it. One such was the circle of Adlerian psychologists.

This school has become known as Individual Psychology, a fitting description. The starting point of Adler's thinking was the realization that not all people fall victim to the same diseases, even though they may be equally exposed to the same dangers. In fact, some *individuals* seem more prone to sickness than others. But while individualism was Adler's starting point, it had of course nothing to do with his fame as a psychologist. What constituted Adler's starting point *in psychology* was his insistence upon the inferiority feeling by which this individualism was mediated. The feeling of inferiority always demanded that the individual sought to overcome the feeling by compensation, and thus Beethoven might be said to have become a composer not despite, but because of, his deafness. It should be noted that this feeling, because universal, was in itself neutral.

Up to this point the Adlerian outlook had many similarities with the Nietzschean. Both were prepared to consider a system which was beyond good and evil and which left the way open to the assertion of personality. There were, too, in Adler implications of an aristocratic kind. He did express an admiration for aristocratic virtues, and he carried these beliefs over to account for the later rise of Hitler; it was

[23] NEW 30.7.36.

inevitable, he thought, in a country "with all those insurance societies. People should take care of themselves; but the German people always want it done for them." But in 1916 Adler developed an aspect of his psychology which caused the Nietzscheans to withdraw in a body and which prevented any further claim that Adlerianism was a morally neutral system.[24] In that year, under the impact of the war, Adler announced his belief in *Gemeinschaftsgefühl*, and so gave a clue to the real significance of his inferiority complex theory. The nature of the compensation was now particularized; if it was self-directed, said Adler, then the individual was neurotic, and the extreme case was when a person experienced pain which was in fact self-inflicted. If, on the other hand, the compensating impulse was other-directed, that is, directed to the good of society, then that man was sane. Individual Psychology was now revealed as a system with a transcendental goal, completing the immanence of the earlier gropings.

What has been said so far in respect of Adler's view of man and society applied equally well to the methods by which he worked. Just as man's purpose could be made intelligible only when considered against the background of the whole society, so could a patient's psyche be understood only in its entirety. The term *psychoanalysis* was not for Adler; rather, in its determination to find, not "the cause of [a] particular symptom, but what was the aim of the total personality," Individual Psychology aimed at *psychosynthesis*.[25] This was not to say that Adler had come to believe in a purely idealistic method of approach, for the earlier starting point in inferiority had of course stressed organic inferiority. With Adler, then, the idealism was a superstructure raised upon a materialistic basis and could be seen as the synthesis and corrective of the nineteenth-century overinsistence upon materialism. In this way Adler fell into that body of thought begun by Sorel and Bergson which insisted upon a "vital" interpretation of life's purpose, yet which likewise acknowledged the mechanistic factors in any problem.

Adler emphasized the implications of such thinking in his own religious life. He was of Jewish stock and had been brought up in that faith. But later he became a Protestant, because he disagreed with the exclusiveness, not to say selfishness, of the Jewish concept of God.[26] It must be confessed that the Bellocs and Chestertons, the

---

[24] P. Bottome, *Alfred Adler* (London, 1946), pp. 43, 107, 111.

[25] L. Way, *Adler's Place in Psychology* (London, 1950), p. 57.

[26] Bottome, p. 44.

de Maeztus, and even the Comteans, perhaps, would have preferred a Catholic conversion.

Adler's first visit to England was in 1923 and passed off without any notable stir, his impact being lessened by a poor command of English. But in 1926 a second and more successful visit was undertaken. A great deal of interest was aroused, which led to the setting up of the club in Gower Street which held almost nightly meetings during the summer and autumn of 1927. The lead in this enterprise was taken by Mitrinovic, and the two most active co-workers were Philip Mairet and Alan Porter. When a little later Symons and Demant became interested, the awareness of the Chandos Group, and hence of Social Credit, was inevitably aroused.[27] The connection between Individual Psychology and Social Credit was expounded in many different ways. There were direct references, and even discussions, in the *New Age* until, it seems, Brenton objected and they abruptly ceased; Mairet published *The A.B.C. of Adler's Psychology* and later a book entitled *Aristocracy*, where the aim of "forecasting the function of aristocracy in the society of the future" was undertaken on the assumptions of Individual Psychology; Porter was responsible for editing a selection of Adler's work; and Symons contributed articles to various journals, some of which were gathered up into a book, *The Coming of Community*.[28]

But the main channel of Adlerian–Social Credit ideas was the quarterly *Purpose*, a publication which had developed from an improbable, but revealing, background. In the mid-twenties a monthly, *Focus*, had been founded to further the Nature movement. Along with a vaguely Theosophical outlook and a rejection of much of existing society, notably the party system, went an interest in the simple life much on the lines of the Penty-Distributist critique. The editor of *Focus* had earlier brought out the *Healthy Life*, to which Hargrave had been a contributor, and it was not long before a series of articles on the need for a reformed credit system began to appear and something of the Douglas analysis to be included. A little later, Symons took over the series and naturally began to feature Social Credit in its entirety. The paper showed every likelihood of becoming a useful one to the movement, and Professor M. A. Canney, of Manchester

[27] Bottome, pp. 209–11; NA 15.12.27, 7.2.29.
[28] Mairet's first was published in London, 1928; his second, London, 1931 (the quotation from it is on p. 10); A Porter, ed., *What Life Should Mean to You* (Boston, 1931); W. T. Symons, *The Coming of Community* (London, 1931).

University and later of the Monetary Reform Association, began to contribute.[29] Although *Focus* came to an end with the death of the owner-editor in 1928, the journal was revived as *Purpose*.

The fact that *Focus* had been founded to treat problems "synoptically,"[30] and the fact that Symons had become prominent in its affairs, meant that the way had been prepared for the acceptance of just such a philosophy as Adler's, a philosophy which insisted upon the totality of experience. From the very first issue, then, *Purpose* was a journal of Adlerian psychology, and when soon afterwards Symons and Mairet became joint editors, the way was also open for a discussion of its implication for Social Credit.

The Chandos Group members, and others of the Social Credit–*New Age* background who turned to Adlerian psychology, did so for reasons which operated on two levels. To begin with, there were basic similarities in their analysis of the world. Both Social Credit and Adlerianism were technical solutions which could be applied at once without reference to the future or the past. That Douglas accepted the great bulk of the existing economic system and demanded but a minor accounting change has been made clear. Adler, in his own way, shared this outlook. The impulses of man could be accepted as given and basically sound, and the only problem was to ensure that they were organized in the right way. To this end no major rebuilding of the foundations would be necessary; it would be enough to restructure the surface, or as Mairet put it, "to train the individual to feel the community as his own self-fulfilment." Mairet also brought out another facet of Adlerian thinking on this point by contrasting it with Freudian psycho-*analysis*. That doctine might be true and yet miss the point, for "the Source of sanity is not in the past. . . . It lies in social vision."[31] In other words, for the Adlerian the here and now was the important thing, not a crying over spilled milk. Symons saw a connection between Douglas and Adler in that both took "the world as it is for a starting point" and accepted the past. It was for this reason, he thought, that the left had rejected Adler and Douglas alike; both postulated "no strife, no revenge."[32]

Another point of agreement between the two outlooks was a belief in the organic. The Adlerians had their counterpart to the Social

[29] *Focus,* 1.26, 2.26, 5.26, 8.26, 4.27, 7.27.

[30] *Focus,* 1.26.

[31] P. Mairet, *The A.B.C. of Adler's Psychology* (London, 1928), p. 93.

[32] Symons, p. 325.

Credit Cultural Heritage and National Dividend, for to an Adlerian such as Mairet "not only science but even intelligence itself is the result of the communal efforts of humanity." He went on to claim that the Adlerian was "the first modern psychology to be categorically and practically social."[33] It was Symons who brought out most clearly the connection between Social Credit and Individual Psychology. "The Adlerian restatement of man's essential nature is of profound importance in the realm of economics. . . . Property is egoistic safety, violence is egoistic protest. The individual can attain health only by abandonment of both, in an act of faith." At the same time it was also Symons who showed how the trace of Nietzschean thinking, common to the backgrounds of Adler and of Orage, was not to be forgotten in the organic ordering. "Adler and Douglas find the world stood on its head by neurotic perversion. They seek to re-establish man in recognition and enjoyment of his common value, and thereby free his particular value—the aristocrat in him—for unrestrained and healthy expression."[34]

The second level on which Adlerianism appealed to Social Credit ways of thinking was a negative one. Individual Psychology provided an attractive explanation for the thinking of orthodox economists of all levels and also for the resistance which Social Crediters experienced in trying to convince the oppressed of the truth which would set them free. Adlerian psychology had shown how it was possible for a patient to suffer the worst agonies of ill-health without having anything organically wrong with him, the sickness being but a product of the mind and made possible by a wrong way of looking at things. The similarity between such an explanation and that which Social Crediters would be obliged to give to explain why so many people seemed to prefer to disregard Social Credit and so suffer poverty, degradation, and ill-health must have been evident, even though it was never expressed in print. What was expressed, however, was the explanation which Individual Psychology furnished for the other side of the coin, so to speak, of why the few in possession of the goods were so reluctant to adopt a scheme which promised, in the words of the Green Shirt slogan, "not less for some but more for all." The point about the inferiority feeling giving rise to antisocial and neurotic compensation quite evidently could be pressed into the service of Social Credit to explain why people thought as they did about wealth

[33] Mairet, *The A.B.C. of Adler's Psychology*, p. 10; NA 4.10.28.
[34] Symons, p. 323; *Purpose*, 1.29.

and property. The words of Symons already noted, "Property is egoistic safety," will bear repetition in this context. On another occasion
Symons took the argument still further, to bring out the vicious aspect
of the financial power, "Douglas in the economic sphere has made
precisely the same discovery that Adler has made in the psychological
sphere, viz. that power over other men is the aim of the neurotic
individual; . . . the device by which this aim is pursued in the social
life is the financial system; [whereas] Adler deals with the individual
unconscious, Douglas deals with the collective unconscious."[35] Mairet was not prepared to be so extreme in his analysis, but he agreed
that money itself was a form of neuroticism.[36]

Before leaving Individual Psychology it is interesting to note that
Douglas himself was an instinctive Adlerian. In an article which he
wrote many years after interest in Individual Psychology had waned,
he quoted the view of an eminent surgeon, "It is the business of the
physician to treat a patient, not a disease." Consequently, he responded favourably to the interest in Adlerianism and acknowledged
agreement "with the main thesis, that the craving for power is the
focus of the world's ill health," adding, "I said so in the plainest terms
ten years ago." His only doubt concerned the dangers of an approach
"independent of, or superior to, physiology."[37]

The Chandos Group also provided a link with the Sociological
Society. The interest which the society and its more Comtean associates had taken in monetary matters on the eve of Social Credit's
appearance has been described. In this postwar and post-Douglas
period the *Positivist Review*, the orthodox Comtean organ, was in its
dying stages. But it was alive to Social Credit and similar notions, and
in its last gasp, under the new title, *Humanity*, it was edited by F. J.
Gould, who had followed his admired Orage into complete acceptance of Douglas.[38] The Ethical movement also kept up its interest in
such matters and devoted a winter session to an extended discussion
of monetary reform; it was noted that there was a higher-than-average
attendance.[39] But as might have been expected, it was the Sociologi-

[35] *Purpose*, 1.29.

[36] NA 4.10.28.

[37] C. H. Douglas, *The Big Idea* (Liverpool [1942]), p. 58; NA 4.10.28.

[38] Personal communication from Miss H. Corke, 1967. Gould edited *Humanity*
from 1924 until its death in 1925. Earlier he had bracketed Orage with Comte and Marx
as his heroes; see his *Labour's Unrest and Labour's Future* (London, 1919).

[39] G. Spiller, *The Ethical Movement in Great Britain* (London, 1934), p. 107.

cal Society which was most aware of the question. Indeed, so much a part of the society's thinking had monetary reform become that Mrs. Victor Branford could refer to Social Credit's being taken up by the Douglasite "sect."[40] Discussion of such topics could always be heard at society meetings, and the educationalist Helen Corke, still today a leading member of the Social Credit Co-ordinating Committee, remembers discovering the doctrine at one of their meetings.[41]

The link with the Chandos Group was a close one. Mumford was for a while editor of the *Sociological Review*, Demant was sufficiently prominent to be elected a member of the council, Davies became subeditor of the *Review* in 1927, and Mairet was not only so close to Geddes that it was he who was asked to write the official life, but he had taken a leading practical part in the setting up of Le Play House. Given such a close connection, it was not surprising that Chandos members could always count upon good reviews for their writings, slanted as they were toward Social Credit.[42]

However, it was not simply a question of interesting another group in Social Credit. The Sociological Society had its own effect upon Social Credit and played a part in the development of that movement. For with the leaven of the Sociological Society, a new congeries of societies was formed from the Social Credit–Chandos–Adlerian groups. At 55 Gower Street, which had been the headquarters of the Individual Psychology movement since 1927, no less than four groups grew up, different variations upon a basic membership. One was the International Society of Individual Psychology; another was the Eleventh Hour movement, whose title drew attention to its belief in the imminence of disaster; the third and fourth were facets of an identical tendency—one, the New Britain Group, calling attention to the part Britain was to play in giving the world a lead, the other, the New Europe Group, applying this belief in the larger context of a Europe under Britain's leadership. The essential unity of these groups, which may have had no real separate existence, was indicated by the fate of their publications. *New Britain*, after temporarily becoming the *Eleventh Hour Bulletin*, absorbed *New Atlantis*, edited by Mitrinovic (does the title point to Baconian-Comtean associations?), and its successor, *New Albion* (on which Orage worked), and its successor,

---

[40] *Sociological Review*, 1924, p. 128.

[41] Personal communication from Miss H. Corke, 1967.

[42] P. Mairet, *Pioneer of Sociology* (London, 1957), p. 204. *Sociological Review*, 1921, p. 136; 1927, p. 351; 1931, p. 55; 1932, p. 220.

New Europe. It was a welcome simplification which ended the annoying practice of reprinting blocks of one publication in another. In all this the significance of the Sociological Society was symbolized in the appointment of Geddes as president of the New Europe Group, a position which he held until his death; he was succeeded by Kitson and then by Delahaye.[43]

The interest which Geddes, Branford, and their followers had taken in devolution, in regionalism, and in the importance of the land encouraged the New Britain Group to take up the ideas, no doubt sufficiently attractive to Mitrinovic and Orage on account of their mystical presentation, of Rudolf Steiner. An Austrian, and at one time a Theosophist, Steiner had been influenced by the anarchists.[44] Later, he had broken away from Theosophy to form his own movement, more man-centered, to which he gave the title Anthroposophical Society. Independently of the English discoveries, Steiner had come to conclusions similar to guild socialism, which he published in a book translated into English under the title *The Threefold State*.[45] Using the analogy of the human body, which is composed of three systems (head, digestive, circulatory), each with its independent controls, Steiner argued for a body politic similarly constituted; here the systems would be the economic, the political, and the spiritual. Each of these, though functioning best when in proper relationship with the other two, only functioned at all when its own purpose was recognized and catered to first. At the same time it was noted that the concepts liberty, equality, and fraternity were only useful when applied to a single sphere; equality was the aim of the political sphere, liberty of the economic, and fraternity of the spiritual. Steiner's world would organize itself in these three divisions, and each division would deal directly with the corresponding division of another country; thus the attack upon the idea of the state was, if anything, more thoroughgoing in Steiner's than in the Guild Socialist view.

The New Britain group put out a cryptic creed which revealed the prominent place given to Steiner's views. They declared for "1, Social Credit. 2, National Guilds. 3, the Threefold State. 4, National, Imperial, European and planetary; federation in devolution and

[43] Mairet, *Pioneer of Sociology,* p. 210; *New Britain,* 10.32, 12.7.33.

[44] T. A. Riley, "New England Anarchism in Germany," *New England Quarterly,* 1945, p. 31.

[45] London, 1920. Steiner was known to the *New Age* readership; see NA 3.11.21, 8.12.21, 12.6.24, 23.7.25, 8.3.28, 26.6.28.

devolution in federation."[46] After this, Adler, not wishing to be involved in politics, withdrew his blessing from the venture, and psychology began to fall into the background. When Delahaye and Professor John MacMurray, the philosopher and student of communism, began to drop out, their places were taken by S. G. Hobson and G. D. H. Cole.

The reappearance of these two old Guild Socialists was something of a surprise. Hobson had been very taken by communism and had been scathing about Social Credit. Cole, not so taken by the Russian experiment, had been very hostile to Douglasism. But the years had brought changes, and Cole was now prepared to come much closer to a Social Credit position. The attitude of Hobson was curious. He still continued his guild agitation, though it was via the House of Industry League, which planned to convert the Lords into a chamber to regulate industrial matters. At the same time the functionalism of de Maeztu had finally asserted itself and appeared in a most extreme form. Hobson summarized this position as follows: "1, The final and supreme values are . . . moral satisfaction, scientific discovery and artistic creation. 2, The instrumental value, *par excellence*, is man and his associations and institutions. 3, The instrumental values for the instrument, man, are those which may be called by the name of economic values; power, wealth, pleasure, etc."[47] On this basis Hobson concluded that function demanded the complete overthrow of the financiers, for their purpose in life, coming low in the third category, gave them no title to control something which came in the second category, man himself.

Although Hobson and Cole had come a long way from their initial response to Social Credit, they were not prepared to be outrightly converted. For Social Credit advocacy within the New Britain movement, it was necessary to look to Bonamy Dobrée and Eimar O'Duffy, "an uncompromising supporter of Major Douglas,"[48] to Orage and Mitrinovic, and to Douglas's own views, which were included there. As time went on, however, and especially after Orage's death and the decline of the movement after 1935, Social Credit purity began to be watered down. The early rejection of "one dogmatic system of Social Credit"[49] became stronger as Soddy and Kitson became more and more prominent. Eventually even O'Duffy felt obliged to sink his

[46] *New Britain*, 8.8.34.
[47] *New Britain*, 1.33.
[48] *Eleventh Hour Emergency Bulletin*, Easter 1934.
[49] *New Britain*, 10.32.

purity in an agreed minimum programme, which made the following statement:

> Firstly and most vital, we are agreed on the absurdity and injustice of the system of issuing all new money in the form of a debt by the community to a handful of private monopolists; and on the urgent necessity of restoring to the Crown the right to issue and control all forms of money. Secondly, we are agreed that a monetary system base on gold is totally inadequate to the requirements of modern civilization and that the proper basis for the community's money is the real wealth at its disposal. Thirdly, we are agreed that the issue of fresh money must be accompanied by some check to prevent inflationary tendencies—in other words that prices must be controlled. Fourthly, we are agreed that so-called unemployment is not an evil to be cured but a benefit to be exploited. Recognizing that the increasing use of machinery must entail an increasing displacement of human labour, we agree that purchasing power must be distributed by some method supplementary to wages and salaries.[50]

Because politically the New Britain movement stood for a new beginning which would transcend the old party divisions, it attracted a good amount of support, and its periodical was soon boasting a circulation of 32,000 copies a week. This support was attracted equally from right and left. Harold Macmillan, then a lone figure on the left of the Tory party, contributed an article entitled "A Plea for an 'Above Party' Policy" and Bertrand Russell one entitled "Why I Am Neither a Communist nor a Fascist." This minor confrontation of right and left was carried further when the articles of Odon Por were contrasted with those of J. T. Murphy, the former shop steward, sympathetic critic of guild socialism, and one-time Communist, or the article of C. M. Grieve with that of T. S. Eliot.[51] On balance, and despite the prominence given to Horsfall Carter, it is fair to sum up the New Britain movement as one of the left, as, in fact, a recent commentator has done.[52] Yet, the wide nature of the appeal did not

[50] *Eleventh Hour Emergency Bulletin,* 10.7.35.
[51] *New Britain,* 26.7.33, 4.10.33, 17.1.34, 31.1.34, 28.3.34, 25.7.34.
[52] N. Wood, *Communism and British Intellectuals* (London, 1959), p. 57.

help for long. As a political movement it was short-lived, and only one national conference was held. By this date, 1934, there were some Adlerians left—such as Delahaye, who was elected one of the leaders. But the Chandos–Social Credit interest had all but departed, and the only Social Crediter, apart from Delahaye, elected to the board was the Reverend A. D. Belden, the unorthodox Congregationalist (who will be met with later).[53] From the mid-thirties on, the Social Credit intellectuals were to withdraw to the shell of the *New English Weekly.*

The intellectual response to Social Credit was varied and shifting. But it did have a thread. There was the continuity provided by membership, a matter above all of the Chandos Group, although it included several figures from the *New Age*–Guild Socialist circles and their fringe associates. And there was, too, the continuity provided by approach, for these varied groupings shared many of the same assumptions and preoccupations. A more precise evaluation of this aspect of the problem, however, will be reserved for the concluding chapter.

[53] *New Britain,* 11.4.34.

chapter nine

SOCIAL CREDIT AND THE POLITICIANS

At first glance, a discussion of Social Credit and the politicians would seem to be fruitless. Douglas himself, in a more than usually sibylline pronouncement, said, "My political sympathies, if any, are Tory, possibly because there is no Tory party in this country."[1] In the light of this statement it would seem that his electoral advice not to vote at all was not a limited response to a specific electoral situation but a reflection of a deep-seated rejection of the political process as such. This conclusion on Douglas's part would be only too understandable. His scheme was essentially a technique; it owed nothing to faction and was capable of being implemented by any party. Indeed, it *demanded* to be implemented by all parties. When, on tactical grounds, he had approached the Ministry of Reconstruction and then the Labour party and had been turned down, a native dislike of politics had been bitterly reinforced.

His following shared the same antipathy towards politics. Those who had been involved in the guild movement had come to distrust any very direct involvement in politics. They remembered the fate of the National Guilds League, which had borne out Orage's fears only too well. Moreover, almost all converts to Social Credit, whatever their background, felt that their new understanding of credit and prices had reduced any specifically political allegiance to a minimum.

[1] C. H. Douglas, *Warning Democracy* (London, 1931), p. 162.

On the few occasions when politics were referred to within the movement it was only inclinations which were commented upon, and then only to be played down. Thus, at a *New Age* dinner it was considered noteworthy that the toast to the success of the movement should be proposed by J. S. Kirkbride and seconded by Symons; the former had proclaimed his Tory leanings under the nom de plume "Old and Crusted" when writing for the *New Age*, while Symons was a socialist and member of the ILP.[2] On another occasion the Chandos Group convened a private meeting at which the question of political approach was discussed.[3] Mairet, who called himself a Socialist, and Mrs. Tait (wife of the Socialist, Fred Tait, of whom more below) opted for approaching the Conservatives. The appeal of Labour was upheld by B. J. Boothroyd. The Liberals, even at this date (1933), were not considered.

Yet, the political response requires discussion. If the attitude of Social Credit to politics was negative or indifferent, that of politicians and political thinkers towards Social Credit was otherwise. The way in which they responded says much about the contemporary evaluation of the doctrine, and it also provides pointers to a more general characterization of Social Credit.

One broad section of political opinion could hardly avoid being swept up in a discussion of Social Credit. Within the left the authority of Orage and the *New Age* was such as to command a respectful hearing—far wider, in fact, than the mere circulation of the paper seemed to warrant. At the same time, the *Monthly Circular*, the organ of the Labour Research Department, the radical offshoot of the Fabian Society, was being edited by the Coles. Besides helping to spread awareness of Social Credit by including references to it, this paper traced the ways in which the hard-core *New Age* circle was reaching left-wing opinion. The lectures of Reckitt on credit were noted; the decision of the National Union of Clerks to ask the government for an inquiry into the Douglas–*New Age* proposals was reported.[4] It was hardly surprising, then, to find the *Labour Leader*, the paper of the ILP, admitting that Social Credit had "brought more letters . . . than any other question since the war." Nor was it surprising that the *New Statesman* had to overcome the evident reluctance

---

[2] NA 11.2.26, 25.2.26; personal communication from W. T. Symons, 1966.

[3] Report of conference, 1–2.4.33, in Reckitt's papers; the *New Age* had earlier opted for the Conservatives, NA 5.1.28.

[4] Labour Research Department, *Monthly Circular*, 10–12.21, 7.22, 8–9.22.

of its editor and discuss the scheme. "A considerable number of our readers have written to us asking us to express our opinion upon the merits of the Douglas Credit Scheme . . . we must make the attempt since Douglasism . . . is becoming a religion."[5]

One branch of the left wing wasted no time in responding to Social Credit and in doing so in unmistakable terms of outright rejection. The newly formed Communist party, the success of which had been responsible for disrupting the Guild Socialists, was quite clear in its attitude to Douglasism. Or at least Maurice Dobb, the Communist economist, was quite clear, and his views continued to serve as Marxist orthodoxy upon the subject right down into the thirties. His early article "Does the World Need More Money?" was expanded and refurbished in 1933 under the title "Social Credit and the Petit Bourgeoisie" to do duty against the second wave of Social Credit which was rising at that time. When three years later it was felt that another statement of the Communist line was called for, this basic article was issued yet again, this time under the title "Social Credit Discredited"; later it was included in shortened form in *Discussion*, the official Communist Party of Great Britain monthly. Though the work was that of one pen, this criticism represented the Communist thinking.[6]

It was a twofold attack. The technical onslaught was directed at the A + B argument; it amounted to the bald statement that B payments ultimately became A payments. The notion of time was brought in with the somewhat mysterious announcement that, if anything, such an argument worked against the Douglas scheme. In the later versions, it was suggested that in putting forward the A + B theorem Douglas was deliberately setting out to fool the people. This first argument, then, was perfunctory, but this mattered little when the second line of attack became evident, for it was on a quite different level and made its impact in a totally different way.

This second method was to introduce two innuendoes. The Social Credit ideas were inflationary. "The Douglasites cannot have it both ways. *They cannot both inflate credit and deflate prices*." This charge sounded serious, but it was one which, in the absence of a discussion, at least, of the Just Price mechanism, was not entirely fair. It failed even to consider the claim that under Social Credit, money would be

---

[5] *Labour Leader,* 27.10.21; *New Statesman,* 18.2.22.

[6] *Communist Review*, 5.22; *Labour Monthly*, 1933, p. 552; *Discussion,* 1.36. The pamphlet was published in London in 1936.

added to circulation only in respect of proven capacity to produce an increased amount of goods and services. And what made this charge all the more objectionable was the hypocritical statement—*after* the introductory condemnation, "Douglasism is merely a modern version of the Inflationist fallacy"—that in fact Douglasism was not inflationary, but its popular appeal was! This criticism ended with the emotional plea, "Douglasism is the pitiful attempt of the petit bourgeoisie and the bourgeois serving intelligentsia to save Bourgeois Democracy by fettering the power and depredations of Imperialist Finance Capital." And for good measure, the cause of the slump being experienced at that time was identified as that pointed to by the most reactionary of the orthodox. "Europe lived on its capital during the war and was generally impoverished."

This same technique, damning by association even if the association had to be fabricated, emerged in the later attacks by Dobb. By the thirties the fascist danger was revealed, and it suggested a stick with which Social Credit could be beaten. The connection of Mosley with Social Credit was noted, as was that of Ezra Pound; Wyndham Lewis had written a favourable book on Hitler and had included references to T. S. Eliot, who was known to be a crypto–Social Crediter—a somewhat tendentious argument, but no matter, for could it be denied that "the fascists on the Continent . . . made a big use of ideas and demands of a Social Credit type?" There again followed that misleading, malicious profession of fairness which had been used in connection with the jibe about inflation. "In saying this we are not trying to label the Social Credit Movement in this country as fascist, still less to describe the numbers of sincere believers and followers of the movement as fascist either in influence or intention. . . . But Social Credit holds the serious danger that it may easily be used by fascism to draw middle class elements and even workers *away* from the working class movement and *away* from the struggle against capitalism . . . and if notions of this sort are used by Hitler and Mosley, is that not a very strong reason on the face of things to suggest that they are aimed, not at the true, but a fictitious foe?" (If it would have been any consolation to Douglas, he could have reflected that soon afterwards Keynes was singled out for the same treatment. The possibility of Keynes's views being "simply a more academic version of Social Credit theories, capable of serving fascist ends," was erected into another straw argument, he was connected with Gottfried Feder, and then he was graciously dismissed with a caution.)

This, then, was one reaction: instant identification, arraignment, and condemnation. Yet other left-wing groups were more ambivalent in their response. Thus the Social Democratic Federation's paper, *Justice*, contained a fair measure of support, or at least consideration, for Douglas, even if the official verdict was hostile.[7] The *Clarion*, representing undogmatic socialism, was prepared to go a good deal of the way with Social Credit. As early as the beginning of 1919, a correspondent was asserting the need of money "made . . . as we went along," as happened during the war; he also distinguished between what was possible for an individual and what for a nation. Included in these suggestions were demands for the demonetizing of gold and for the replacement of wages by dividends. The editor, Robert Blatchford, accepted the principle of the State Bonus League. However, Douglas himself was never accepted. The leading monetary reformer on the paper found "the bowling . . . altogether too awful" and saw B payments dissolving into A payments. Not surprisingly, a letter from Douglas stressing "flow" did not enlighten the expert.[8]

A most significant socialist response, however, came from the Plebs League. The two papers just mentioned represented movements which died in the interwar period. But the Plebs League, Marxists in economics and stridently proletarian, matched the mood of the times. The league had been founded in 1909 by a group of Ruskin College students who felt that the college had sold out to the middle class. It thus predated the Communist party and did not feel bound by that dogmatic line favoured by the Comintern. "There is a decided need," it noted, "for a plain examination of banking in everyday language, and the ideas of Marx need a modern setting." Such a willingness to be open meant that when Mark Starr, the leading Plebs polemicist, brusquely dismissed Social Credit, he was taken to task by correspondents. When a weak condemnation of the doctrine, making use of the similarity between Douglas and the Chartist Attwood, Proudhon, and others appeared, the ineptitude of the attack was soon commented upon. Eventually, the Executive Committee of the Plebs League felt obliged to make an authorative statement. After making the usual claim that all B payments eventually became A payments, it centred the attack upon the tactical danger of reducing working-

[7] *Justice*, 13.1.21, 19.1.22, 12.10.22, 16.11.22, 23.11.22, and 21.12.22 are pro–Social Credit. The rejection was signalled by the acceptance of Hobson's views, 23.11.22.

[8] *Clarion*, 31.1.19, 4.6.20, 14.1.21, 4.2.21.

class solidarity. But before the official condemnation, the impression had emerged from the freer atmosphere of the league that a good measure of sympathy for Social Credit was felt.[9] And it ought to be noted that somewhat later a Communist did advocate Social Credit—the Scots poet Hugh McDiarmid, alias C. M. Grieve.[10]

A more complex, but possibly more deadly, reaction was that of the Labour party, which seemed to keep an open mind on the subject but was quite incapable of coming to terms with the implications. As it happened, the path of Social Credit to the Labour party had been smoothed by the consideration, at the 1919 Labour party conference, of two items bearing on finance. The first was a resolution moved by no less a person than Snowden—before he became chancellor of the exchequer, it goes without saying—which condemned the inept handling of war financing, the creation of "fictitious credits by borrowing thousands of millions at unnecessarily high rates of interest" instead of a more stringent taxation policy, and which advocated the setting up of a "National Bank for national service with branches in all centres."[11] The resolution was adopted without debate. But more significant was the motion by the Chesterfield Trades Council "to give careful consideration to the State Bonus Scheme as outlined by Mr. Dennis Milner." It too was adopted. Clearly, then, the party conference was interested in, and prepared to discuss, financial methods for improving conditions. The following conference showed that this interest had increased. In 1920 Milner appeared in person as the delegate from the Hendon Labour party to move for the practical application of his State Bonus Scheme; it was referred to the Executive Committee. There was also a motion from the Sheffield Trade and Labour Council for the establishment of municipal currencies, to be issued interest-free upon the backing of municipal credit. And in 1921 no less than three motions favouring some form of the State Bonus Scheme, one including the idea of underconsumption, were put forward. However, the same year saw the appearance of the Executive Committee report on the Scheme; it rejected Milner's idea, on the ground that it sought to "raise money without any regard to ability to pay and to distribute it without any regard to need." The real meaning of the rejection becomes plain when it is noted that its

[9] *Plebs Magazine*, 4.20, 8.21, 10.21, 11.21, 12.21, 2.22, 4.22, 5.22.

[10] NEW 27.4.33.

[11] The Labour Party, *Report of the Annual Conference* (London, 1919), pp. 146–55c. (The bound copies contain reports of the Conference, Executive, and Agenda Committees proceedings; these have separate pagination and so are referred to here by the additional letters *c, e,* and *a* respectively.)

author's claim that 90 percent of the population would get more out than they put in was not considered, thus weakening the first contention, and when it is remembered that the Bonus Scheme was a minimum upon which any manner of further reforms could be imposed, thus disposing of the second objection. When in addition the executive observed that the new wealth would cause great problems and that the old Labour standby, the Right to Work Bill, would cover what Milner wanted anyway,[12] it revealed itself as fundamentally hostile to the root idea of Douglasism, that basic remuneration should not be a function of scarcity and toil, but of citizenship. That this attitude was typical of the party at that time was confirmed by the comment of Snowden when the Municipal Currency idea was put forward. It was reported that he had said that "he never expected to see a resolution like that brought forward seriously." He referred the motion back to the Executive Committee, where "he knew the reception that such a resolution would receive at the hands of men who had even an elementary knowledge of the subject."[13]

There was, then, about this time a split within the Labour party between a rank and file which was eager to discuss novel financial ways out of an ever-deepening industrial depression and a leadership which was not sympathetically inclined towards them. Almost inevitably a motion dealing with Social Credit would come up to be discussed. This, in fact, happened at the 1921 conference when the South Hampshire Divisional Labour party made the following motion: "That this Conference, recognizing the great service rendered to the Labour Movement by *The New Age* in formulating and persistently advocating the National Guild ideas, is of the opinion that the further proposals now being made by *The New Age* for the completion of that scheme of Social organization deserve the fullest and most sympathetic consideration, and therefore instructs the national executive to arrange . . . for a thorough investigation . . . of the Douglas–*New Age* scheme for the democratic control of credit." The appeal to past services is unusual and strikes an almost apologetic note, as though the movers suspected the reception which they might receive. In the event they need not have worried, for as Sidney Webb pointed out, a committee had already been charged with the duty of examining Social Credit.[14]

[12] Ibid., p. 174c; ibid. (1920), pp. 184–86c; ibid. (1921), pp. 24a, 60e.
[13] Ibid. (1920), p. 185c.
[14] Ibid. (1921), pp. 212c, 30a.

Rather earlier, the attention of the Scottish miners had been aroused in Social Credit. The second half of *Credit-Power and Democracy*, which appeared in 1920, was the outline of how Social Credit could be applied to one particular industry, coal mining. That this appendix had been written by Orage gave it a clarity and cogency which other expositions to date had lacked. In September 1920 a subcommittee of the Scottish Labour Advisory Committe had two interviews with Major Douglas. As a result of these discussions, they decided to "recommend that the Executive of the Miners' Federation of Great Britain be asked to investigate Major Douglas' scheme for introducing credit reform *via* the mining industry."[15] This, Douglas claimed, took place during January 1921.[16] However, the executive of the Miners' Federation preferred to turn the task over to the executive of the Labour party, which in turn appointed a subcommittee. When this committee was set up is not known, but Douglas was to claim that it must have been appointed about April 1921.[17] From this beginning, the examination and the report were in every way unsatisfactory.

It began with a wrangling between the *New Age* people and the Labour subcommittee. Douglas and Orage were invited to give evidence before the committee. They refused. The reason given was their opposition to the composition of their examining body. They claimed that of the eleven members only one, Frank Hodges, the miners' leader, had any notion of practical industry and that three who had come out against Social Credit were included.[18] It was a disastrous decision, for it could be suggested that Douglas and Orage were afraid of being pressed about their scheme. This was not a justifiable taunt, of course. Douglas had already been to the Ministry of Reconstruction and was to go before the Canadian banking inquiry in 1923 and that of Alberta in 1934, as well as appearing as a witness before the Macmillan banking inquiry of 1930. There was, too, his radio debate.[19] And Orage had for years mixed with the leading socialists of his day and never been inclined to run; in particular he had to his

---

[15] *Forward,* 15.1.21.

[16] C. H. Douglas, *The Labour Party and Social Credit* (London, 1922), p. 20.

[17] The Labour Party, *Labour and Social Credit* (London [1922]), p. 1; NA 20.7.22.

[18] NA 18.8.21.

[19] This debate was against D. Robertson, and it took place on 21.6.33; see NEW 29.6.33. Douglas had also taken on Hawtry at Birmingham; see NEW 6.4.33.

credit a notable victory over Webb, when he proved that paragon of exactitude wrong over a comma.[20] The explanation may lie in a clue provided by "Rob Roy," writing in the Glasgow *Forward* (the pseudonym was no doubt that of Tom Johnston, editor of the paper). After reading *Economic Democracy*, he suggested that Douglas give evidence before the Labour party, with which, as editor of an important paper, he had some influence. He added that Douglas and Orage and others of the paper had been eager to do so, but they had been intrigued out of the opportunity.[21] If this were so, the refusal to go before the committee may have been a mark of pique—a very foolish one. The committee was forced to rely upon the two books, the incidental observations in the *New Age*, and a smattering of other writings, not all of which would be endorsed by Douglas. They acknowledged in their report that they found such evidence unsatisfactory.

The next unsatisfactory element was the way in which the report appeared. It was not printed until July 1922—a gap, as Douglas pointed out, of some sixteen months. It professed, too, to be an interim report, but although a final report was promised it was never forthcoming. There was in the opening lines a tribute to "the active cooperation of an experienced bank official"; he remained anonymous. Douglas made capital of this admission, which seemed to justify his objections to the membership of the committee. And when in its perfunctory way (the part dealing with Social Credit was only eleven pages long) the report came down to an analysis of the scheme, its shortcomings were cruelly exposed.

The criticism began by an exposure of the claims of the A + B theorem. This was swiftly done, for in quoting from *Credit-Power and Democracy* the crucial sentence, "The product of any factory may be considered as something which the public ought to be able to buy, although in many cases it is an intermediate product of no use to individuals but only to a subsequent manufacture," was omitted. The theorem was thus reduced to an extremely crude form and was easily despatched. The significance of this omission is serious. Either the committee had not grasped its importance, in which case they did not see what Douglas was getting at, or else they deliberately left out the passage in order to distort the meaning. Either way, it was a damning omission. Nor was this all. The further arguments were weak in the

[20] Mrs. C. Chesterton, *The Chestertons* (London, 1941), p. 9.
[21] *Forward,* 22.1.21.

extreme. How was it possible, it was asked, if the Douglas analysis were correct, to account for the fact that real wages had been steadily increasing since the 1850s? There was no attempt to determine how much wages might have risen but for the impediment which Social Credit alleged existed. The price ratio, it was claimed, would lead to inflation, but no serious examination of this statement was attempted. The scheme would give no control of the mines to the miners—a criticism which sounded ill coming from the party which had shown an instinctive horror of syndicalism. Finally, the report included an error of fact when it claimed that Douglas was opposed to any measure of nationalization. The passage relied upon for this statement was one considering the implication of nationalization without any change in methods of financial accounting; it has been quoted above in chapter 5. Moreover, the committee had ignored the passage in *Economic Democracy* in which the nationalization of the railways and of the electricity supply had been allowed for because these were services which could not be efficiently run by individuals.[22]

The report, then, was a sorry production. And there is some evidence that the party felt this too. It was never hawked about, and when it went out of print no attempt was made to reprint, even when revived interest in Social Credit in the 1930s suggested it should be. At the party conferences of 1922 and 1923 no references to Social Credit were made, and in commenting upon the inquiry, a writer could only damn Douglas by comparing him with previous monetary reformers whom everyone knew, of course, to be cranks.[23] It must be pointed out that Douglas himself contributed to this unsatisfactory state of affairs. He naturally made a counterattack upon the report. But he scorned the obvious method of attack, which was to make an assault on specific items of misrepresentation, and he never took up the question of the omitted passage in the A + B theorem. He felt, one suspects, that it was much more intellectual and grand to look for the philosophical reasons for the Labour party's finding as it did. This was not for him a difficult task; the Labour party's findings showed the inevitable effect of organization, which brought about a split between the leadership and the rank and file. "It is an important report," he wrote, "as a concrete instance of the defective working of Labour Party organization; defective that is in the sense that the aims

[22] C. H. Douglas, *Credit-Power and Democracy* (London, 1920), p. 22; idem, *Economic Democracy* (London, 1920), p. 18.
[23] *Labour Magazine*, 8.22.

of the rank and file and the Central Executive have not so much in common as those of the Central Executive and their alleged adversary the 'Capitalist'."[24] From this statement Douglas went on to criticize democracy as it was practised and to attack the London School of Economics. The Douglas–J. A. Hobson argument in the *Socialist Review* likewise suffered from this unwillingness to come down to specific criticisms.[25]

But after all, what kind of response was to be expected from a party whose spokesmen could speak as they did over the State Bonus Scheme? It was an attitude which was seen to even better advantage when Snowden became chancellor and had the May committee inquire into means of cutting down spending still further. It was to be seen when a fresh attempt at a scheme along Social Credit lines was repudiated at the 1933 party conference. There the following motion was made: "This conference instructs the National Executive Committee to prepare . . . a scheme whereby socialized credit applied to retail prices may be used to enable the home market to absorb as much as it needs of the home industry's output of consumable goods so that the standard of living may be substantially raised. . . . With the program the Labour Party would sweep the country and this plan would mean the final establishment of Socialism and the Socialist Commonwealth." The seconder pointed to the disappearance of £ 180 million which had been taken out of circulation since 1920. Norman Smith, the prospective candidate for Faversham and a "convinced believer in Social Credit," added the typical Social Credit observation, "Industry exists, not as the National Executive appeared to think, to find work, but to deliver to the people the consumable goods that they want." The reply to this was as brutal as Snowden's had been thirteen years before. The official spokesman asked that this resolution be rejected and that no time be spent upon it, because the conference had "already declared a policy . . . providing for the extension of purchasing power." The accepted policy to which he referred merely held that "the aim of monetary policy should be to stabilize wholesale prices at a reasonable level."[26]

The interest of the rank and file could not be killed completely, even despite such reactions. At the 1935 conference this continuing interest was acknowledged. Although it was reported that the 1922 pamphlet

[24] Douglas, *The Labour Party and Social Credit*, p. 17.

[25] *Socialist Review*, 2–4.22.

[26] The Labour Party, *Report* (1931), p. 195; ibid. (1933), p. 176.

was out of print and an official inquiry was safely pedalled, those interested in learning of Labour party reaction to Social Credit could choose from the reports of Gaitskell, of Durbin, and of Hiskett. These examinations were all full accounts; Gaitskell's, as was pointed out by John Lewis, a Marxist critic of Social Credit, was full to the extent of manufacturing cases which Social Credit had never remotely considered.[27] But they all relied upon disproving the A + B theorem by the usual method of showing that the B payments eventually became A payments. In any case, the Labour party did not need to worry now. By the mid-thirties the internal dissensions of the Social Credit movement had reached such a pitch that the movement began more to repel than to attract. The Labour party, safe in the backing of an unimaginative Trades Union Congress (TUC), was to be no more troubled by such notions.[28]

And yet there was interest in, and sympathy for, Social Credit on the left. It was to be found in the ranks of the ILP. Since its foundation the ILP had stood for a thoroughly proletarian socialism, a socialism which had intensified as the Labour party had increasingly settled for meliorism, especially after the Labour party reorganization of 1918 had transferred the focus of individual members' loyalty from the constituent organizations to the party itself. This socialism had been strongly pluralist, and at the 1922 conference the party accepted the guild philosophy. In the years immediately after the war the ILP enjoyed a tremendous popularity, though by the end of the decade the uncompromising extremism of Maxton and his backers had gone far to wrecking the party. The centre of this force was Glasgow, and the importance of this city was signalled when at the 1922 election a body of some forty ILP members from the west of Scotland, directed by a core of Glasgow members, arrived at Westminster to become known as the Clydesiders.

These Clydesiders could draw upon a rich tradition of extremist revolt. At the turn of the century Kropotkin had been a visitor to the area, and his views had been passed on to John Maclean, a leader in the wartime strike movement, and through him to Guy Aldred, who

[27] H. Gaitskell, "Four Monetary Heretics," in *What Everybody Wants to Know about Money*, ed. G. D. H. Cole (London, 1933), and E. F. M. Durbin, *Purchasing Power and Trade Depression* (London, 1933), were the first into the field. Durbin added *The Problem of Credit Policy* (London, 1935) to the attack. W. R. Hiskett, *Social Credits or Socialism* (London, 1935). J. Lewis, *Douglas Fallacies* (London, 1935), p. 2.

[28] The TUC *Reports* are silent on the subject of Social Credit.

from Bakunin House preached anarchism until well into the twenties. Maxton, too, had been influenced by Kropotkin. Even before the war the shop steward movement had been simmering. The Socialist Labour party, one of the chief constituents of the later Communist Party of Great Britain, was active in the city, as was the British Socialist party, the other main source for the Communist amalgamation. And of course during the war the revolt broke out into the open. Kirkwood, MacManus, and four others were deported from the Clyde, and Maclean, Gallacher, and Maxton arrested. In 1919 these individuals were again to be leaders in the Glasgow riots of 27 January, when the Red flag was raised in the city. The whole of this mood of violence and extremism was channelled through the Glasgow weekly, *Forward*, one of the most successful and outspoken of socialist papers. This paper had been founded in 1906 by Tom Johnston, an ILP member; it was the paper which had been suppressed in 1915 when it printed the truth about Lloyd George's failure to win over the striking Glasgow workers.[29]

Amid this welter of anarchic revolt three sources stood out as predisposed towards credit reform. Of these two have been mentioned already. Johnston himself was interested in financial matters, and a useful by-product of this concern was a book he published chronicling the major financial swindles of the twenties. More importantly, he had busied himself with the question of municipal banking. Under the influence of Neville Chamberlain this movement had gained a measure of success in Birmingham. But the act of 1919 had been restrictive rather than helpful to the spread of this kind of banking. In 1920 Johnston spotted a loophole in the act and saw how any council could run such a scheme, and under his leadership a bank at Kirkintilloch, Dumbartonshire, was established in that year.[30]

Secondly, the Guild Socialists had been very active on the Clyde. The Glasgow branch was the one which founded the *Guildsman* in the middle of the war and was at the forefront of guild theorizing. There was a branch at Paisley, too. Both these groups were early seceders from the National Guilds League when its negative attitude

[29] R. K. Middlemas, *The Clydesiders* (London, 1965), pp. 22 n. 1, 48, 50, 55, 80; H. Pelling, *The British Communist Party* (London, 1958), pp. 6–10; B. Pribicevic, *The Shop Stewards' Movement and Workers' Control, 1910–22* (Oxford, 1959), chap. 5; D. Kirkwood, *My Life of Revolt* (London, 1935), p. 112.

[30] T. Johnston, *The Financiers and the Nation* (London, 1934); G. White, *The Council as Bankers* (London, 1930), p. 8.

to Social Credit was made plain. The leading Guild Socialist–Social Credit light on the Clyde was H. M. Murray, the only writer on Social Credit to whom Douglas awarded his imprimatur.[31] Murray found a ready platform in *Forward*.

The third source was perhaps the most interesting, for although it did not appear in the guise of out-and-out Social Credit, it was responsible for concrete, practical measures which were on the lines suggested by the doctrine. John Wheatley was a Catholic miner of Irish descent. After a first venture into politics in 1906, when he began the Catholic Socialist Society in Glasgow, he went on to join the ILP. From the first his interest had been in housing and he later became minister of housing in the first Labour government and did excellent work to repair the ravages caused by the failure of Addison, his predecessor in office. In examining the problem of housing, he became aware of the crippling effect which high interest rates could have upon any scheme for low-rent cottages. In 1914 he put forward a local scheme for cottages at eight pounds a year, provided they could be financed at a cost of only 2 percent per annum. He was prepared for the views of J. A. Hobson, who became popular in ILP circles just after the war, and in 1922 Wheatley "enthusiastically adopted the Hobson underconsumption thesis as an explanation of the post-war slump." It was Wheatley who was the real leader of the Clydeside brigade, though he chose to push Maxton to the fore as the figurehead. It was disastrous, then, when Wheatley died relatively young in 1930 and his guiding hand was removed. Social Crediters realized their loss, too, for if he had never publicly declared for the idea, it was thought that he was nonetheless a convinced believer obliged by his position to conceal his true beliefs.[32]

Important though the Glasgow contingent of the Social Credit–inclined ILP was, it did not totally overshadow the English activity. W. T. Symons has already been noted, but his friend and colleague, Fred Tait, was more important when it came to ILP work. Tait, from the north of England, was to the left of the party, known as "comrade" in the years after the war when this form of address was not common among the ILP. A recent historian has described him as "the Communist Tyneside school master," and in 1932 he was one of those who favoured the disaffiliation of the ILP from the Labour party on

---

[31] See Douglas's endorsement in H.M.M.'s *The Outline of Social Credit* (London, 1929), preface.

[32] Middlemas, especially pp. 35–40; NA 5.6.30.

the ground that the Labour party had ceased to be socialist.[33] He became prominent in the northeast region in party work, and he represented that area on the National Administrative Council in 1924.[34] In 1927 his region began to put out its own monthly news-sheet, *The Northern Democrat*, and he used it as a vehicle for Symons, who contributed many articles on Social Credit before the paper folded in 1928 after little more than a year. Party interest, and Tait's especially, continued to show itself, however, in a series of pamphlets on monetary questions which the ILP published during the later twenties and early thirties.[35]

In addition to this activity at the top there was a widespread interest lower down. Branches showed a great keenness to hear Social Credit speakers. Reckitt gave many talks to such groups, and in 1921 he was invited to speak to the ILP Summer School. Douglas himself ad-dressed the Bristol ILP branch. And the ILP paper, the *Labour Leader*, featured articles of a Social Credit or at least of a financial reform kind. In particular, G. O. Warren, who had links with the prewar Individualist-Anarchists, ran a series on the ability to issue paper money keyed to productive capacity, insisting that "houses are not built with money—they are built with labour. Nor are people ever paid with money, but with things they get for their money." Milner was given the chance to outline his scheme. Kitson, too, wrote in the paper.[36] Not surprisingly, the reports of the ILP conferences bear witness to the interest which the Social Credit proposals aroused.

The Social Credit assault upon a party receptive to the ideas of monetary reform began in 1923 when the Gateshead branch, in the person of Tait, moved the following resolution: "That this Conference believes that no scheme of socialism can succeed unless it allows for, 1. The joint control of the National Credit by the Nation and the producer, 2. A system of fixing prices and regulating currency, so that

[33] Middlemas, p. 265; The Independent Labour Party, *Annual Reports* (1932), p. 55.

[34] The Independent Labour Party, *Annual Reports* (1924).

[35] G. White, *The Council as Bankers* (London, 1930); J. Wheatley, *Socialize the National Income* (London [1927]); F. Tait, *The Douglas Theory and Its Communal Implications* (Gateshead [1932]); F. Tait, *The Jugglers of Finance* (London, 1932); T. Stairs, *Money and Credit* (London, 1932).

[36] Labour Research Department, *Monthly Circular,* 10.21; *Labour Leader,* 19.12.18, 16.1.19, 2.3.22; for Warren, see R. Rocker, *Pioneers of American Freedom* (Los Angeles, 1949), p. 151; *Labour Leader,* 30.1.19, 27.3.19, 3.4.19, 1.5.19, 15.5.19; R.E. Dowse, *Left in the Centre* (London, 1966), gives too much emphasis to Hobson, and Douglas is mentioned in a footnote reference but is not adequately identified or explained.

the money distributed to the people will be sufficient to buy back all the consumable goods they may produce, 3. An industrial system so organized that the benefits of science and invention will be reaped by the producer in shorter working hours without any reduction in his standard of living and by the consumer in lower prices." The motion was not carried, but the difference in temper between the Labour party discussion and this one was that Tait's outspoken claim that "it was not work they wanted" was loudly cheered.[37] The following year Tait, seconded by Symons, moved for an inquiry into the Douglas system. Better fortune attended the move this time. Despite the attempts of some to block the suggestion on the grounds that the party, having been involved in the expense of fighting three elections in three years, should only undertake the most pressing of inquiries, the motion was successful.[38] What may have been crucial in swinging the decision was the advocacy on the side of monetary reform of a meteoric new recruit to the ILP, Oswald Mosley. Mosley, who had joined the party two months after the formation of the first Labour government, and his lieutenant, John Strachey, were to be very important in moving the ILP in a direction not too different from Social Credit. The close connection of Strachey with the Ludlamites, which was soon to develop, has already been described.

Mosley himself led the way at the 1925 conference and followed this by an address to the summer school, held in August. These ideas were then embodied in a pamphlet, *Revolution by Reason,* and their endorsement by the Birmingham ILP Federation and by the Birmingham Borough Labour party led to the plan's being called the Birmingham Proposals. Sweet to the ears of Social Crediters must have been the central claim, "Demand must precede supply," and the claim "Absence of purchasing power is the central problem." Also attractive must have been the proposal for the establishment of machinery to estimate the gap between actual and potential production, and the issuing of consumer credits. However, the specific remedies were not so acceptable. Mosley, the politician, would go no further than piecemeal grants, and these would be kept on the small side— a question of sixpences rather than of pounds—in order to avoid inflation (or rather, the public fear of inflation). There was no system in this, merely the arbitrary selection of minimum wage levels in arbitrarily selected industries. But these shortcomings were not so

[37] The Independent Labour Party, *Annual Reports* (1923), p. 129.
[38] Ibid. (1924), p. 105.

serious as they might have been, because it was known that Strachey, the intellectual lieutenant of Mosley, was bringing out a more extended treatment of the theme under the same title. Dedicated to Mosley, it appeared later in the same year.

The statement "Capitalism is in a blind alley" was Strachey's starting point, and he went on to argue, as Douglas would himself, that the only way capitalism had of saving itself was to engage in cutthroat, and eventually ruinous, competition, or in imperialism, or in what was perhaps the worst evil of all, a state tyranny working through gigantic combinations. This last horror, Strachey noted, was condemned by Lord Hugh Cecil and Karl Marx alike, an observation which pointed to Strachey's Tory past and (temporary) communist future, for in his twists and turns he was as agile as his leader, Mosley. But even a socialist government ran the risk of playing into the hands of a state tyranny if it did not take steps to avoid the fate of the late Labour government, which had disappointed so many of its supporters, that is, the dictatorship of the few working through the power of high finance. It was this that the Birmingham Proposals were designed to prevent. As it was put in the Proposals: "1. A public banking system capable of giving such accommodation to industry as will enable it to increase the purchasing power of the workers, so that new home markets can absorb industry's real productive capacity; and 2. an Economic Council for the coordination and control of that productive capacity . . . would give a Labour Government control of the economic system." Care was taken to point out that this Economic Council would not be given legislative powers, and so there would be no possibility of a thinly disguised state tyranny operating through such a board. Finally, the hopes of Social Crediters must have been raised once again when Strachey acknowledged that the whole scheme would depend upon the National Credit, which was "directly proportionate to the national capacity to produce wealth."[39]

Among the ILP, however, Social Credit did not have things all its own way, for the sympathy for monetary and economic reform was shared by another analysis. With this quickening of the debate, battle was joined within the party between two forms of underconsumptionism, Douglasism and Hobsonism. The latter was in a strong position. Its founder was a member of the party's Living Wage Committee and a lucid writer, unorthodox yet without seeming, like Douglas, to be

[39] J. Strachey, *Revolution by Reason* (London, 1925), pp. 87, 126, 129, 132, 156.

perverse. It had been his philosophy which gave rise to the Living Wage concept. The idea was that a minimum wage for the whole of industry would stimulate consumption, and hence production, and so eventually finance the cost of yet another, higher, minimum wage; it was an approach within the tradition of British pragmatism and caution. It also infuriated Social Crediters by choosing to talk of a wage at all. A high-powered committee was set up to investigate the Living Wage concept; it included Brockway, the pacifist, Hobson himself, Maxton, soon to be leader of the party, Mosley, and Shinwell. The Douglasites could not summon such support. Their committee, the Finance Enquiry Committee, consisted of Symons, Cousens, and Strachey, with three others of little standing. Only Strachey was a well-known figure, and soon the committee was allowed to lapse. More extreme statements from Strachey ("The Major is perfectly right. There is nothing whatever, at bottom, the matter with his economics") and the protestations of Wheatley ("Under the new system there will be no bounds to the purchasing power of the people except their power of efficient, organized production") could not save the day.[40]

The outright confrontation came at the 1929 conference when Tait spoke against the Living Wage Programme. This was, he said, a plan erected upon a money base, whereas it should be upon a goods base—a clear rejection of the Hobson version and a useful reminder that, appearances to the contrary, Douglasism was not a money scheme at all but a tickets scheme to real wealth. Tait's objection was rejected, and later the ILP consensus upon monetary reform was given as follows: "1. That the total volume of the purchasing power (money and credit) should expand to keep pace with every increase in production. 2. That this purchasing power should be distributed in such a way that a due proportion shall obtain between expenditure on instrumental goods and expenditure on consumable goods. 3. To bring about this due proportion the inevitable tendency of every capitalist society to expand savings more rapidly than it expands consumption must be corrected by a diversion of income from the savers to the consumers, from the owning class to the wage earners."[41]

Nineteen thirty-one provided the Social Crediters within the ILP with their last chance to stage a rally. Under the stress of mounting

[40] The Independent Labour Party, *Annual Reports* (1927 and 1928); *New Leader*, 10.6.27, 5.4.29.

[41] *New Leader*, 4.11.30.

unemployment, financial orthodoxy from Snowden of the most reactionary kind, and evidence of a bankers' ramp over the gold standard, the 1931 conference heard Tait move an amendment for "the control of prices on a scientific basis by the community" to a resolution for the abolition of bankers' control of credit. The amendment was lost after a speaker had pointed out the antisocialism of Douglas. (It was ironic that this "socialist" speaker, E. F. Wise, should choose to resign from the National Administrative Council of the ILP when the party decided to withdraw from the Labour party on the ground that the latter had ceased to be a socialist organization; Tait, on the other hand, was to make a speech in favour of the disaffiliation.) A second amendment offered by Tait was also lost.[42] There was no further chance for Social Credit in the ILP. The failing party was fully occupied now with the Fascist threat, and after 1933 even the Living Wage Programme gave way before the need to organize a national front against the right.

At the same time the appeal of Social Credit shifted, for as Mosley moved from the ILP to the New party en route to the British Union of Fascists, so too did the appeal of Social Credit move from the left to the right. How did British fascism look upon the Douglas doctrine?

British fascism contained two waves, each coinciding, as might have been expected, with one of the two European movements, that of Mussolini and that of Hitler. These two waves should be kept distinct, for just as there was a broad difference between the two original impulses on the continent, so too was there a difference in the ways in which their imitators in England looked upon the doctrine. Broadly speaking, the second outbreak was much more opportunistic than the first, concerned more with the Fascist methods of gaining and holding power. There were, of course, signal exceptions to this generalization, such as A. Raven Thompson, an intellectual and convinced believer in the corporate state, who threw in his lot with Sir Oswald Mosley, and A. K. Chesterton, the nephew of G. K. Chesterton. (Incidentally, the Fascists had no use for GKC, whom they dismissed as "that human mountain of hot air" and whose early distrust of Hitler they castigated as "unreasonable." When it came to recognizing allies among the Distributists, they chose to pick out Penty, whose later work they praised enthusiastically and whose son, Michael, contributed a series of articles to the Fascist press.)[43] And

[42] The Independent Labour Party, *Annual Reports* (1931), pp. 48–49.
[43] *Blackshirt*, 22.7.33; *Action*, 18.6.36, 22.5.37, 18.11.37, 12.3.38, 16.4.38.

just as the two waves differed, so too did their response to Social Credit.

The earliest of the Fascist organizations in Britain was the British Fascists, set up in 1923. No notice was taken by this group of Social Credit until two years later, when W. H. Walkinshaw wrote an article in their paper. Walkinshaw was a schoolmaster of Comtean leanings. The article was preceded by an editorial which professed "an absolutely open mind on the subject," but which went on to note that any scheme advocating boom was to be congratulated, because it lessened the danger of communism. The editorial also contained reference to the *Protocols of Zion* and to Kitson's conspiracy views, which reflected the British Fascists' vague distrust of things foreign; to speak of anti-Semitism as it is generally understood would be misleading. It would seem to be this element of fascism which had attracted Walkinshaw to the paper. In his own writings he betrayed the same confused sense of conspiracy, though he tended to attribute the evil to Romanism rather than to Jewry, with which on the whole he sympathized. These views earned him the disapproval of the *New Age*, which had its own far-from-consistent outlook upon cosmopolitanism and conspiracy.[44]

Walkinshaw's article itself was the usual exposition of the subject for new audiences, and it produced some correspondence. But the paper remained cool and later began to turn against Social Credit when the arch conspirator-hunter, Mrs. Nesta Webster, headed a crusade against all esoteric movements, especially "the menace," Theosophy. In this connection the Kibbo Kift, just then accepting Social Credit, was singled out for condemnation.[45] Interest in Social Credit evaporated.

The British Fascists were never a force, and the twenties saw the movement splinter into smaller and smaller sections. But one group stood out, for though tiny it never lost its identity, and its characteristics made it an earnest of things to come. This was Arnold Leese's Imperial Fascists. The pattern of contact with Social Credit was rather different from that of the British Fascists, for Leese was invited along to the *New Age*–Social Credit discussion group to speak on his aims and beliefs. Leese's version of the meeting was that of the thirty-odd members present, only one was hostile. The *New Age* reported matters rather differently: it noted his belief in a strong executive

[44] NA 15.1.25, 26.3.25; *Fascist Bulletin*, 15.8.25; W. H. Walkinshaw, *The Solution of Unemployment* (Newcastle-on-Tyne, 1924), pp. 210–12, especially p. 212.

[45] *Fascist Bulletin*. 7.11.25, 16.1.26, 29.5.26; *British Lion*, 9.27.

and approved it, but it feared that Fascist thinking would leave the central problem of a bankers' control untouched, and on the whole it was not impressed. Of the two accounts, the *New Age*'s would seem to be the more accurate, for as time went on, Leese turned increasingly against the Social Crediters. The system was labelled "fantastic," and the connection with the occult was condemned. In particular, Leese's deepest suspicions were aroused. His sole real belief was in the menace of the Jews, and he even condemned Mosley as being in their pay. For Leese it was intolerable that the *New English Weekly* was against anti-Semitism, and of Douglas's portrait he added darkly, "It gives us to think."[46] (He was not the only one to suggest that Douglas had a Jewish background; P. Selver, seemingly not troubled by Semitic–anti-Semitic considerations, mentioned this in connection with the major.)[47] On the negative side, the Imperial Fascists soon settled down to a diet of Kitson, and on the positive side, they chose producer credit schemes of 50 percent advances on the value of productive enterprises, that is, the Stoll system.

The second wave of fascism is by far the better known, since it coincided with the Nazi seizure of power and was led by a man of outstanding political gifts, Sir Oswald Mosley. This wave, channelled via the British Union of Fascists (BUF), was much more in touch with Social Credit and other monetary reform thinking. As has been noted, Mosley himself had gone near to Social Credit in the mid-twenties, and when Ludlam joined Mosley, there was for a short while in existence a specialist Fascist financial paper and an "expert" to lead Fascists in studies of the economic malaise.

In the beginning, then, there were important points of similarity between the Fascist and the Social Credit analyses. In particular, they both began from the all-important postulate that the world of the 1930s was a world of plenty. The BUF's intellectual, Raven Thompson, put the matter beyond doubt when he wrote, "The class war becomes a sheer absurdity in an age of plenty, for what object can there be in struggle between the classes when there is plenty for all?" And if they agreed with Social Credit in refusing to find the obstruction to plenty in the class exploitation, they further agreed in what they did identify as the cause of continuing scarcity. The bankers were a group of irresponsible, antisocial men holding the country to

[46] *Fascist,* 10.29, 2.33, 5.33, 6.35, 11.35; NA 29.8.29; C. Cross, *The Fascists in Britain* (London, 1961), p. 82.
[47] P. Selver, *Orage and The New Age Circle* (London, 1959), p. 28.

ransom. To the Fascists, "the Treasury was the West End Branch of the Bank of England." And this power of finance was far more powerful, far more evil, than was generally supposed, for it amounted to a conspiracy on an international scale. The real rulers of the world were a few cosmopolitan bankers. There was further agreement with Social Credit that deflation had been a deliberate policy pursued after the war as a means of tightening the bankers' grip. A conclusion from all this was yet another point of contact with Social Credit. Democracy was a sham, and it must be replaced by a government of technicians. It is important to note, however, that when Mosley stated that the only dissent should be "the constructive criticism of technicians," he was taking the analysis a step further than Douglas would have allowed; for Douglas, the "aristocratic hierarchy of producers," it must not be forgotten, was always to be "accredited by, and serving, a democracy of consumers."[48] There is a world of difference between the two conceptions of technician.

And so, too, in spite of the points of similarity, there was a great difference between the two philosophies. On the technical aspects of the analysis there was disagreement. Inevitably A + B came in for harsh treatment and was summarily pushed to one side. But there were other disagreements. One writer went so far as to call into question what might have been presumed to be a natural corollary of the age of plenty, that consumption and not production was the more important consideration. This writer categorically stated, "It is not consumption that regulates production but production that regulates consumption." No reason for this statement was given; to him it was an axiom. Another writer actually stood Douglas on his head in accounting for the lack of purchasing power. Where Douglas had supposed that the logic of capitalism forced manufacturers to ask what the market would bear, using supply and demand to find a price at which all money would be removed from the market, thus leaving none over to buy the excess production of the next cycle, Thompson believed in real competition among the producers, competition so real in fact that prices were beaten down, in this way reducing purchasing power.[49] Thompson, then, had not grasped the idea of a dynamic system of industry whose profile was constantly changing.

These differences were basic, and yet not so great that in theory, at

---

[48] Cross, p. 72; *Fascist Quarterly,* 1.35; *Blackshirt,* 30.12.33; Douglas, *Credit-Power and Democracy,* p. 94.

[49] *Age of Plenty,* 7.34; *Fascist Quarterly,* 1.35, 4.35.

any rate, their authors might not have come round to a Social Credit analysis in time. That they were never inclined to do so was due to the fact that there were deeper grounds of incompatibility between the Fascists and the Social Crediters. For those attracted to fascism, the *feel* of Social Credit was wrong. It was a wrongness which showed itself most plainly in the attitude to work. It is quite clear that Douglas and true Social Crediters regarded work as an old-fashioned concept. Indeed, they went further and realized that there was no ground for making basic income depend upon effort. This was something which neither the first nor the second wave of Fascists could stomach. The British Fascists could see in a boom only a means of smashing communism, and their sketchy outline of financial reform was based upon an Individualist foundation in the Spencerian sense. The Imperial Fascists were more explicit; coupled with their denial of the justice of a scheme which gave benefit to all went a repudiation of the accompanying doctrine of the "good man." Mosley's followers were equally determined to advocate the claims of effort. An article on which no Social Crediter could look without a shudder appeared in *Blackshirt;* its caption was "Work not Maintenance." And the *Age of Plenty* change of face was signalled when the following revealing sentence was included, presumably from the pen of Thompson. Rejecting the idea of a National Dividend, he wrote, "The only possible objection . . . will be on political grounds, for the National Dividend is based upon a Democratic, if not Marxist, doctrine of social equality." The most touching comment, however, came from one of the rank and file. After noting the similarity of fascism and Social Credit, the writer felt obliged to point out the distressing tendency for Social Crediters to be antiwork; this puzzled and upset him, but he ended on a brighter note by showing that things could not be so bad as they seemed, for he had observed Social Crediters in action, and they were certainly a busy lot. So deep did this worship of effort go that even Pound, who should have known better, wrote to reassure Fascists that Douglas intended the Dividend to go only to those who agreed to work.[50] This was not accurate; Douglas always intended the Dividend to be a birthright, though during a transitional period adjustments might have to be made.

Such a divergence was fundamental, and it was not to be bridged. Kitson was taken up, but never Douglas personally, and significantly

[50] *Fascist Quarterly,* 10.36; *Fascist,* 10.29; *Blackshirt,* 6.7.34; *Age of Plenty,* 7.34; *Action,* 11.9.37.

he never wrote for a Fascist paper, even though he had agreed to write in socialist and other journals. Douglas could, and did, congratulate himself on having identified the evil of effort long before it was made into a cult by the totalitarianisms. Some years previously he had travelled on the same ship as Kipling, and he claimed to have spoken with the writer. Douglas came to understand and to repudiate Kipling's philosophy, which he identified as "the glorification of creative activity . . . at the expense of freedom and individual development."[51] Without raising the question of whether Kipling was a Fascist, it is clear that the person who rejected him on these grounds was definitely not predisposed in that direction.

It remains to note the response of the two traditional parties, the Conservatives and the Liberals. This can be quickly done. The Liberals never bothered with Social Credit, and this was only to be expected. Helped on by Keynes, Lloyd George had launched his expensive series of inquiries at the end of the twenties. The results were early expositions of deficit spending, and they contained enough promise to enable the Liberals to ignore Social Credit newfangledness. The Conservatives managed to ignore the new currents even more completely, putting their trust in hard work and retrenchment. Only in 1936 was any notice taken of Douglas, when he was invited to speak at the Conservative centre, Bonar Law College, Ashridge; even this degree of interest amazed the Conservative party archivist. The *Ashridge Journal*, the organ of the college, did not feel it worth while to print Douglas's speech, and the summary given in *Social Credit* indicated that Douglas gave his by then habitual speech to doubting audiences.[52]

Thus, an examination of the political response to Social Credit illustrates a fact which has already emerged about the doctrine—that its appeal was to the extremes, leaving the centre untouched. With the exception of the Communists, who possessed a dogmatic framework which made no provision for monetary reform, and for whom tactical considerations were paramount, it was among the further left, and not among the moderates, that support for Social Credit was to be found. Then comes a gap along the political spectrum until once again interest is found, this time among the far right. Traces of an even starker contrast in a response to Social Credit, however, can yet be found, and this response, the religious response, is to be the subject of the following chapter.

---

[51] NA 17.2.27.
[52] Personal communication from G. D. M. Block, 1967; *Social Credit*, 14.8.36.

chapter ten

SOCIAL CREDIT AND RELIGION

When Hugh Gaitskell wrote his chapter, "Four Money Heretics," for Cole's *What Everyone Wants to Know about Money*, in which he criticized Douglas and Social Credit, he pointed out that when Douglas was heard by the Macmillan committee it was on the initiative of the Social Service Section of the Congregational Union; and it was with an air of surprise that Gaitskell added, "Douglas' views are popular in other clerical circles."[1] Just why Gaitskell should have been so surprised is not clear. As an economist he should have been aware, along with Keynes, that clerics had always been prominent in the development of economic theory.[2] And in addition there were surely good grounds for supposing that the churches would interest themselves in a system which, if correct, would inevitably make a tremendous difference to a religious approach to economic, and hence to social, questions in general. In fact, as will be seen, there were other reasons why certain religious minds should find Social Credit attractive, reasons which related some of the deeper implication of the doctrine to basic theological presuppositions.

It must be immediately acknowledged that Congregational interest

[1] G. D. H. Cole, ed., *What Everyone Wants to Know about Money* (London, 1933), p. 347.

[2] This observation is noted in J. D. Carmichael and H. S. Godwin, *William Temple's Political Legacy* (London, 1963), p. vii.

in Social Credit did not run deep and may be quickly dismissed. Only two Congregational ministers supported the doctrine, and one of these, Rev. A. D. Belden (already mentioned in connection with the New Britain movement, and of whom more later), was an untypical Congregationalist to say the least. The other, Rev. Malcolm Spencer, was a leading member of his church, however. Before undertaking parish work in the poorer part of Manchester he had taken a first in mathematics at Oxford.[3] By the early thirties he had come to accept the view that "from the very beginning of our Machine Age there has probably been a disproportion in the division of the profit derivable from the Machine, too little being assigned to the immediate spender and too much assigned to the would-be investor." This was not the A and B theorem in its usual formulation, but since Spencer explicitly rejected the Hobson heresy of oversaving, it was clear that he was proposing a form of Social Credit, that is, a chronic and inherent shortage of purchasing power. Although by 1936 Spencer had come to believe that Douglas was "technically wrong," he still believed that Social Credit had been useful in that its supporters had "called attention to some profoundly important principles," and he added, "The release of free credit which they advocate must be and can be secured on other lines."[4]

Earlier, the General Assembly of the Congregational Union had endorsed, in the vaguest manner possible, a demand of a Social Credit kind for increased leisure and improved standards of living.[5] But with Spencer recanting, no advance was made upon this position, and Congregational interest in Social Credit faded away. This passing phase indicated, in fact, no fundamental Congregational identity with Social Credit, but merely the temporary influence upon that church, via Spencer, of a brand of Anglican thinking. For about this time Spencer was a member of the Christian Social Council, the forerunner of the present British Council of Churches, and there he came into close contact with an Anglican source of Social Credit propaganda. But before the connection of Anglicanism with Social Credit is examined, it is necessary to sketch the development of its background, the socialist wave within the Church of England.

[3] M. Lawson's *God's Backroom Boy* (London, 1952) is the nearest to a biography of Spencer.

[4] M. Spencer, *Building on Sand* (London, 1936), pp. 8, 68; idem, *Economy and God* (London, 1936), p. 8.

[5] *New Britain*, 9.5.34.

Anglican interest in socialism had originated, in this more modern period, in the Guild of St. Matthew, begun in 1877. Neither this Ruskin-Morris-mediaeval organization nor the more restrained Christian Social Union of 1889 proved to be successful. But in the wake of the 1906 election the Church Socialist League was set up, and it flourished until the outbreak of war. People as diverse as George Lansbury, later the pacifist leader of the Labour party after the 1931 débâcle, and Cecil Chesterton were members, and the clergy included Conrad Noel, the aristocratic eccentric originally connected with the Labour Church movement, P. E. T. Widdrington of Coventry, Paul Stacy, Widdrington's curate and eventual successor at Coventry, and Egerton Swann; membership around 1912 may have been as high as twelve hundred. Yet even this more modern group felt the powerful and, in the end, victorious tug of mediaevalism. It was at this time that John Neville Figgis, a member of the Anglican monastic community of Mirfield, was following the lead of Maitland and Gierke to draw attention to the dangerous implications of contemporary legislation, in particular the French Association Laws and the Free Church of Scotland case, both of which threatened to end the organic autonomy of the church.[6] In a slightly different way the same lesson was being driven home by Rev. William Temple, then vicar of fashionable St. James, Piccadilly, but later successively Bishop of Manchester, archbishop of York, and archbishop of Canterbury. Under Temple's leadership the Life and Liberty Movement was formed to bring the laity into a more active partnership with the clergy in the running of the church. Although this movement was ultimately successful, and the Enabling Act, 1919, gave Temple what he wanted, the fact that an appeal had to be made via Parliament had underlined the subordination of the religious to the secular. It was a development which, in fact, provided a foretaste of worse to come. In 1927, Parliament, a body which contained many, if not a majority, of non-Anglicans, threw out the new prayer book which the church itself wished to use.

Even before these later developments the war had been for many of the Church Socialist League a last straw. The war came as a profound shock. The belief in state socialism, never strong, was shattered. One writer retracted his earlier views in anguish. "We were all

<hr />

[6] J. N. Figgis, *Churches in the Modern State* (London, 1913), pp. 18, 24–31. The law case in question had ruled that when a majority of a corporation agreed to a new line of development, the legal entity, and hence the property, was preserved in the unchanging rump.

wrong before the war. We see it all now. We had neglected vital factors. We had been relying either on vague sentimentalisms, or on one-sided deductions from abstract economic analyses."[7] In the shock of disillusionment the tendency towards mediaevalism became more pronounced. Figgis himself had earlier stressed Catholicism when he attacked the Nonconformist demands for nondenominational schooling as springing "quite naturally from that passion for state absolutism which is the child of the Renaissance and Reform and the grandchild of the Pagan State."[8] Now his fellow thinkers were prepared to be more extreme. "Protestantism has made no distinctive contribution to the Christian religion," wrote one, and continued, "It invariably tends towards either complete atheism or the Catholic Faith."[9]

For a while, it seemed that the Guild Socialist philosophy could provide a haven for the League, and in 1914 the league did decide against affiliating with the Labour party and threw in its lot with guild socialism. But it was an alliance destined to have but a short life, for by the end of the war the movement had broken apart. A few league members were prepared to go along with the Russian experiment, the force which had disrupted guild socialism, and Rev. Conrad Noel was a notable example. This priest seceded in 1918 to begin the Catholic Crusade, in which ritual and Lenin were equally important; the climax of this unorthodoxy came when he hung his parish church with the Sinn Fein and the Red flags. The parent body continued for a while longer under the old league name, until an intensifying Catholicism, but growing repudiation of socialism, led it in 1923 to change its name to the League of the Kingdom of God. In itself this grouping was never able to capture the allegiance of a sizable body of opinion, either in the church or out of it, and its quarterly was obliged to close down after a short while, owing to lack of support. But a further development out of this background did live on—the Anglo-Catholic Summer Schools of Sociology, which were founded in 1925 and continued to meet regularly thereafter. The Anglo-Catholic Congress was the official name of the organization which took the leading part in running these conferences, but it has been better known as the Christendom group.

This group, which was one of the leading centres of Church of

[7] *Optimist*, 1914, p. 215.
[8] Figgis, p. 47.
[9] *Optimist*, 1914, p. 220.

England opinion in the period between the wars and which, under the wing of Temple, played the directive role in the great Malvern conference of 1941,[10] took its name from the periodical *Christendom, A Journal of Christian Sociology*, which was edited by Reckitt with the assistance of Demant, Widdrington, and Ruth Kenyon. (The last gave lip service to Social Credit, but evidently did not fully understand it.) Even before the first appearance of *Christendom* in 1931, the Anglo-Catholic Congress had sponsored the pamphlet *Christian Vocation in Industry and Marketing*, by T. M. Heron, in which Social Credit had been advocated and Douglas mentioned by name. Clearly, the Christendom group was in large measure the Church of England side of Chandos, even down to the inclusion of T. S. Eliot. But it did include those who were not in the Chandos Group but who yet did advocate Social Credit. The Reverend W. G. Peck, of whom rather more in the final chapter, was one such.

The most fruitful field of Chandos-Christendom activity was through the Christian Social Council. The council was set up towards the end of 1928, with representatives of nine denominations, to consider how Christian principles could be applied to the day-to-day social problems of Britain. Almost inevitably the council was dominated by the Church of England, which secured thirty of the seventy-two seats, eighteen more than the next most heavily represented, the Methodists. And in turn the Church of England section was dominated by an Anglo-Catholic group, of which Reckitt was the unofficial leader. The position of this group was made even stronger when the Department of Research was established, for this department came to exercise a commanding influence over the council as a whole. What gave Reckitt, Demant, and through them the Chandos and Christendom groups their tremendous pull was the appointment of Demant as director of the department. And when money was lacking to continue this work, Reckitt came forward with the offer to pay Demant's salary for three years (£ 1,200). From this position of influence Reckitt and Demant could bring in convinced Social Crediters, who made their impact felt in the subcommittees set up under the aegis of the Research Department. Thus the Anglo-Catholic, T. M. Heron, and Hilderic Cousens, another Chandos member but not an Anglican, were co-opted to the Research Department. The height of Chandos influence came when its position was formalized by the decision of the

[10] H. Davies, *Worship and Theology in England, 1900–65* (New Jersey, 1965), p. 199.

department that a subcommittee should work with the Chandos Group on the problem of Christian conscience in politics. Incidentally, the influence of Social Credit, as distinct from that of Chandos, was also to be seen in the co-opted membership of two adherents of Douglasism, the Marquis of Tavistock, from the Evangelical wing of the Church of England, and J. E. Tuke, representing the Quakers.[11]

The strength of this centre of Social Credit has already been hinted at; it was from this source that Spencer had taken his short-lived commitment to Social Credit. In addition, the Christian Social Council was responsible for enquiries which were later published as books or as pamphlets. Such a one was *The Just Price*, in which Douglasism was hinted at in the most discreet fashion: "From all sides we find a consensus of opinion that somehow the purchasing power of the community . . . is inadequate to allow it to buy all it could produce." Douglas himself was relegated to a footnote. But a year later a second publication, *This Unemployment: Disaster or Opportunity?* appeared which included a section openly espousing Social Credit. In the pamphlet *Monetary Policy* the complete repudiation of the gold standard and the use of index numbers were insisted upon.[12] Another way of taking the message of Social Credit to the people, or at least to a certain section of them, was the series of visits undertaken by Demant and Spencer to the universities to make contact with the leading men.[13] The council also arranged or took part in conferences, for instance in the interdenominational conference at High Leigh, 26–29 April 1935, which called for a "planned increase of the purchasing power of the people" on the Douglasite basis that "the supply of legal purchasing power should be regulated in the fullest possible accordance with the nation's capacity to produce real wealth in desired goods and services."[14] And then there were the close links which the council maintained with the working-class-oriented Industrial

---

[11] I am grateful to the British Council of Churches, successor to the Christian Social Council (hereafter referred to as CSC), for permission to search the records. CSC, 25.2.29, 17.9.29, 25.9.31, and membership list, 1932; also CSC Research Department Minutes, 28.5.29, 26.11.35.

[12] V. A. Demant, ed., *The Just Price* (London, 1930), p. 119 and note; idem, *This Unemployment: Disaster or Opportunity?* (London, 1931), pp. 121–31; the pamphlet was published in London, seemingly 1936.

[13] CSC, 2.5.33.

[14] CSC, *The Christian Approach to Economic Reconstruction* (London, 1935), p. 6 (this work may be seen in the CSC files).

Christian Fellowship. The Fellowship ran a series of study circles through this period, and in their discussions relied heavily upon the Research Department, in particular upon Demant's *This Unemployment* and Spencer's *Building upon Sand*. In the opinion of the Fellowship, "Various schools of financiers and economists differ in their views as to the reasons for financial chaos . . . [but] all . . . admit that the financial system is not working as it should; and all agree that the main trouble lies in the credit system."[15]

In addition to these institutional ways of spreading Social Credit there were the efforts of other Anglicans working independently. For instance, there was Rev. W. G. Peck, who found an outlet for his views in Eliot's paper, the *Criterion*, and who brought Douglas into the tradition of the church by including the Social Credit message in his book, *The Social Implications of the Oxford Movement*. And there was, too, Dr. Hewlett Johnson, who broke with the Church Socialist League and embraced Social Credit before returning to a more straightforward socialism by supporting the Russian Communists and becoming known as the Red Dean. But even then he did not repudiate his Douglasism.[16] The greatest acquisition for Social Credit, however, was undoubtedly William Temple. It is not certain that Temple ever admitted to being a complete believer in the Douglas analysis. A hostile account of his political views states that he "was greatly influenced by the Social Credit line of thought." T. M. Heron claims that Temple admitted in private to the Chandos people that he was a Social Crediter, that his position prevented his saying so openly, but that he would do what he could towards smoothing the path for them.[17] Certainly he was very sympathetic to Social Credit and he showed this in the twenties when he edited the periodical, *Pilgrim*. An early editorial proclaimed: "We believe that Major Douglas and *The New Age* are doing a great service in calling so insistently for attention to the manipulation of credit. . . . We are not advocating the 'Douglas Scheme'. It may be sound or it may not. . . . If it is even partially correct it brings before us matters of vital importance which ought to be worked out in the fullest public discussion."[18] Such a discussion did, in fact, take place in the pages of the *Pilgrim*, where favourable

[15] Industrial Christian Fellowship, *Study Circle Outlines*, 1935 (in the CSC files).
[16] For his Social Credit phase, see *Pilgrim*, 4.22.
[17] Carmichael and Godwin, p. 20; personal information from T. M. Heron, 1967.
[18] *Pilgrim*, 1.22.

articles by Egerton Swann, Reckitt, Demant, and Spencer were featured. In addition Temple did come out during the war with speeches
which were very akin to Social Credit, and in a book published in 1942
he did take Social Credit as the example of "a particular economic or
political innovation" the effects of which he was considering.[19]

Evidently a significant section of Anglo-Catholic belief was committed or was at least sympathetic to Social Credit, and it is now
necessary to account for this interest. Certain connections may be put
aside, on the ground that they were in the nature of "accidents." Thus
the mediaevalism which was such a strong feature of Anglican socialism linked up easily with the similar elements in Social Credit. The
attraction which the Just Price, that basic belief of Social Credit, had
for the Anglo-Catholics was to be seen in its use as a book title.
Leisure, believed to be a characteristic feature of mediaeval society,
was another such element; Widdrington claimed that "Mediaeval
Christendom, whatever its shortcomings, did not encourage over-
work," and he pointed out that a decretal of Gregory IX had ordained
no less than eighty-five days of obligation, to which must have been
added the local feast days.[20] In these Anglo-Catholic circles much
store was put by Thorold Roger's *Six Centuries of Work and
Wages*, with its portrayal of the late Middle Ages as a time of high
prosperity for the average man.

There was another aspect of mediaevalism, however, which appealed at a deeper level of significance and pointed the way to essential
connections between Anglo-Catholicism and Social Credit. Just after
the war, one of the Church Socialist circle, but not a Social Crediter,
developed the mediaevalism implicit in that background and showed
how the capitalism to which they objected was essentially connected
with the Protestantism they increasingly repudiated. This, the Tawney variant of the Weber thesis, originally given as the first Scott-
Holland lecture, was later printed as the book *Religion and the Rise
of Capitalism*. This line of thought provided an attractive explanation
of modern developments which heavily qualified the Marxian interpretation and was understandably popular in Anglo-Catholic circles.
When in 1930 the English translation of Weber's *The Protestant Ethic*
at last appeared, Demant gave it an enthusiastic review in the *New

[19] For a speech at the Albert Hall see F. A. Iremonger, *William Temple* (Oxford,
1948), p. 579; W. Temple, *Christianity and Social Order* (London, 1942), p. 35.
[20] *Christendom*, 6.31.

Age, and when in 1949 he himself gave the Scott-Holland lecture, he chose to speak upon the state of the Weber-Tawney thesis. He concluded that, broadly speaking, the thesis remained valid, and he suggested that recent attacks on capitalism could more truthfully be represented as a return to old ways rather than as a novel departure into the unknown.[21]

Demant also pointed out that classical liberalism was only possible while people believed in an infinite world, so that exports and the balance of power could be extended without limit.[22] And here he drew attention to another aspect of the attraction of the Middle Ages—that its static quality seemed more in touch with the conditions of the twentieth century than did the dynamism of the period just ended. Here was one of the paradoxes of Social Credit. That doctrine assumed, as few previous doctrines had, the tremendous dynamic power of the machine. But it took that production to the point of satiety. Now a world which knows no demand because supply is infinitely great approaches very closely a world which knows no demand because the supply is infinitely small, as was the case in the mediaeval world, in which a certain standard of living had been accepted as inevitable. In both systems, therefore, it was possible to dispense with economic debate and, incidentally, with politics as such. The deeper identity of Social Credit and Catholic thought now begins to emerge.

Social Crediters rooted their system in realism. As a correspondent in the *New Age* put it, with that pomposity which was an unfortunate feature of post-Oragean writing, "*The phenomenon of the physical universe as translated to the consciousness through the five senses must be taken for granted as absolute reality.*"[23] In this same tradition Anglo-Catholics hailed Douglas's writings as "a criticism of finance by an engineer . . . in the line of Catholic realism."[24] What the writer of the article from which this quotation was taken was claiming was that both capitalism and Marxism were to be rejected because both tried to work on the assumption that individuals were basically good, and hence need only to be allowed to be free in order to come to perfection. In other words, the Catholics were claiming that the essential concept of original sin would find a place in a Social Credit

[21] NA 23.10.30; V. A. Demant, *Religion and the Decline of Capitalism* (London, 1952).
[22] Demant, *Religion and the Decline of Capitalism*, p. 25.
[23] NA 15.8.29.
[24] *Christendom*, 9.35.

state and that a Social Credit state would equally demand some notion of original sin.

This point requires some clarification, because Douglas himself rejected with force the idea of original sin, and so on the face of it the two formulations seem to be totally opposed. But Douglas did not mean original sin in the theological sense at all; what he intended to say was that he did not accept the view that man, without the constraint of poverty and the need of work, would inevitably abuse his freedom and turn to licence and degradation. When Douglas used the term "original sin," he was not using it correctly and should have stuck to the alternative which he sometimes used, "puritanism."[25] The people whom he objected to were the people like the Webbs, who according to Orage, had understood the technique of Social Credit and agreed that it was feasible, but had rejected it because, "touched to their puritan quick," they disagreed with the aim.[26] The doctrine of original sin does not claim that man is inherently evil, and its disagreement with the Rousseauesque idea of the good man is only on the ground that that view goes too far the other way. Demant made the position quite clear. "Catholics believe in 'original sin' (not in human malice) and in consequence believe that unless an organized human activity is kept to its true function by a social philosophy politically and economically embodied it will run amok and assume the direction of human life."[27]

This aspect of Social Credit should not be lost sight of. It is customary to concentrate upon the individualism of Social Credit, and certainly this was a crucial consideration, not only for Douglas but also for this very Anglo-Catholic section. At the same time, however, both Social Credit and Anglo-Catholicism stressed the equal importance of the individual and of society. In his insistence upon the belief that "Man is naturally and inevitably social," Temple was even prepared to acknowledge that the Fascists had to their credit an emphasis upon the organic, as opposed to the individualism of the communists. (This, incidentally, was written as late as 1942.)[28] And in truth, before this individual freedom could be conferred, the organism in which these individuals were articulated had to be so organized and directed that economic plenty could be produced. It was an essential part of the

[25] *Social Credit*, 24.8.34; NA 1.11.28, 30.10.30.
[26] NA 8.4.26.
[27] *Christendom*, 9.35.
[28] Temple, pp. 46–50.

Social Credit case that the benefits were social benefits, for was not the title *Social* Credit? Moreover, the continuance of the Social Credit benefits demanded "organized human activity . . . kept to its true function," as Demant had called for (see footnote 27). In this Catholic scheme of things the Unearned Increment served not only as the beacon which guided man in his pursuit of the social function but also as the gauge by which the success of his pursuit could be checked. Should it be lost sight of, the Just Price would rise until it coincided with the cost price.

Such an insistence upon original sin gave rise to conclusions which fitted in with Social Credit in other ways. In the first place it was agreed that because of original sin property had been instituted, for as Temple said, "Private property is lawful as an accommodation to man's sinful state."[29] Thus while the Anglo-Catholic school was opposed to capitalism it did not rush to the conclusion that nationalization of everything was called for. In this respect it was very close to Douglas, who wanted to keep the technical apparatus of capitalism but so transform it by socializing credit and by making possible low prices that its evils would be taken away; he, too, accepted the feasibility and advisability of retaining private property.

Secondly, a belief in original sin demands a neutral individual; man is neither damned, as the Calvinist would have us believe, nor eternally blessed, as Rousseau suggested; rather he contains the potential for both good and evil, and salvation or damnation depend upon his reactions to situations, in other words, upon free will. (One is here reminded of a background strain of Social Credit, Orage's Nietzschean "beyond good and evil" outlook.) As Reckitt put it, the connection between Social Credit and Catholicism on this point was a particularly close one; to him national dividends were "an economic expression of the vital truth of free will."[30]   In making this point Temple was even more outspoken. While he agreed that "the whole conception of personality requires that there shall be what is necessary to some measure of personal life secured to everyman before he begins to do anything at all, if this can be contrived," he also believed that "there must be the freedom to abuse the property if it is to be all it should be in the Christian scheme."[31]   Thus it was not surprising to

[29] Temple, p. 28.

[30] R. Kenyon, ed., *The Catholic Faith and the Industrial Order* (London, 1931), p. 105.

[31] Anglo-Catholic Congress, *Report of the Third Summer School of Sociology* (London, 1928), p. 33.

find certain writers putting forward the fact that Social Credit would not abolish inequality as an added benefit rather than as an inevitable flaw in the scheme.[32] This Catholic quality of *acceptance* was also to be seen in connection with group diversity. "Difference and diversity," Demant wrote, "are aspects of creation and they are as much the grounds of co-operation, interdependence and functional service as of dissension. It depends entirely upon the things men do and say whether separateness or closeness makes more for unity or for conflict." This was very far from fascism, however, for in that system the process had been taken too far, so that " 'the social organism' is considered not only as a fact of existence but as a moral goal."[33] This was clearly unacceptable.

The way in which realism bound together the Catholic and Social Credit patterns of thought may be illustrated once more by noting the following application of the notion of acceptance. Catholic thought demands that the "here and now" be considered more important than the problematic future. In a scathing denunciation of the alternative, Demant wrote: "A Christian knows that every moment and event has its moral quality, and will never allow that a false move can make for a true society at an undated millenium. Starvation today for the sake of plenty the day after tomorrow (Capitalism); the Servile State today for the sake of the glorious freedom of Anarchist Communism in the days to come (Communism); toleration of injustice for the sake of 'pie in the sky when you die' (Pietism) are wicked deceptions with which a Christian will have nothing to do."[34] Douglas's claim that with his system the world could be changed overnight on the basis of the present benefits of the machine, ignoring past claims either for privilege or for compensation, springs irresistibly to mind.

The following quotation from the pen of a leading member of the League of the Kingdom of God may be given as a convenient summary of this thinking:

> The Catholic theory of freedom . . . corrects the
> individualism of Mill's *On Liberty* no less than the *Etatism*
> of Hobbes' *Leviathan*. But by what name may this

---

[32] M. Spencer in *The Just Price*, ed. V. A. Demant, p. 132; also Demant in *Christendom*, 9.35.

[33] V. A. Demant, *The Christian Doctrine of Human Solidarity* (London, 1940), pp. 4, 11.

[34] Ibid., p. 18.

philosophy be recognized? Surely, the obvious name for it is
Toryism. Toryism stands for the subordination of material
to moral values; it takes a realist view of human nature
(which is neither wholly bad nor wholly good) because it
dates from a working political machine under the King, and
not from the coherent intellectual system of some political
philosopher; it knows of no short cuts to Utopia, although
it is animated by a passion for social righteousness, for
equity, in social relations and in business dealings; its sense
of social partnership, of the whole community, renders it
implacably hostile to class and sectional interests—hence its
devotion to Church and Crown, which together, standing
above such interests, and attempting to envisage the country
as a whole, provide a true focus of loyalty; while sensibly
attached to order and privilege it lays its emphasis upon
obligation, and is sceptical of 'rights'.[35]

In this formulation may be seen elements of the thought of the *New
Age*'s Tory radicalism, the monarchical attachment of Hargrave and
the later Belloc, Penty's belief in fascism as the product of action, not
of abstractionism, and finally elements of the "anti-rights" notions of
Hulme and de Maeztu. There were, then, many grounds on which
Social Credit and Catholic outlooks coincided. Therefore it would be
reasonable to expect Roman Catholics to turn to Social Credit. What,
in fact, was the response of that church?

As early as 1921, a Catholic priest, Father Drinkwater of Birmingham, had written to the *Christian Democrat*, the monthly organ of the
Catholic Social Guild, asking for "some cognizance of *The New Age*
proposals for Credit Reform." But the editor was content to rely upon
the advice of "many able economists of different schools of thought"
who all, he said, admitted that they were themselves mystified, and
nothing came of the suggestion.[36] From time to time Catholic writers noted the doctrine and gave accounts without coming to any firm
conclusion either way. There was a spate of articles in the early
thirties in the *Clergy Review* in which Drinkwater joined. Father
Watt, S. J., had contributed to *The Just Price* and Father Coffey to
the *Fig Tree*, Douglas's own short-lived quarterly. Then, too, the
Catholic convert and writer, Christopher Hollis, wrote on financial

---

[35] D. J. Symon, in *Christendom*, 6.31.
[36] *Christian Democrat*, 8.21.

matters from a quasi–Social Credit point of view.[37] But in sum the response was disappointing and lagged far behind the Anglo-Catholic lead.

However, it should be noted that many Catholics who might have given some attention to Social Credit would be attracted to the basically similar and competing doctrine of distributism being advocated by the leading Catholic writers, Belloc and Chesterton. At the same time it is to be noted that Belloc agreed with the technical case for Social Credit and disagreed only on the moral and ethical level. Also many a Catholic pen was directed to analysing and commenting upon *Quadragesimo Anno*, the papal encyclical of 1931 which commemorated the bull *Rerum Novarum* of 1891, and both of these contained much which was similar to, or at least sympathetic with, credit reform; Drinkwater often used the encyclical as a peg on which to hang his Social Credit sermons. Above all, the Catholic Social Guild was unfortunate in being dominated about this time by Henry Somerville, a man of no breadth of mind and no intellectual daring who was content to snipe at any suggestion while taking refuge in a vaguely Catholicized liberalism.[38] Of the church's response it can only be said that no official voice denounced the doctrine.

Another religious group to show an interest in Social Credit was the Society of Friends. The way had been prepared for the reception of these ideas when early in the war the Quakers set up a Committee for Social Reconstruction. The journal of the committee revealed how the notions of credit reform were being discussed. The ideas of Arthur Kitson, considered by many a St. John the Baptist to Douglas, were a topic of interest, and the State Bonus Scheme was there defended by its author. In addition Milner was invited to address the War and Social Order Committee, and a subcommittee was appointed to consider the plan. In its report the subcommittee commented favourably on the intention to "provide the bare means of subsistence to every citizen irrespective of any return in the form of service." Two articles in the journal attacked the bank monopoly and, noting the 1914 crash, advocated a commodity standard in place of the gold standard.[39] From 1921 onwards the claim of Douglas received a friendly and at

[37] *Fig Tree*, 12.36. C. Hollis, *The Breakdown of Money* (London, 1934), especially p. 119; idem, *The Two Nations* (London, 1935), p. 85.

[38] His *Studies in the Catholic Social Movement* (London, 1933) exposes his limitations.

[39] *Ploughshare*, 2.18, 7.19.

times favourable hearing, since between 1922 and 1934 the War and Social Order Committee was chaired by J. E. Tuke, a Social Crediter, who could get Douglas himself to address the committee.[40] In the report written by M. L. Rowntree for the committee, the doctrine was considered. He noted with approval, "The aim of the Douglas *New Age* scheme is freedom for every individual," and although he was not completely convinced of the validity of Social Credit, he acknowledged that if it should prove to be correct, then it would answer all problems.[41] In the following year the same committee gave "a full session to the consideration of the Douglas scheme of credit control." Later, Quakers recorded the following conclusion: "We think that some other method should be found of issuing purchasing power than that solely of a wage or salary for work done. We are of opinion that as credit is a social product and as the control of it tends more and more to be concentrated in the hands of a comparative few, it is essential that it shall be democratically controlled in the interests of the community and of the individual."[42] And the bibliography which the Industrial and Social Order Council (the successor to the War and Social Order Committee) put out in 1935 included works by Demant, Douglas, and other monetary reformers and Social Crediters.

In addition to these institutional expressions of Quaker interest there were the individuals who participated in Social Credit activity or were active on the fringes. The two leaders of the Social Credit party, John Hargrave and Philip Kenway, had been brought up as Quakers. S. G. Hobson, the Guild Socialist pioneer who later came close to Social Credit, was another ex-Quaker, as was Montague Fordham, also an ex-guildsman and semi-Distributist. Reckitt, Ezra Pound, and the minor imagist poet, Basil Bunting, who ran the London University Social Credit study circle, were all Social Crediters from Quaker backgrounds. The Reverend Malcolm Spencer's mother was a Quaker. Tuke still was one.

The deeper reasons for this identity must be postponed for a while, but it is easy to see that in Social Credit there were elements which

---

[40] War and Social Order Committee Minutes, 7.1.22, 8.11.24, 30.11.24. I am grateful to the Society of Friends for permission to search their records.

[41] M. L. Rowntree, *Social Freedom* (London, 1921), p. 122.

[42] Society of Friends, *Social Thought in the Society of Friends* (London, 1922), p. 28; Conference of Quaker Employers, *Quakerism and Industry* (London, 1928), p. 64.

would appeal to the Quaker mind and tradition. The attractions of an individualism bordering on anarchism were naturally strong, and it was this aspect which Tuke commented on when he endorsed the movement. To him Douglasism stood for the "perfect freedom of the individual."[43] At the same time, the antistate corollary of this attitude fitted well with a movement of which the origin and history confirmed the evil of authority in many cases. And on a more mundane level, many a Quaker of small-scale industrial background (Tuke was one such) must have been struck by the Social Credit denunciations of twentieth century banking. Within the close-knit Quaker community, banking on the old family scale had been an important activity, and Fordham, looking back to his ancestors' banking days, lamented its passing.[44]

The only other religious groups to show a marked interest in Social Credit were the Theosophical. The early and continuing prominence of Orage in Theosophical and Social Credit circles would in itself, perhaps, point to an essential connection between the two ways of thinking, for Orage had a flair for spotting the currents of the day and for seeing their interrelatedness. That Steiner, still within the broad Theosophical framework, despite the change into anthroposophy, was so popular with the New Britain group and known to *New Age* and Sociological Society circles was another pointer. Other points of contact were many. The Theosophical Order of Service and the Centre Party, another Theosophical organization, gave backing to the League to Abolish Poverty. In Sheffield, a hotbed of Theosophical activity, the separate Theosophical Social Credit Study Circle flourished in the early period; Theosophical influence in the Kibbo Kift had always been strong; Major C. F. J. Galloway, the Social Credit author and speaker, was a Theosophist, as were A. E. Powell, another Social Credit writer, Oscar Köllerström, connected with the New Britain movement, George Hickling of Coventry, the founder of the first Green Shirts before their absorption by Hargrave, and T. Kennedy, organizer of the Belfast and Dublin Social Credit Study Circles. Finally, J. M. Cohn, speaking in 1967 and looking back to the mystical circles in his Cambridge of the early twenties, made a special point of connecting Theosophical and Social Credit thinking.[45]

---

[43] *New Britain,* 16.5.34.
[44] *New Order,* 10.37.
[45] See the references to Sheffield in W. C. Hartmann, ed., *Who's Who in Occultism.*

This, then, was the nature of religious interest in and support for Social Credit—Anglo-Catholic, Roman Catholic, Quaker, and occupying an indeterminate position, the Theosophists. At once two puzzles become evident. In the first place, in Alberta the religious appeal was of quite a different kind. In England, the appeal was through sophisticated forms of religion, whereas in Alberta the appeal was via the fundamentalist sects. This is not the place to examine this particular puzzle. But what must be looked at is the discrepancy between the kinds of support which Social Credit received in England. There is a great gulf between the Catholics at one end of the ecclesiastical spectrum and the Quakers at the other, and apart from the ephemeral Congregational interest, there was nothing in between. For wherever the Theosophists are put, it is clear that they must go to one or the other flank and that they do nothing to fill in the gap. But the clue to this polarization, which has been noted in other contexts, will be postponed to the final chapter.

Yet before this estimation is attempted, one further point should be made about the Catholic and the Quaker responses. There was a marked difference between the two. Whereas the Anglo-Catholic Social Crediters were men of some substance religiously speaking—in Temple they had a sympathizer among the very establishment, and Hewlett Johnson was later dean of Canterbury and Demant professor of moral theology at Oxford—the Quakers who declared for Douglas or sympathized with monetary reform were of little consequence when compared with the Cadburys and the Rowntrees; indeed many of them had left their Quaker background. May one conclude, then, that the Catholic response was the more "logical" and fitted more closely into the Social Credit pattern of thought, and that Social Credit was more of a Catholic than a Quaker way of thinking?

(Jamaica, New York, 1927); NA 9.6.21, 19.1.22, 7.2.24, 14.1.32; for Galloway, who wrote: *Poverty amidst Plenty* (Sheffield, 1928), see *News and Notes of the Theosophical Society,* 14.1.32; Powell wrote *The Deadlock in Finances* (London, 1924), and *The Flow Theory of Economics* (London, 1929). For the others, see *News and Notes of the Theosophical Society,* 3.29, 4.30, 10.30; Hartmann, p. 64; J. M. Cohn, "The Spiral Path," BBC Third Programme, 1.4.67.

chapter eleven

CONCLUSION

This examination of Social Credit in the country of its origin has revealed two problems which, on the face of it, are puzzling to the point of paradox. To begin with, Social Credit was a doctrine which gloried in being a realistic, indeed self-evident, *via media*, rejecting alike the pitfalls of the left and of the right. And yet it has been shown that where there was any positive response to Social Credit it tended to come from the fringes of both right and left of the various compartments of thought which were affected. This claim to represent sanity and reasonableness is one almost always made, of course, by a doctrine seeking public acceptance, and it is almost always equally true that such an appeal misses its target. But there can be few instances of an appeal's landing so far from the centre, of being so impartially wide of the mark, as was the case with Social Credit. For there was not just one example of this polarization; it was to be found in all instances considered.

The second puzzle is connected with this first point. At the outset Social Credit made a significant impact, and the Labour party into the thirties found that the subject could not be ignored. Through most of this period, the cause of Social Credit enjoyed the services of two papers of distinction, the *New Age* and the *New English Weekly*, and in addition rested secure in the knowledge that several figures of importance gave either outright support or at least qualified approval. Today, fifty years after the first appearance of Douglas's ideas in print, and despite the shadowy existence in England of three varieties of organized Social Credit activity, it is impossible to disagree with Reckitt's conclusion that 1936 marked the end of the movement, at least as far as England is concerned. Why, then, was the Social Credit movement such a seven-day wonder? Was its diversified appeal a source of weakness, in fact, rather than of strength?

And what, taken together, do these two questions and their possible answers signify? For while these are the important questions to emerge from the account of Social Credit in England, there is a third question which can hardly be avoided. Beyond England, Social Credit did not fail, or rather, did not fail in quite the same way. In Canada, it has been a topic of discussion, and of anxious discussion, since Aberhart's brand captured Alberta. The spread of the doctrine to British Columbia, and its appearance in Quebec, where the appeal of Caouette has added another dimension to the problem, has kept Social Credit a topical issue. The comment is frequently heard in Canada that Social Credit is fascist, and although this term is never defined, it is clear that it is used pejoratively and that the unspoken charge is that of totalitarianism, more particularly, totalitarianism of the National Socialist pattern. The threat which is held to exist is often sharpened by asking what would happen should depression once again return to Canada. In introducing this wider consideration, however, the original limits of the account are not left too far behind. For it has been remarked how, as early as 1923, the extreme left fastened this reactionary smear onto Social Credit and how at intervals thereafter this charge was repeated. Therefore this third question, of the implications of Social Credit thinking, should be added to the first two. Together they may be summed up in one overriding question which, if a simplification, does not do too much violence to the problem of Social Credit's life and death in England: Was Social Credit a sinister development and one whose eventual failure was to be welcomed?

Reference has been made to the diverse nature of the Social Credit appeal. But that observation could, with point, be extended. The predominant impression to emerge is not simply one of diversity, but rather of contradiction. And it was not restricted to the unfolding of Social Credit itself, but ran through its background and its fringe associations as well. In the underworld of monetary thought, from Ruskin, who could proclaim himself a Communist *and* a Tory, the sources of inquiry had been two—the Individualist and the anarchist; from Comte, who could insist upon order *and* progress, the sources of inspiration had been two—the forward- and the backward-looking. The same split was to be found among the more political inhabitants of the underworld. There was a time when the *New Age* seemed on the point of declaring for Tory radicalism, while the political philosophy which was eventually chosen, guild socialism, was a more or less consciously made attempt to bring together two warring viewpoints, the anarchist and the socialist. In this connection it is useful to remember Hobson's avowal that in writing *National Guilds* he had set out to build a bridge. Inevitably when the breakup came, guild socialism split into two quite distinct and antagonistic camps. The sister movement, distributism, likewise concealed a deep division of opinion within the ranks, between the out-and-out rejecters and the cautious accepters of twentieth-century technology.

Within the Social Credit movement itself these dichotomies were, if anything, even more clearly marked. In the religious sphere, the juxtaposition was that of Anglo-Catholic and Quaker-Theosophist; in the political, it was the ILP and the Facists; while the general intellectual interest spanned Ezra Pound (who could with justice be called a Fascist) and C. M. Grieve (who was a member of the Communist party) and embraced support of early Nazi Germany along with that of Republican Spain. Moreover, the individuals connected with Social Credit and its allied movements exhibited the same uncertainty. Most of them changed their political allegiance, sometimes in bewildering fashion: Herbert was successively Conservative, Liberal, and Individualist; Meulen completed the swing by joining the anarchists; the Distributists came as refugees both from liberalism and from socialism; Orage and Reckitt were two who began public life as socialists but who passed through to something else; and to look slightly ahead, there were the twists and turns of Mosley and Strachey. Moreover, many of these participants showed the same tendency to change their positions when it came to religion. Finally, and above all, G. K. Chesterton's love of paradox pointed to an even deeper-seated uncertainty.

In such a welter of contradiction it is not easy to find a common denominator which could serve as a clue, pointing to a way through the labyrinth. There is such a thread, however, one which appears in the earliest background and which can be traced through to utterances made on the eve of the failure of 1936. This thread is anarchism.

It has been shown how the early monetary reformers were close to an anarchist position. Kropotkin, in particular, approached very closely to a Social Credit position, and later Social Crediters were to refer favourably to him. The Sociological Society thinking, which likewise tended towards the Douglas analysis, was heavily influenced by anarchism. Even the Individualists found themselves pushed into that direction, while the disciples of Ruskin found it difficult to avoid an anarchist resting place; Morris was all but in that camp, and the

Distributists almost entered too. The peak of the anarchist wave came in the last years of the nineteenth century, and although it thereafter declined it never entirely disappeared. Its underground continuation was to be seen in the *New Age*.

Orage himself, whose socialism stemmed from the semianarchist Tom Mann, was quite clearly attracted by anarchism. His untypically passionate involvement with the fate of the anarchist Ferrer was an indication of this, as was his commitment to guild socialism, especially the manner of that commitment. Among those who skirmished on the flanks of guild socialism were many whose incipient anarchism was plain; an example would be the Clydeside–Shop Steward movement, and significantly Glasgow was both an anarchist and a Social Credit stronghold. Another and very important indication of the *New Age*'s instinctive anarchism would be the view expressed by its philosopher, T. E. Hulme, who came close to accepting political anarchism when he acknowledged the importance of Sorel and of Proudhon.

From Social Credit itself the scent of anarchism emerged unmistakably, even though the term was hardly ever used. There was the detestation of the state, which appeared frequently in the guise of a rejection of liberal political parties as well as of single party alternatives. The belief which Douglas voiced that no organization was to be trusted if it had over three thousand members was a pointer to a conclusion which one early observer did draw: reporting a meeting which Douglas had held in Oxford, he noted, "The substance of Social Credit is an exposition of the way that 'anarchism' can be applied economically even to a highly industrialized community like England."[1] Further clues of the almost subliminal way that anarchist thought had penetrated Social Credit writing abound. For instance the novelist Storm Jameson's championing of Social Credit from a leisure angle was entitled *The Soul of Man in the Age of Leisure*, which took as its inspiration the title of the book by the quasi-anarchist Oscar Wilde, *The Soul of Man under Socialism*. And the revival of anarchism in the 1930s was connected with Social Credit in the person of Herbert Read, who in 1935 wrote *Essential Communism*, in which he declared both his belief in "the economic analysis of Douglas and Orage" and also his belief in anarchism.[2] It is unfortunate that the low state of anarchism in England in the years between the wars

[1] NA 27.5.20.
[2] H. Read, *Essential Communism* (London, 1935), p. 20.

should have meant the impossibility of continuing the pioneer work of the eighties and nineties, and of tracing the response of anarchism to Social Credit.

The frequent references to individualism in this account should not be taken as weakening this case too much, for they cannot be thrown into the scale against anarchism. Indeed, quite the reverse, for on most occasions they only help to strengthen the case for anarchism. Thus, the Individualist monetary reformers did not challenge the anarchists in too fundamental a manner, and once the reactionary wing of the Liberty and Property Defence League had been shaken off, most of the Individualists felt the inevitability of slipping away from their liberal heritage. That the latter-day individualism was totally unconnected with the Spencerian variety was indicated by its attachment to some version of the Nietzschean system; men such as Orage, Levy, and Ludovici, and even Mairet and Symons, always put individualism in a very different and less simplistic setting. Levy, for example, looked to a Renaissance joie de vivre, in which all men could, he believed, be aristocrats.[3] More soberly the same plea was made by Symons in *The Coming of Community*, in which he spoke of liberating the aristocrat in every man. It is to be noted that anarchism and aristocracy have been recognized to be compatible outlooks.[4] It is not straining matters, then, to make use of certain Individualists as part of anarchism.

If this suggestion of the link between anarchism and Social Credit is accepted, the analysis can be taken another step forward. For if anarchism remains one of the most perverse and ill-defined philosophies which have ever been seriously canvassed, at least enough is known of its history to venture certain judgements. A most significant point about anarchism is its geographical setting. In contrast to its great rival, social democracy, anarchism is a southern, not a northern, European movement; whereas social democracy has had its strength in Germany, Scandinavia, and England, anarchism has flourished best in Spain, Italy, France, and Russia. An economic explanation has been used to account for this fact and to show why the doctrine should contain such contradictory elements. In the southern countries, it is claimed, the conflict between old and new was far harsher than in the northern countries. There had been no blurring of the old ways, no

---

[3] O. Levy, *The Idiocy of Idealism* (London, 1940), p. 71.
[4] G. Woodcock, *Anarchism* (Harmondsworth: Penguin, 1963), p. 30; NA 1.11.34.

transitional liberal era, so that when capitalism did eventually come, it did so in an advanced, fully developed, and frighteningly efficient guise; at the same time, it encountered an essentially feudal system still retaining much that was vital. When protests arose, therefore, against the new capitalism, they had a tendency to be violent, as violent as the new intrusions. Moreover, they tended to be rooted in a still-living past, the good elements of which were thought to be worth saving. (That Orage should have been inclined towards Sir Francis Fletcher-Vane's feudally inspired outlook was therefore not surprising.) The only step necessary to usher in the utopia was the removal of the exploiters, and given the feudal background, this was held to mean a struggle against the state rather than against any class as such. Finally, the attraction of a feudal past led anarchists to ignore the methods and preoccupations of the liberal era which they had never known. Thus, democracy was valued less than the social element, and the basis of any system was taken to be, not that liberal construct, the naturally good man, but rather the social feeling, which was thought of as an innate characteristic of man but one which left room for some antisocial manifestations.

Such an argument is sound as far as it goes. It begs the question, however, of why the confrontation had to be a sudden one—why, in fact, the liberal era was so late in coming and so transitory when it did arrive. Again the answer is suggested by considering the setting in which anarchism did best. That was a Catholic setting. Anarchism was an apocalyptic creed which was naturally at home in an apocalyptic view of the world. For the Catholic the preoccupation is with the Incarnation, with the Day of Judgement, with the contrasts of before and after, while for the Protestant the interest is in the day-to-day winning of salvation; the very name Methodism is the fitting culmination of this approach.

The key to the anarchist mentality would seem to lie less in the problem of change than in the manner in which change was to come about. It would be more accurate, therefore, to refer to anarchism as a cast of mind than as a political philosophy. Clearly it will be a cast of mind not frequently found in its purity. Those able to accept the full implications of such an outlook will always be a minority. At times, however, there will be those who, while not accepting the whole of the anarchist case, will allow its presuppositions to colour other, more orthodox, views. Is it possible to identify such traces in the background to Social Credit and in the doctrine itself? If they can be found there, they will add confirmation to the tenuous identification so far built up.

As it happens, the *New Age* at the very moment of its rebirth under Orage was provided with the opportunity of making clear its thinking in this respect. Although the terms in which the discussion was carried on were not identical with those used up to this point, they were part and parcel of the same overall way of looking at the world.

Just before the failure of the old *New Age*, the temporary editor had ventured a judgement. "The three signs of the times," he proclaimed, "are the Labour Movement, the New Theology Movement and the Woman Movement."[5] These three movements were not a fortuitous grouping, but they had an inner consistence. For the labour movement and the woman movement were, in the *New Age*'s eyes, linked together as visible signs of progress along that spiritual advance of which the New Theology was the embodiment. Where Rev. Lewis Donaldson had said, "Christianity is the religion of which socialism is the practice," the *New Age* was now claiming in effect that the New Theology, that nine-day wonder of Rev. R. J. Campbell, was the true sect of that religion. Its starting point was too ready an acceptance of the fruits of modern science and of the higher criticism, and its clarion call was the belief that "it is as immanent that God becomes known." Week by week, the Reverend Mr. Campbell thundered forth from the City Temple, the main Congregational church in London, his emphasis upon the "fundamental axiom, the unity of God and man," and he reiterated his belief in the "fundamental unity of the whole human race" to the pitch that in reply to his own rhetorical question, "Where . . . is the dividing line between our being and God's?" he could reply only, "There is no dividing line."[6] When it was protested that this was pantheism, and when that liberal churchman, Bishop Gore, wrote a book to prove the charge, such accusations were brushed aside.[7] But for all the high hopes of the New Theology (which led Shaw to give his guarded blessing to its offshoot, the Progressive League),[8] it was a movement way behind the times, out of date before it was born. As far back as 1879 Balfour's *Defence of Philosophic Doubt* had

[5] NA 4.4.07.

[6] NA 3.1.07, 24.1.07; R. J. Campbell, *The New Theology* (London, 1909), p. 29; see, too, A. H. Wilkerson, *The Reverend R. J. Campbell: The Man and His Message* (London, 1907), and G. S. Spinks, ed., *Religion in Britain since 1900* (London, 1952), p. 53.

[7] C. Gore, *The New Theology and the Old Religion* (London, 1907).

[8] Details were included in Campbell, pp. 223–44.

foreshadowed the reassertion of the claims of transcendence; in 1907 the bull *Lamentabile* had condemned the modernism, so similar to that of Campbell, of the Jesuit, George Tyrrell. This repudiation of immanence was to culminate in Rudolf Otto's *The Idea of the Holy* and in Karl Barth's *Commentary on Romans*. The New Theology, and the mentality of the Clayton *New Age*, were in fact but the last flicker of Nonconformist thinking, and like the last seeming health of a consumptive, a mockery of the true state.

Immediately on becoming editor, Orage repudiated all three movements. The pages which had been full of Campbell, immanence, and letters of support, ceased abruptly. The woman movement was mentioned only to be scorned, which happened so often that one reader was brought to protest, "Really, you are becoming as sensitive about your virility as an old maid about her modesty."[9] And the labour movement was ignored in favour of an insistence upon socialism, a very different matter to the *New Age*. For Orage sensed that the woman movement and the labour movement were based upon nothing more than a vague brotherly feeling, which looked to no transcendental purpose for its validity. These three movements were the culmination of the immanentist philosophy, and for that reason the repudiation of the Clayton heritage had to be a total one.

The dichotomy of immanence-transcendentalism is an extremely useful one. Transcendence evidently encompasses that key characteristic of anarchism, its apocalyptic outlook. From such a point of departure it is now possible to go on to examine the attractiveness of Social Credit.

It can be illustrated in two ways. It can be shown that the interests which considered sympathetically, or took up, Social Credit were those which themselves exhibited this need to move from an immanentist basis to a transcendental. Such an argument, though circumstantial, would be a strong one. But not a complete one. It would be a half-argument, showing why these interests were inclined to take up monetary reform, perhaps, but not why they chose Social Credit. After all, Douglas was not the only monetary reformer at this time. One writer on monetary thought in this period claims to have found over twenty thousand schemes in Germany alone, and Cole himself received several hundred suggestions. To take but two examples: why did Kitson never form a movement, although he had been writing long before Douglas, his understanding of the machinery of credit was

[9] NA 1.8.12.

superior to Douglas's, and his exposition was much easier to understand; and why did Soddy fail to take? Should Gaitskell be correct in his judgement, that a certain amount of mystery is necessary to launch a successful monetary movement, it may be true that Kitson was too straightforward; but on the other hand, Soddy contained enough intricate matter to stock any number of movements.[10] For all its overall failure, Social Credit was a success when set alongside the other similar movements. It will be necessary to show secondly, then, the qualities by which Social Credit rather than the others satisfied the demands of the situation.

The attempt to combine the best of two outlooks, by synthesizing the immanentist and the transcendental, does not begin with the twentieth century. The earliest example in the modern period comes, hardly surprisingly, in the wake of the first triumph of the outrightly immanentist creed, the French Revolution. And that example was positivism. This system of thought, its branches, and its associations have been outlined, together with their commitment to monetary reform, and above all to Social Credit kinds of thinking.

This synthesis was an early one and its transcendence kept within limits. In England its claim to be a religion was muted; perhaps Huxley's comment, that positivism was "Catholicism without Christianity," had been too devastating. But parallel with positivism ran other movements which exhibited a more thoroughgoing transcendentalism. Spiritualism, which experienced a tremendous popularity at the turn of the century and enrolled in its ranks such notables as Conan Doyle, F. W. Myers, and Sir Oliver Lodge was an example of this trend. Its use of scientific, and hence essentially immanentist, techniques to study nonmaterial, and hence transcendental, phenomena was a classic instance of the collision of two patterns of thought. Spiritualism, it must be confessed, had no interest in monetary reform, and it was a spent force by the time that Social Credit came along. But Theosophy, which began about the same time, was clearly cast in the same mould. By going to the East for inspiration it underlined the need for European thought to strike out on a new line. It emphasized extrasensory perception and added a belief in reincarnation. In stressing this last point it was indicating its determination to act as an accommodating bridge between the two outlooks,

[10] M. G. Myres, *Monetary Proposals for Social Reform* (New York, 1940), p. 22; M. Butchard, ed., *Tomorrow's Money* (London, 1936), p. 177; G. D. H. Cole, ed., *What Everybody Wants to Know about Money* (London, 1933), p. 369.

for reincarnation both retained and surpassed man as the centre of the system. The close connection of Theosophy, in its original form and in its Steiner variant, with Social Credit has also been remarked. Finally, it may be noted that some Theosophists were consciously undertaking a bridge-building exercise. One wrote, "If there is one function that can legitimately be ascribed to all Theosophists it is that of bridge building."[11]

Lest it be thought that this swing was confined to the fringes, leaving the main body of orthodox religious opinion untouched, the general observations made in connection with Barth and Otto may be amplified with observations drawn from the sphere of orthodox religious interest in Social Credit. It will have been noted that among the Chandos Group, converts were dominant: Reckitt was from the Quakers; Demant was from a Positivist background; Heron had been a Presbyterian; T. S. Eliot had been a Unitarian; Geoffrey Davies and Mairet, while not religiously inclined, were connected with the Sociological Society, which may be looked upon as a kind of substitute Catholicism. (It may also be noted that other converts connected with Social Credit and its associates were Chesterton, Pound, and Ruskin.) To these instances may usefully be added the Reverend W. G. Peck, who supported Social Credit from within the Anglo-Catholic wing of the Anglican church. Although not a member of the Chandos Group, he did write for T. S. Eliot's *Criterion*.

Peck began his religious life as a Methodist, influenced by Campbell. But towards the end of the war he took a leading part in the Free Catholic movement. This odd and short-lived movement was, as its name suggested, a bridge, too. It had been brought to life by W. E. Orchard, another ex-disciple of Campbell and preacher in the City Temple, who had moved to the uniquely ecumenical atmosphere of King's Weigh House Church. In this once staunchly nonconformist chapel, all manner of religious expressions had been allowed, including, interestingly enough, the Bahai movement of semi-Mahometan inspiration. Orchard's interest was not Islam, however, but mediaeval Catholicism, and from this there developed a fusion of ritualism and nonconformity which filled the chapel with incense and put a Free Catholic monk onto the roads of England. The fortunes of this ever-diminishing band of Free Catholics, fated to be absorbed into established religious groups, may be followed in two slight but interesting

[11] *News and Notes of the Theosophical Society*, 12.33; also see NA 4.4.12 for a Theosophical restatement of the Comtean blending of progress and order.

publications, the *Crusader* and the *Free Catholic*. The former was a platform for Peck, Egerton Swann, Fordham, and Rev. A. D. Belden, the only other Congregationalist besides Spencer who was sympathetic towards Social Credit and whose connection with the New Britain movement has been mentioned. The latter attracted the attention of Penty for a while, and it also featured Social Credit discussion. When the movement eventually split up, Orchard joined the Roman Catholic church, but Peck, like Campbell before him, went no further than the Church of England. There he found what he could not get from his original background and in particular from socialism. "Socialism," he concluded, "appeals to no ultimate and transcendent dogma concerning man's spiritual end."[12]

Attention has also been drawn to Quaker interest in Social Credit. A closer examination of the position of Quakerism at this period throws some light, perhaps, upon their interest in the doctrine. During the late nineteenth century the level of Quaker thought and practice had fallen away alarmingly. In part this decline was connected, whether as cause or as effect, with the emergence of Quaker families as members of the establishment. Not surprisingly, there had begun to develop a reform spirit, which almost inevitably went on to question the basic assumptions of Quakerism. At the same time it was almost equally inevitable that it took note of the new spirit of the age. Quaker outlook had been immanentist. With the turn of the century it began to swing to the transcendental.[13] And a member of the Society of Friends and convinced Social Crediter, none other than Philip Kenway, put his finger on this truth and its implications. Writing of his religion in the early years of the twentieth century, he commented, "We were only a little creedless company in the main body of Liberal Evangelical Nonconformity."[14] Although he did not say so, it was evident that he feared that unless something were done the Quakers might go the way of the Labour church and be swallowed up in a

[12] W. G. Peck, *Catholicism and Humanity* (London, 1926), pp. 2–5; idem, *Christian Faith and Social Order* (London, 1926), p. 35. The Society of Free Catholics had been founded as far back as 1907 by Rev. J. M. Lloyd-Thomas, a Unitarian; see H. Davies, *Worship and Theology in England, 1900–65* (New Jersey, 1965), p. 359. But it was Orchard who breathed life into the venture; see W. E. Orchard, *From Faith to Faith* (London, 1933), pp. 98, 112. B. Findlow, "The Free Catholic Movement," *Transactions of the Unitarian Historical Society*, 1958.

[13] M. A. Creasey and H. Loukes, *The Next Fifty Years* (London, 1956), p. 26.

[14] Kenway, *Quondam Quaker* (Birmingham, 1947), p. 137.

larger movement. It is suggested that Social Credit was seized upon by a questioning section of the Friends because it enabled them to alter their position in some fundamental way which, if concentrated in a purely religious context, might have given rise to problems too stark and too daunting to be accommodated within the existing framework. The point has been made that much of the Quaker interest in Social Credit was apostate Quakerism; such an observation lends weight to the suggestion. At the same time it may be noted that Quakerism is but the refined culmination of a pattern of thought which gave exaggerated importance to the idea of an apocalyptic "renovatio" and that it is at this point that Quakerism approaches most closely to Catholicism.

Any consideration of bridge building between an immanentist and a transcendentalist outlook need not be restricted to the religious sphere. By taking the dichotomy in the wider sense it can be seen that the swing was in operation in other spheres, too. The extreme immanence of the early Kibbo Kift movement was patent, as was the realization that this outlook quickly became a dead end from which only a basic reappraisal could point the way. In psychology the fact that it was Adlerianism which was taken up by Social Crediters was significant. Against the immanentism which any psychological system must stress, Adler balanced the importance of the *Gemeinschafts-gefühl*, marking a fundamental antagonism towards the atomized individualism of the liberal creed. Indeed the *Gemeinschaftsgefühl* was, as it were, the antidote to a state which could be understood as the result of original sin. Yet further to point up the bridging character of Adlerianism was the fact that the alternative name for the doctrine was Individual Psychology.

The circumstantial case now having been outlined, it is necessary to indicate tne way in which Social Credit was equipped to fulfil the needs of the time. By its supporters, Social Credit was frequently reduced to the three elements—the Cultural Heritage, the National Dividend, and the Just Price—and it will be convenient to conduct the next stage of the examination under these three headings.

It is impossible to read Douglas and fail to be struck by his obsession with the need to free the individual from the tyranny of a system, the means by which the few sought to gratify their lust for power. In this emphasis his individualism tended to appear as a simple, almost naïve, form of immanentism. The idea of endowing any group with attributes beyond those immediately necessary for the discharge of its purpose went flatly against the one notion which Douglas had seen fit to accept from the guild heritage and which he applied in a most restricted manner—functionalism. Once, he dismissed the more extreme organic interpretations with the sneer, "We can, I think, safely leave the group consciousness to look after itself."[15] Even so, within the doctrine lay elements which could be given a different emphasis. The basis of the whole concept was the increment of association, which was clearly rooted in man's endeavours and, owing nothing to any loyalty beyond man, was immanentist. In some way, however, it was evident that the Cultural Heritage came to overshadow man himself. It was such an imposing structure that it came to have a life of its own. An interesting interpretation of the Cultural Heritage was given by the Anglo-Catholic, Father Demant. As a Catholic he recognized the need for a transcendental purpose beyond man, for a "social philosophy politically and economically embodied" which would keep "organized human activity . . . to its true function." He claimed to find what was needed in the Cultural Heritage. And significantly, Symons, who was not a member of a formal religious group, saw the Cultural Heritage in the light of a mystery, to be referred to in terms of awe, and in fact he did liken it to the Mass.[16] In all this there was evidently a link with the Vitalists, who have earlier impinged upon this account. Just as the Bergsonian *élan vital* was embedded in life itself and derived from it alone, so too did it somehow transcend the limitations of mere life.

The National Dividend fitted smoothly into the pattern, and brought out another facet of this immanentist-transcendentalist swing. Once again there was the immanence which appeared in a joyful acceptance of the fruits of modern technology. But to offset this was the principle on which these fruits were to be distributed. The Dividend was intended for everyone without exception. Except possibly as a tactical exercise, and then only temporarily, it was not to depend upon contribution, nor even upon need, but was to be perfectly equal. To translate this into theological terms is to bring out the implications in terms of the dichotomy under discussion. It was in respect of the sonship of the Lord who provides, rather than of the brotherhood of those who work, that the Dividend was given.

It was the Just Price, however, which best illuminated the blending

[15] NA 30.12.20.
[16] Demant, *Christendom*, 9.35; W. T. Symons, *The Coming of Community* (London, 1931), p. 24.

of the two outlooks. In its purity, the Just Price means the flat rejection of the liberal notion that nothing has any more value than can be got in the open market. As in mediaeval times, the doctrine has the implication of an absolute standard, and for this reason it would have appealed immediately to Hulme. But the Social Credit use of the term was a happy compromise with the mediaeval doctrine and the relative notion of the liberals, which managed to retain elements of both in a way which would have delighted Comte. In this connection the views of Cousens were significant. In a chapter in *The Just Price* he argued that the Just Price was a device for maximizing total satisfaction (i.e., a form of an absolute), and this, in the conditions of the Middle Ages, had meant that both producers and consumers were satisfied in any bargain. At the price of a certain static quality, this had been accomplished. But to bring the doctrine forward into the twentieth century was to discover that if the Just Price was one that operated satisfactorily for both consumers and producers, then prices were not just. "They certainly fail," he said, "to get rid of the available goods at the optimum rate for growers and manufacturers."[17] Implicit in this argument was the assumption that in the dynamic conditions in the modern world a transcendental goal was better brought about by applying social tests rather than individual ones. This neat work of accommodation was reinforced by an article in the same book by Father Watt, S.J., who argued that the mediaeval doctrine had never been based on any kind of labour value but had depended upon the principle of utility.[18] Besides being a rebuff to the Marxists, it pointed to the fact that it was possible to discipline the market, and to do so without doing too much violence to the principle of free bargaining, and so arrive at a compromise not only social but also individual.

So far the term "apocalyptic" has been used to draw attention to an either/or outlook, a concentration upon states of mind. The same term can also be used to highlight methods of thinking, for in its processes anarchism was the reverse of social democratic ways. The latter may be termed sequential thought. Its characteristic is the emphasis which it gives to orderly progress, or to put it in terms of the political philosophy of the nineteenth century, the dialectic. The former may be called nonsequential, for in tune with its transcendental outlook it prefers to approach its goal by big jumps rather than by

---

[17] V. A. Demant, ed., *The Just Price* (London, 1930), p. 108.
[18] Ibid., p. 61.

cumulative small steps. It is a contrast which emerges unmistakably when the natures of the anarchist and the Marxist revolutions are compared. It is a feature of the anarchist system that the revolution will be a sudden, swift event which will immediately and of itself usher in the millennium; its adherents are all-or-nothing revolutionaries. The Marxists, on the other hand, have always considered the revolution, whether bloody or not, whether revisionist or otherwise, as essentially a process. It is because of this difference that anarchist thought tends to put such a misleading emphasis upon destruction. And it is also because of this difference that Lenin's painstaking, remorseless *What Is to Be Done?* and *The Development of Capitalism in Russia* could be countered by Kropotkin only with such books as *The Conquest of Bread*, in which the successful outcome of the revolution is made to depend quite literally upon the organization of a food supply at the moment of insurrection.

Many instances of the nonsequential may be found in Social Credit and its associated patterns of thought. A good example would be in Theosophy. The aim of that philosophy is to bring the initiate to a sudden awareness of the truth which lies beyond the veil of appearance. In a slightly different way, Theosophy showed its nonsequential character in the ready way in which it took to the theory of relativity. For people used to Theosophical thinking, Einstein was not so revolutionary. And a similar readiness to adopt the theory of relativity was shown by Frederic Harrison, who welcomed it in the *Positivist Review*.[19] That such an old man should take to what was still a new philosophy was a tribute to the essential modernity of Comtean thought.

Mediaevalism was another outlook in which nonsequential thinkers could find a haven. Mediaevalism must be seen not merely as a refuge for escapists but rather as an attractive realm for some of those alive to the implications of the times. Penty's repudiation of Parliament was based upon the awareness that the dialogue of debate was inherently dialectical, and so out of place in a truly ordered society. And if it was thought that Penty's dislike of the progressive was too unreasonable, as Orage did in fact think, then it was possible to turn to Hulme, whose revolutionary content could not be denied. Hulme, too, had spotted the necessity for a break with post-Renaissance notions of

[19] *Positivist Review*, 1.20; *Theosophical Review*, 7.25; A. E. Powell, the Theosophist, entitled a book on monetary reform *The Flow Theory of Economics* (London, 1929), and there drew attention to Einstein, p. 3.

time. A leading article of his had been devoted to this problem; he had roundly declared that "one of the main achievements of the nineteenth century was the elaboration and universal application of the principle of continuity." And he had added, "The destruction of this conception is, on the contrary, an urgent necessity of the present." He followed up this observation by identifying Darwinian evolution with romanticism, that is, process, and he was delighted to be able to contrast Darwin unfavourably with De Vries, who was reemphasizing the importance of sudden mutations. This rejection of constant and progressive, cumulative change had restored classicism to evolution.[20]

There was another way in which Hulme was significant in this respect. Although he did not live long enough to come up against Social Credit, it is to be remembered that his disciple, de Maeztu, was later claimed as a believer in Douglas[21] and that his editor, Herbert Read, did become a Social Crediter. Moreover, he was very closely linked with one whose advocacy of Social Credit was passionately wholehearted—Ezra Pound. The two knew each other in London at the time when both were contributors to the *New Age*, but a more meaningful way of connecting them would be through their participation in the imagist movement. It had, in fact, been Hulme, a poet of slight achievement but of much promise, who began this movement when he founded the Poets' Club in 1908; later Eliot's paper, the *Egoist*, had served as a platform for the movement. As a movement, imagism was not long-lasting, but its elements passed into the tradition of twentieth-century literature in a most influential manner. What was striking about imagist poetry, and was to be seen in exaggerated form in the later Pound writings, was the rejection of the idea of development, and a compensating emphasis upon the immediacy of experience. As Pound himself said, "An 'Image' is that which presents an intellectual and emotional complex in an instant of time."[22] In the search for this complex, Pound was led on to a study of Chinese thought, and especially of Chinese writing, the characters of which possess an immediacy strange to Western patterns of thought. It was significant that the minor imagist poet, Basil Bunting, was also attracted to Social Credit, and he organized the London University Social Credit study circle in the early period of organized activity.[23] A step removed from the imagists, but betraying traces of

[20] T. E. Hulme, *Speculations* (London, 1936), pp. 3, 117.
[21] *Fig Tree*, 9.37.
[22] Quoted in S. K. Coffman, *Imagism* (University of Oklahoma, 1951), p. 9.
[23] NA 12.5.21.

that influence, were Eliot and Grieve, both of whom were Social Crediters. (It may also be worth noting that Hulme's acceptance of the importance of Cézanne was shared by Clive Bell and Roger Fry, members of the Bloomsbury group, from which emerged the academically respectable version of the underworld, Keynesianism.)

Yet other examples of nonsequential thinking which turned to Social Credit abound. For instance, Demant's insistence that the Catholic–Social Credit philosophy demanded enjoyment in the here and now, not in the problematical future, has been mentioned. The Adlerian interest held much the same notion. The other forms of psychology current at the time stressed the importance of *tracing back* symptoms to root causes in childhood, and so showing how successive impulses—now cause, now effect—contributed to the moulding of character. Such methods were essentially sequential. Adler's method was in dramatic contrast to this. For him the totality of a person in the here and now was the important thing, not the past development. It is well to remember a Social Crediter's summary of Adlerianism, "The Source of sanity is not in the past. . . . It lies in social vision."[24]

Douglas himself showed that he was aware of the importance of nonsequential thought. Social Credit made no appeal to the idea of development, other than to acknowledge with gratitude that today's technological blessings amounted to a state of plenty. There was no need to bring the balance of the past into present calculations. A world of plenty meant that sequential thought had no part to play. As Douglas never tired of insisting, a system of rewards and punishment (and such a system was sequential) was meaningless in such an environment; it had meaning only amid scarcity. A Social Credit world would inevitably be a world of material anarchy at least.

It will be appreciated that an inevitable consequence of the nonsequential approach is an emphasis upon the totality of experience. This, too, has been met with at every turn in this examination, though probably nowhere more touchingly than in connection with *The Healthy Life* and *Focus*. Totality is important because it points to an understanding of the paradox which had underlain so much of Social Credit and its associated underworld. From Comte onwards it has been common to find demands for absolute standards. This insistence, which at first sight appears out of place in a nonsequential world, is in fact the necessary corrective without which anarchy would become

[24] P. Mairet, *The A.B.C. of Adler's Psychology* (London, 1928), p. 93.

chaos. The concluding portion of chapter 2 in this account summarized the different ways in which the underworld insisted upon an absolute standard. Douglas, too, was in this tradition; indeed, he could claim to have given the world its first true definition of price. To state that the price of anything was the cost of consumption was to go well beyond the previous gropings of a Kitson or a Donisthorpe, whose price indexes, though an advance, were still tainted with the relativism of the market place.

Social Credit was never anarchism in the classic sense. That characteristic of anarchism, a contempt for wealth as such, had no place in Douglas's thought. "I have no intention of being poor," he had declared,[25] and his disciples went further in emphasizing the material benefits. Rather, Social Credit sprang from the same kind of background as had anarchism, and it was the application to postwar England of an attitude. Thus, the Social Credit attitude to wealth could be accommodated to the traditional anarchist distrust; in the nineteenth century world of scarcity, anarchism was bound to renounce the concept which on the face of things was responsible for suffering. The twentieth-century updating at the hands of Social Credit was comparable with, and as justified as, the Quaker acceptance of abundance, so long as that doctrine implied abundance for all.

Social Credit may be accepted, then, as within the broad anarchist stream. Once this identification has been made, a pointer has been given to the answer to the question, Why did Social Credit make such an initial impact only to fail so signally? Anarchism flourishes only at the moment of maximum conflict, and even the partial solution of the crisis can cause a collapse of anarchism. It seems that Social Credit came at the very worst possible time. Anarchism in England had been at a peak in the 1880s and after that had faded, to return only with the onset of depression in the 1930s. Douglas began to advocate his views in the trough between the peaks. And although the postwar situation was bad, the experience of wartime control led critics to expect a solution more along the lines of orthodox socialism. Had Douglas come at an earlier, or better still, in view of his fundamental break with sequential-immanentist thought, at a later, date, it may have been that a greater swell of dissatisfaction would have taken up the idea. It may also have been that such a hearing would have been sufficiently respectful that the later unfortunate developments of Douglas's thinking might never have been called into being. As it was,

---

[25] *Millgate Monthly*, 8.32.

the wave of discontent of the thirties had been so discredited, and Douglas so driven to cranky solutions, that the opportunity had passed.

It may have been that the possibilities mentioned above would have happened—but it is doubtful. For while the *mood* of anarchism will probably be an eternal one, recurring whenever tension is particularly marked, it seems to be equally true that any particular *manifestation* of the mood is fated quickly to pass away. The experience of the Social Credit form of anarchism well illustrates this lesson. Towards the end of the period examined here, Pontifex summed up the state of the Social Credit movement. He bemoaned the inability of Social Credit to attract the leading writers of the day and added that it was false to claim that the nature of Social Credit did not permit its effective propagation.[26] This was an interesting comment, for evidently Pontifex was responding to a criticism which had, in fact, been made of the movement. And such a criticism, despite Pontifex's disavowal, had every justification. Even a bare outline of the fortunes of the movement is sufficient to show that the organized movement was a very weak affair indeed. To one side there was Hargrave and his backing, whose attachment to the creed, while not insincere, was not fully disinterested either, and whose eventual impatience with the movement was made brutally clear. On the other side stood the intellectuals. While some of them wrote in support of the doctrine, and some took part in organized work through the Chandos Group, too many were content to rest satisfied with an almost languid endorsement of the message. (In all this, Pound is always excepted.) Typical of the intellectual response was that of Herbert Read. He had been connected with the *New Age* so must have been caught up in the discussion of Social Credit at an early stage. He found in the doctrine nothing to quarrel with, and for one who had anarchist sympathies which were later to turn into outright acceptance, this was not surprising. Yet, it was only in 1935 that he declared his acceptance of Social Credit, and even then his declaration was made en passant.[27]

The truth was that the nonsequential basis of Social Credit cut off would-be propagandists from their potential audiences. This inability to communicate was seen in two ways. To begin with there was the inability, or unwillingness, of many to see what Douglas was calling for. Nowhere was this made plainer than in Douglas's brush with the

[26] NEW 25.5.33; *Purpose,* 1936, p. 90.
[27] Read, p. 20.

Macmillan committee, in particular with Mr. R. H. Brand, who recoiled at the idea of paid idleness, and with Professor T. E. Gregory, who seemed quite unable to see that Douglas made the aim of his economics not work but consumption.[28] If people at this level were sceptical of the purpose of the scheme, how much the more would be the ordinary man in the street. But beyond this there was the more troublesome fact that once the technical possibility of ushering in a world of plenty had been established, there was little else to write about. The jump into a new dimension was so complete, so little connected with the present, that it was at once too easy and too difficult to describe it. Like science fiction in the realm of literature, it never quite achieved respectable autonomy. The Leisure Society had a weaker life than most of the Social Credit organizations. One can imagine how easily the meetings must have become a mixture of the repetitiously obvious and the undisciplined guess at the future. And when such academics as Professor Dobrée, or novelists such as Storm Jameson, came to write on Social Credit their works were so disappointing. D. H. Lawrence's confession of ineffectualness in this respect has already been noted. In the supine acceptance rather than challenging advocacy of Social Credit by the intellectuals can be seen the initial strength and the eventual weakness of the doctrine, the quickly aroused sympathy with a nonsequential way of thought which is inherently incapable of maintaining itself for long. Mairet had some inkling of this when he complained of the lack of a Social Credit dynamic. He advocated the use of nationalism to supply this need.[29]

It is for this reason that the other grounds for the failure of Social Credit may be discounted. The inability of Douglas to provide acceptable leadership is one such. Until 1934 he held back, perplexing a following eager to be given a lead. Thereafter he dictatorially intervened and offended many an erstwhile supporter. Finally, he broke up the secretariat. There was in addition a lack of understanding between Douglas and his most influential group of supporters, Chandos. The black-and-white approach of the major drove a wedge between them, and it enlarged differences which could have been smoothed over. Douglas always had a disproportionate influence within the movement, and this was something more than the respect paid to the originator. It was due to the lack of an effective membership, and given the nature of the doctrine, it was impossible to build one.

[28] The Macmillan Committee, *Report* (London, 1931), paragraphs 4513, 4521.
[29] *Purpose*, 1930, p. 10.

Bruce Glasier, a member of the early Independent Labour party and a close friend of William Morris, had this to say of the anarchists whom he had got to know at close quarters: "The anarchist is either a socialist who has got muddled with individualist ideas, or an individualist who has got muddled with socialist ideas."[30] Although such an opinion does not do justice to the anarchist position, it does draw attention to the truth that anarchism was a "bridge" philosophy. But if Social Credit was, as a brand of anarchism, a bridge, which way was the traffic flowing? Was it, as Dobb's implied claim made out, a traffic bound for reaction—a reaction, some would claim, of a totalitarian kind? On this showing, Social Credit failed because it was opposed to the current of history. Inevitable rise and inevitable fall are neatly taken care of by such an interpretation.

To approach the question in general terms would be to lend weight to this argument. It has been pointed out that the American Populist movement, which contained much monetary reform in an attempt to reestablish a vanishing society undermined by big business and international finance, gradually became more and more crotchety until it sank to Jew-baiting and Daytonian fundamentalism. This line of reaction has been traced down through the Longs and the Coughlins of the thirties to the neo-fascists of the postwar scene. The view advanced by J. S. Schapiro in his article "Pierre Joseph Proudhon, Harbinger of Fascism" brings the charge nearer home.[31] His argument can be widened by drawing attention to the influence which Sorel had upon Mussolini. Arguments such as these rely upon one of the two possible ways of providing the point. No attempt is made to fasten upon the accused an avowed aim of establishing elements of what today would be called fascism, or totalitarianism. Rather, efforts are directed towards uncovering the less conscious drives which animated the leaders and the movement, seeking to show that behind the open declarations lay hidden, less acceptable goals and motivations. The argument may even admit that these preconceptions are not in themselves objectionable, only that the attempt to translate theory into practice leads to ends not wished for. Since this last method was one used by Douglas (and by his mentor, Belloc), it is only fair to apply the test to him too. At the same time, the first argument may

[30] J. B. Glasier, *William Morris and the Early Days of the Socialist Movement* (London, 1921), p. 125.

[31] V. Ferkis, "Populist Influences on American Fascism," *Western Political Quarterly*, 1957; J. S. Schapiro, *American Historical Review*, 1945.

be dismissed, since on no occasion did Social Credit consider a fascist-totalitarian solution.

The case for applying the Schapiro-Dobb interpretation to Social Credit looks a strong one. Douglas himself had all the signs of an unsure person, increasingly driven into a compensationally dictatorial manner; his retention of his wartime rank would be merely one indication of this need for reassurance.[32] The concluding cranky pronouncements and the emerging anti-Semitism would be further pointers in this direction. Then, too, his associates were men who either showed many of these traits or could be suspected of harbouring them. The traces of resentment in Orage and the adherence of Lords Tavistock and Tankerville, representing a dying class, are examples that could be presented in this light. Reckitt could be brought in together with the Anglo-Catholic wing to confirm this impression. The *New English Weekly*'s economic nationalism could be described as a response to Britain's fading imperialism, while the Green Shirt militants could be seen as an even more extreme instance of the same tendency. To some critics the fact that Social Credit remained solidly middle class, even in the case of the Green Shirts, who set out to be proletarian, would be damaging; that so many were schoolmasters would, *pace* Shaw, be even more so.[33] The inclusion in the major's ranks of failed businessmen, such as Kitson, would clinch matters.

Yet this argument has never been a strong one. The Populist-derived argument has been met on its own ground by Pollock and rebutted.[34] Schapiro's article would have been more convincing had it not appeared in 1945, when the intellectual manhunt was in full swing and the process begun by which almost every intellectual current had been identified as a constituent of fascism-totalitarianism. The root objection to most of these exercises in ideological paternity is to the practice of assuming that *anything* advocated by fascism-totalitarianism must be evil and then identifying such characteristics as the same as those in previous philosophies. Too often this

[32] It was a practice shared, among monetary reformers, by Galloway and Powell (majors) and Adams (captain).

[33] J. Strachey, in| *Social Credit: An Economic Analysis* (London, 1936), p. 19, showed that he had learnt the communist style when he accused Douglas of unreality by speaking of the "weekly household bill" in connection with the spending habits of the majority of the people. For the high incidence of teachers see *Broadsheet*, April, 1928.

[34] N. Pollock, "The Myth of Populist Anti-Semitism," *American Historical Review,* 1962.

identification rests upon surface manifestations only; to take but one example—the too-easy identification of nineteenth-century anti-Semitism with that of Hitler. It is slowly being realized that the supreme evil of totalitarianism is not its content, but its execution. The thoroughness of totalitarianism, its utter ruthlessness—these are what are to be feared. It is the cult of efficiency.

Totalitarianism is the apotheosis of sequential thought, the logical outcome of the whole liberal philosophy of progress which must become the cult of efficiency as the old, ever-expanding world becomes suddenly revealed as a finite, overcrowded globe. In such a world picture, Social Credit has no place. It may, on the other hand, have a part to play in the present. One of the salient characteristics of today's world, and becoming ever more important as the world becomes increasingly technological, is the decline of the idea of sequential process and the corresponding rise of the belief in the immediate, the unconnected. Today's favourite word is "instant."

But, it may be objected, such a total world, breaking down the restraints of the past, encourages totalitarianism. The unconnected world lends itself to manipulation by those in power, the only ones who have the means of structuring the world. The example of totalitarian Germany, where administrative units were gratuitously (and technically inefficiently) multiplied, comes to mind. Douglas himself had a prevision of this in the latter period of his life, and hence his increasing stress upon the organic composition of society as a means of curbing the manipulative power of the rulers. But while it may be argued that totalitarianism is helped by a world organized on an atomistic basis, it is impossible to imagine a totalitarian world maintained by a philosophy equally unconnected. All totalitarianisms are driven by the idea of a process, a progression to some goals, whether that goal be a Jew-free society or a world without capitalists. It is significant that the writer who came closest to a totalitarian standpoint at this time was Wyndham Lewis. What is interesting is that whereas Hulme had welcomed the Bergsonian dissolution of time, his sympathizer, Lewis, took violent exception to the notion. And so too did the fascist writer, A. K. Chesterton, who condemned modern writers (in particular James Joyce) for their failure "to reduce their experience to any kind of order," thus merely flinging back "into the teeth of chaos a still more reckless chaos."[35] These totalitarian sympathizers sensed the inability of such thinking to bring about any

[35] *Blackshirt*, 9.3.34.

emulation of their continental models, for take away the future vision and the sustaining force disappears, and the way becomes open again for the reestablishment of freedom.

Social Credit refused to look to a future utopia; it believed in the present possibility of plenty. It had the daring to root its vision in the here and now and the boldness to make this timelessness an eternal feature of its scheme. This characteristic prevented its taking up that dynamic which would have implied a totalitarianism. For this reason it is possible to minimize the anti-Semitism and the nationalism which, superficially considered, make Social Credit a frightening proposition. Perhaps it would not be too much to say, in paraphrasing the well-known saying, "We are all Social Crediters nowadays." This, rather than the Dobb "failure," may be the correct light in which to see the Douglas contribution.

index